MW00982446

praise for

WHOSE STREETS?

We cannot build a mass movement that is up to the internal as well as external challenges we face unless we collectively and comradely dissect and learn from our struggles. This book is an indispensable resource in applying that basic principle to what happened on the streets of Toronto.

> — **Sam Gindin,** Visiting Packer Chair in Social Justice, York University

Dissenting and marching to voice one's views and to express solidarity are not lost arts or relics of the sixties. They remain at the core of political participation and democratic engagement. *Whose Streets?* celebrates the power of speaking out – let it be widely read and let that power be widely heard.

> — **Nathalie Des Rosiers**, General Counsel, Canadian Civil Liberties Association

WHOSE STREETS?

The Toronto G20 and the Challenges of Summit Protest

Tom Malleson and David Wachsmuth, editors

Between the Lines
Toronto

Whose Streets? The Toronto G20 and the Challenges of Summit Protest

© 2011 Tom Malleson and David Wachsmuth, eds.

First published in Canada in 2011 by
Between the Lines
401 Richmond St. W., Studio 277
Toronto ON M5V 3A8
1-800-718-7201
www.btlbooks.com

All rights reserved. No part of this publication may be photocopied, reproduced, stored in a retrieval system, or transmitted in any form or by any means, electronic, mechanical, recording, or otherwise, without the written permission of Between the Lines, or (for photocopying in Canada only) Access Copyright, 1 Yonge Street, Suite 1900, Toronto, Ontario, M5E 1E5.

Every reasonable effort has been made to identify copyright holders. Between the Lines would be pleased to have any errors or omissions brought to its attention.

NOTICE TO READERS: The views expressed in this book are those of the authors alone and do not necessarily reflect the views or opinions of Between the Lines. Some activities described in this book could, in certain circumstances, involve violations of federal criminal laws, provincial laws, or municipal bylaws, or expose activists to liability in civil actions. Readers are advised to seek legal advice before undertaking any activity that entails a risk of legal consequences. The publisher assumes no liability for the consequences of any activity undertaken by readers.

Library and Archives Canada Cataloguing in Publication

Whose streets? the Toronto G20 and the challenges of summit protest / Tom Malleson and David Wachsmuth, eds.
Also issued in electronic formats.
ISBN 978-1-926662-79-4

1. Group of Twenty (Organization). Summit (4th : 2010 : Toronto, Ont.). 2. Demonstrations – Ontario – Toronto. 3. Police misconduct – Ontario – Toronto. 4. Political activists – Ontario – Toronto – Biography. 5. Anti-globalization movement – Ontario – Toronto. I. Wachsmuth, David II. Malleson, Tom
JC328.3.W45 2011   322.409713'541   C2011–906176–7

Cover design by Jennifer Tiberio
Front cover photo © Arindam Banerjee / Shutterstock.com.
Back cover photo © Vincenzo D'Alto.
Page preparation by Steve Izma
Printed in Canada

SEP - - 2013

MIX
Paper from
responsible sources
FSC
www.fsc.org   FSC® C011825

Between the Lines gratefully acknowledges assistance for its publishing activities from the Canada Council for the Arts, the Ontario Arts Council, the Government of Ontario through the Ontario Book Publishers Tax Credit program and through the Ontario Book Initiative, and the Government of Canada through the Book Publishing Industry Development Program.

Canada Council   Conseil des Arts
for the Arts   du Canada

Canada

ONTARIO ARTS COUNCIL
CONSEIL DES ARTS DE L'ONTARIO

All royalties from this book will be donated to the G20 Legal Defence Fund.

For more information about how you can make a donation or get involved, go to **www.btlbooks.com/whosestreets**.

Contents

Foreword

G20 Trials and the War on Activism

Naomi Klein

The following is an abridged version of a speech delivered by the author on November 11, 2010, as part of a Toronto fundraiser for the legal fees of G20 arrestees.

WE KNOW WHAT HAPPENED IN THIS CITY DURING THE G20 – AND the wrong people are on trial for it. There are police officers who should be facing charges for assault and harassment – and so should any supervisors who enabled or covered over those abuses. So far no one in authority has paid any price for what happened. According to the Parliamentary Committee underway in Ottawa, the worst crime the cops committed was taking off their nametags. And let's not forget that our outgoing city council unanimously passed a motion to "commend the outstanding work of Chief Bill Blair, the Toronto Police Service and the Police Officers working during the G20 summit in Toronto."[1]

But this is not just about the cops. There are also high-level politicians who should be under investigation – for their role in ordering the militarization of our city, for subverting the legislative process to increase police powers, for grossly misappropriating public funds, using them to buy off constituents and grease donors. Not surprisingly, the federal government has not convened an inquiry. Neither has the RCMP. And the Ontario Legislature just shamefully voted against having a public inquiry. In 1998 there was an RCMP inquiry called over the use of pepper spray on peaceful protesters outside an APEC summit. It was known as Peppergate. How quaint by G20 standards.

But the truth is we are not so hardened; we are not blasé about state violence. There are hundreds if not thousands of people in this city who are still traumatized by what they suffered and witnessed that weekend at the end of June. The G20 changed them, changed the way they feel about their country and their city. So let's refresh our memories about what did happen.

Large parts of Toronto were engulfed in a sprawling security zone as an atmosphere of hysteria gripped our city. Residents were subject to arbitrary searches as they went to and from work, discovering that they were in a bizarre rights-free zone.

Bike racks and bus shelters disappeared. Trees were uprooted because, apparently, they could be used as projectiles.

All of this caused frustration to boil, as did the fact that when demonstrations did take place they were suffocated by throngs of police in riot gear and in some cases dangerously "kettled."

As we all saw with our own eyes or on video, peaceful protesters were attacked with rubber bullets, tear gas, and pepper spray. At Queen's Park riot police plowed into groups of people sitting on the grass, flailing their batons and kicking protesters to the ground.

In all, over eleven hundred people were arrested – the largest mass arrest in Canadian history.

From them we have heard many reports of beatings (including beatings of people in handcuffs). Of racist, sexist, and homophobic slurs and threats. Of people being screamed at for speaking in languages other than English. Of strip searches of women by male officers, of groping by police, sexual solicitation, and rape threats. We also heard about the shocking detention conditions: people crammed into cells, unable to lie down. Medicines were denied, as was the right to counsel. I heard from women who were not given sanitary napkins, and from others who were denied water and food for longer than a day.

Before I came here I read some of the testimony from today's hearings, and I have to tell you that it is very painful to read because the memories and the sense of helplessness come back. Just a few hours ago a man named John Pruyn testified. I want to share with you what he said. He said he was arrested and cuffed, and, while he was cuffed, police pulled off his artificial leg. Then they ordered him to put it back on, which he obviously could not do with his hands tied. Then they laughed, dragged him off, and hit him, telling him he should never have come. It goes without saying that no one deserves this kind of treatment, no matter what they did.

But the fact is that the vast majority of those arrests were a complete farce. The proof is that almost all the charges were dropped. In other words, arrestees were abused in this manner simply because they went to a protest – or in some cases because they walked by or near one. Or because they were wearing black. On Queen Street in Toronto. I mean, please.

But the G20 assault on democratic rights did not end there. That's because roughly one hundred demonstrators are being prosecuted with a sense of vendetta and a spirit of vengefulness that is so intense it verges on the pathological. Some are facing charges grossly disproportionate to the allegations – like potential multi-year jail sentences for allegedly breaking a window. No simple vandalism charge will suffice. This is personal. This is a crusade. We see it most clearly in the treatment of the nineteen activists accused of "conspiracy" – an extremely serious charge, with grave consequences if they are convicted.

For months leading up to the protests, police in multiple provinces were engaged in an elaborate undercover operation, involving heavy surveillance and many informants in activist groups. Before the large protests took place during the G20, and well before any glass shattered, conspiracy warrants were issued for this group of people. In some cases, police violently arrested people in their homes pre-emptively. The claim, as I understand it, is that these activists were secretly planning the property destruction that took place after they were in jail. The people who did it were apparently helpless puppets. This narrative of intrigue has been central to Bill Blair's bizarre claim that Toronto was victimized by a "criminal conspiracy" – as opposed to what actually happened: a big protest attended by lots of people, including quite a few very pissed off people.

As you can well imagine, we would have liked to have had one of these supposed conspirators speak to us here tonight, to share their perspective. I am sure you all would have liked to hear that speech. Unfortunately we weren't able to. If we did, there is every chance that the cops would storm in here and arrest them for violating their bail conditions. Maybe scooping up some of us wearing black while they were at it.

But let's talk a little about those bail conditions – because they really are something. Here is a sampling: not being able to speak to any of the other defendants; not being able to go to protests or engage in political organizing; not being able to talk on a cell phone; essentially being under house arrest; and in some cases not being able to post to the Internet or speak to the media. And it must be said that to make these wild allegations and to simultaneously gag the accused is not justice, it's propaganda – not to mention the height of cowardice. Alex Hundert, as most of you know, was "pre-emptively" arrested at gunpoint before the demonstrations took place and he has been re-arrested twice since – once for speaking at a panel at Ryerson. He remains in jail.

So the question must be asked: why? Why these draconian lengths to paint community organizers as terrorist masterminds, why this vendetta? Why, in Toronto, is calling for civil disobedience suddenly criminal conspiracy, with the power to ruin young lives? Let's unpack this a little bit, so we are clear. Part of what is going on is that the police went so over the top that they appear to need these convictions as a form of self-justification. In other words, spending on summit security was so exorbitant, and the systems of entrapment leading up to these arrests were so elaborate, that at the end of the day they need something to show for their billion-dollar budget and their rampant civil liberties violations. A conspiracy – not a movement. And our friends are caught in that maze of self-righteousness, that web of self-justification.

Could it be that the government seized the opportunity presented by the G20 to try to wipe out or at least weaken some of the country's most effective and militant anti-poverty, Indigenous solidarity, and migrant rights groups? Because if we look at those bail conditions, and the massive legal costs ahead, that is exactly what these charges seem designed to do. And they have good reason to want to get these groups out of the way, or at least bog them down in legal hassles at this particular point in history. Because let's always remember that the gravest crimes of that summit were not the fake lake, or the civil liberties violations, or even the security budget. The real crime was what the leaders decided to do while they were being so enthusiastically protected.

Nicknamed the "Austerity Summit," Toronto was where they decided to stick the public with the bill for an economic crisis that began with wild speculation on Wall Street. At previous G20 summits these same leaders failed to close corporate tax loopholes, failed to impose coordinated banking regulation, failed to break up the big banks, refused to impose a bank tax, failed to impose even a miniscule financial transaction tax, failed to eliminate fossil fuel subsidies, and of course resolved to continue waging wars. So how would they come up with the revenue to cover their shrinking tax bases thanks to lay-offs and foreclosures? They would cut social programs, of course. The G20's final communiqué in Toronto instructed governments to slash their deficits in half by 2013. This is a huge and shocking cut, and we all know who will pay the price: students who are seeing their public education further deteriorate as their fees go up, which is why they were on the streets of London, occupying the headquarters of the Tory Party; pensioners who are losing hard-earned benefits, which is why they have been on the streets of France for weeks; public-sector workers whose jobs are being eliminated, which is why we have seen massive strikes in Italy and Spain. And the list goes on.

Here in Ontario, well before the G20, the poor were already paying the cost of the crisis. To cite just one example, this year the provincial government shamefully abolished the Special Diet Allowance – a program that gave people on social assistance with health conditions just a little bit more every month so that they could afford foods that don't make them sick. That program cost $200 million a year. As John Clarke of the Ontario Coalition Against Poverty pointed out during the G20, the cost of security for the summit could have paid for that program for five years. At the federal level, the Tories are on course to slash stimulus spending that includes a billion dollars a year for the construction and renovation of social housing. Meanwhile, they are paying Lockheed Martin $9 billion for new fighter jets, with an antici-pated $7 billion more in maintenance costs.

We gathered on the streets of Toronto during the G20 because we know there are other ways to make up a budget shortfall. Like getting the hell out of Afghanistan, and not building new prisons at a time when Canada's crime rate has been down for a decade. But our politi-cians have chosen a very different route, and that route necessarily means more social unrest. And that has everything to do with why the security costs were so high during the G20. Because much of that money went to arming the police with a new arsenal of weaponry: water cannons, sound cannons, tear gas and rubber bullets, surveil-lance cameras. I fear that we G20 protesters were just the guinea pigs. That those are the weapons of the future, designed to be turned on anyone else in the country who dares to resist the G20's policies.

My point is simply this: our government knows that there are heavy battles ahead. Battles over what kind of country we want. Battles with tens of billions of dollars on the line. These are fights we can win if we build coalitions like the ones we saw on the streets of Toronto during the G20: immigrant rights advocates with anti-poverty activists with First Nations defenders of the land with labour leaders and people who were just fed up with having their city taken over.

Our government fears those coalitions, fears the prospect of a truly mass social movement, and we can see that fear in the arrest and prosecution patterns. It is no coincidence that the people facing the most serious charges with the most restrictive bail conditions are among the most effective organizers in this country. They are precisely the people who build bridges across traditionally separate communities and constituencies, finding common ground where there was often antipathy before. That's what Alex Hundert does at AW@L and Southern Ontario Anarchist Resistance, with his tireless support for the blockade at Grassy Narrows, among other Indigenous struggles. That's what Syed Hussan does as an organizer with No One Is Illegal–Toronto – he fights for the rights of immigrants and refugees. But now, in part because of his G20 political activities, he has been unable to get his work visa renewed and faces deportation himself.

Some of the most effective organizers in the country are being taken out of the game when they are needed most, precisely when the stakes are highest. But here is what the Tories and the cops can't seem to get: their attacks only make us more determined. Our movements are more resilient than they know. And when we refuse to forget what happened here during the G20, when we demand accountability for the real criminals, and the freedom of our friends, we are fighting not just for the past but for the future.

We are saying – with clarity and conviction – that we will not accept this treatment again. We have the right to defend our hard-won social services and meagre refugee protections from morally bankrupt politicians. We have the duty to protect our boreal forests and our pristine waters from dirty oil development. And as we perform these duties, we know that there will be costs – there always are. But we refuse to be vilified as criminals and we refuse to relinquish our rights as Canadians. That is what is at stake in the struggle for G20 justice and we cannot afford to lose.

One final thought: what moved me most during the G20 actions is the way people embodied the kind of world they want in the way they conducted themselves. When police stormed, demonstrators locked arms and often repelled arrest. When someone was snatched, they often were freed by their friends or passersby. When people were loaded onto vans and taken to overcrowded jails, strangers looked after each other, advocated for each other. And outside the jails there were solidarity protests where thousands showed up, despite the fact that some of them had just gotten out of jail themselves and were terrified of being re-arrested. Yet they showed up, brave and loud, week after week.

Tonight is simply a continuation of that spirit. It is about acknowledging the extraordinarily high stakes of this political moment, and treating every member of our movements as if they are precious. Because they are. It is about saying that we will not let media-generated suspicion make us afraid and disdainful of each other. That even when we disagree, we will do so with respect, and will refuse to be divided into categories of good and bad activists. Tonight is about saying: we were together on the streets of Toronto during the G20 and we are together still. We have each other's backs. For the battles ahead.

Preface

Tom Malleson and David Wachsmuth

THE IDEA FOR THIS COLLECTION EMERGED FIVE MONTHS AFTER THE June 2010 G20 protests shook Toronto. The political aftershocks were still rippling across the country, a handful of activists were still languishing in jail, and hundreds more faced farcical charges. We initially conceived of the project as a straightforward fundraiser – we'd get a dozen people to write about their experiences organizing or participating in the protests and sell the result as a short book or pamphlet to raise desperately needed funds for G20 legal fees. Though books are never a great way to raise money, we reasoned that in the face of legal fees expected to surpass a million dollars – for a movement that survives on peanuts – every little bit helps.

Yet as we reached out to activists and organizers, got in touch with demonstrators and passersby, and started hearing their stories, the book took on a life of its own. Beyond the important task of raising money, we started to see three additional goals. First, we wanted to forefront the efforts of on-the-ground organizers. We were wary of creating an academic tome, aloof and abstract; instead, as activists ourselves, we were intent on producing a book that could be concretely useful to other social justice activists in Toronto, across Canada, and abroad. We wanted to highlight the pitfalls and dangers, but also the opportunities and successes that can come from organizing a summit protest. Second, we wanted to provide space for a diverse range of voices of the people caught up in the G20 mayhem, from the singing protester to the angry militant to the innocent civilian caught in the crossfire. The testimonials we collected provide a living memory of the protests and thus may serve as a historical archive and reference point for those wishing to look back, remember, and understand what transpired during those fateful summer days. To this end, we ensured that every single chapter was written by someone who was personally involved with the organizing or was physically on the streets. Finally, we wanted this book to be a political act in itself – to stimulate lively discussion about left politics in Canada, and further the debate about how the global justice movement can move forward in the years ahead – so that progressives can learn from each other, deepen our understanding, and strengthen our analysis.

In order to accomplish these goals we sought out chapters from a wide range of people: from students to radical activists, from community organizers to academics, from protesters to bystanders. Luckily, we found ourselves well-positioned to bring these diverse perspectives together. We are both activist-scholars, with one foot in the street and one foot in the academy. Additionally, we were both intimately involved in the G20 protests. Tom Malleson is an antiauthoritarian social justice activist in Toronto, and was a core organizer with the Toronto Community Mobilization Network, which organized much of the infrastructure for the G20 protests; he is also a PhD candidate in political science at the University of Toronto. Likewise, David Wachsmuth is a PhD candidate in sociology at New York University as well as an organizer with GSOC-UAW Local 2110, the union for graduate employees at NYU; he was also one of the eleven hundred people arbitrarily arrested during the G20. Living in both the activist and academic worlds provided us with the rare opportunity to bring together the wide range of talented authors presented here, which, more than anything, constitutes the singular strength of this collection. While the authors of this book are all progressive, they come from a range of perspectives and disagree about many things. Yet the dialogue that emerges from the varying perspectives – and the very different walks of life – is both inspiring and fruitful. We hope such dialogue will be of lasting interest to progressives in Canada and beyond.

Any collaborative work is inherently a collective project, but this book relied on the work of more people than most – it was made possible not only by the effort of the individual authors but also by the hard work and dedication of activists and progressives in Toronto and across the country who came together to oppose the global austerity agenda and to demand the justice and democracy that neo-liberal capitalism has consistently failed to deliver. In addition to the authors, we would like to thank the following individuals for their help, suggestions, guidance, and support: Patsy Aldana, Neil Brenner, Jeff Carolin, Daniel Aldana Cohen, Juliette Daigre, Emma Hughes, David Hugill, Katie Mazer, Clare O'Connor, Shiri Pasternak, Jen Ridgley, Stuart Schrader, Neil Smith, Richard Swift, Esmé Webb, and Lesley Wood. Thank you!

Introduction

From the Great Recession to the Streets of Toronto

Tom Malleson and David Wachsmuth

Resisting the Austerity Agenda

Only nineteen months separated the first and fourth G20 summits of world leaders, yet a lot changed in that time. In November 2008, when the heads of government representing the twenty most powerful economies on the planet first met in Washington, DC, the US financial system was still in the throes of acute crisis following the collapse of the mortgage market and the bankruptcy of Lehman Brothers. The bank bailouts had just begun. By June 2010, when the G20 world leaders assembled in Toronto for their fourth meeting, the US financial crisis had evolved into a global economic crisis – by most measures the largest downturn in the capitalist system since the Great Depression. Across the world, the neo-liberal response to the crisis was immediate, severe, and sustained: the banks must be bailed out with public funds, while the costs must be covered with austerity measures. In country after country, pensions were being slashed, public employees were sacked, tuition fees were increased, and social spending was curtailed. It was this agenda of bailouts and austerity measures that the G20 leaders were meeting to advance.

It is now abundantly clear that the bankers who played such a central role in causing the crisis will bear little responsibility for paying for it. Instead, we have seen a massive and ongoing redistribution of wealth upwards, as the banks' losses in the crisis are socialized even as their recent profits are privatized. This is a grotesque socialism for the rich, leaving the rest of us stuck with the bill and ushering in what threatens to be a painful and divisive decade of austerity.

But the austerity onslaught has not gone unopposed. From riots in Athens and *indignados* in Spain to student protests in London, from the "Arab Spring" uprisings in the Middle East to the massive mobilizations in support of public-sector unions in Wisconsin, masses of people around the world have taken to the streets to express their anger at austerity and to insist that – counter to Margaret Thatcher's slogan – there *is* an alternative to neo-liberal capitalism.

It was against the backdrop of the latest round of bank bailouts, austerity measures, and anti-democratic economic policies being coordinated by the G20 that thousands of people gathered in Toronto for ten days of action in June 2010. Every day there were protests, teach-ins, debates, direct actions, free meals, and more. Posters plastered the city and people filled the streets. Next door to a legal clinic in the working-class neighbourhood of Parkdale, activists had set up a convergence space, an area where people could eat, rest, socialize, and organize. It was a place of frantic art making, multilingual translation, constant cooking, and the source of dozens of press releases – breathless preparations of every sort amidst the never-ending political discussions and debates. Just inside the entrance, a sign read: "Friends, Welcome to our Convergence Space. You are entering an autonomous zone. The authority of the Canadian State is not recognized. Here the people rule. Come in solidarity and be welcome." These were optimistic and audacious words, particularly since everyone knew that the sign was not preventing the police from videotaping the convergence space from outside, circling it with police cruisers, and infiltrating it with informants and undercover agents.

These ominous manifestations of the state's powers hovered over the demonstrations as a whole. The optimism and determination of thousands of protesters was greeted with arbitrary state violence on a scale never before seen in Canada. In what now stands as one of the greatest security fiascos and the largest mass arrest in Canadian history, the police arrested more than eleven hundred people during the ten days of opposition to the G20, the vast majority on the final two days of the summit. Nearly all were either peaceful protesters who were exercising their right to demonstrate or passersby who were in the wrong place at the wrong time. Nearly all were either released without charges or subsequently had their charges dropped. Despite a widespread public outcry at police and government conduct during the G20, the outcome looks much the same as that of the bank bailouts and the economic crisis: the politicians and police officials have largely managed to evade responsibility for the havoc they caused.

That an official public inquiry into the G20 fiasco has failed to materialize makes it all the more important that the public continue to inquire. Facts remain to be uncovered, questions remain to be asked, and lessons remain to be learned from the organization of and the state's response to the G20 protests. How was the resistance to the G20 in Toronto organized? What prompted the Canadian state to spend a billion dollars on security? Why did the police suspend civil liberties, militarize downtown Toronto, and carry out mass arrests on an unprecedented scale? Most importantly, what lessons can activists and progressives in Canada and beyond learn from the events of June 2010 for future struggles?

The contributors to this book attempt to answer these questions. They are activists who helped organize the mobilizations, demonstrators and bystanders who were arbitrarily arrested and detained, and scholars committed to the theory and practice of confronting neo-liberal capitalism. Through a combination of testimonials from the front lines and analyses of the broader context, they collectively offer an account that both reflects critically on what occurred in Toronto and looks ahead to further building our capacity for resistance.

What Is the G20?

"G20" is shorthand for the Group of Twenty. Strictly speaking, it is a group of finance ministers and central bankers representing twenty of the world's largest and most powerful economies. Founded in 1999 and now in its second decade of existence, it has become the premier intergovernmental organization acting to coordinate and stabilize the functioning of the global capitalist system and is an increasingly important political venue for world leaders.

The brainchild of former Canadian prime minister Paul Martin, the G20 builds upon two similar organizations – the G7 and the G8. The former was convened in the 1970s and consisted of the United States, Canada, Japan, Italy, France, Germany, and the United Kingdom; the addition of Russia in 1997 transformed it into the G8. With the rise of the European Union as an independent power and the genesis in East Asia of a serious economic crisis in 1997, however, the G8 nations recognized the importance of expanding their membership in order to continue to exercise effective control over the global economic system. The G20 was the result; the G8's original membership was supplemented by the wealthiest and most powerful nations from Latin America, Africa, and Asia, along with the European Union. In 2008 it officially superseded the G8 as the chief global economic coordinating body, although the G8 continues to meet alongside the G20.

For all the pomp and circumstance of its meetings, the G20 is characterized by *informal elite decision making* by the world's most powerful political actors. Although the specific agenda of the G20 changes every year, its overarching purpose is to ensure the continued functioning of the global economic system in the best interests of the political and economic elites of the leading capitalist economies while avoiding formal (and therefore accountable) institutional decision-making structures such as the United Nations. And although the informality of the meetings does not noticeably reduce their public cost, it does prove extremely effective at insulating them from democratic accountability and popular engagement. The steel fences, barbed wire, and riot police that enclose the summits are both symbolic and real barriers erected to keep the powerful apart from the population. They are dramatic admissions that the global elite will not tolerate any democratic interference.

Why Were People Demonstrating?

The massive protests against the World Trade Organization (WTO) in Seattle in 1999, themselves inspired by the 1994 Zapatista uprising in Chiapas, Mexico, set off a wave of demonstrations that would crash into every subsequent convergence of the global elite. Meetings of the WTO, the International Monetary Fund (IMF), the World Bank, the G8, the G20, and other financial and political leaders became routine targets for thousands of protesters. These demonstrations lost some momentum in the years following the 2001 destruction of the World Trade Center in New York City and the reaction it provoked, but in recent years the so-called anti-globalization movement has reappeared in force on the streets of cities across the world.

International summits such as the G20 have come to serve as flashpoints for the undercurrents of discontent in rich societies such as Canada. When twenty of the most powerful people in the world step down from their jets to discuss global economic policy, they invariably arrive at the doorstep of some of the very people adversely affected by such policies. And so in June 2010, the arrival of the G20 in Toronto acted as a lens to bring people's anger at neo-liberal policies into focus.

The Toronto G20 demonstrations were broad and diverse, responding to a multitude of oppressions and injustices of global capitalism. There were protests against poverty and climate change, demonstrations for queer justice, migrant justice, and Indigenous sovereignty. There were rallies organized by unions and marches organized by anarchists. The ten days of action reflected the complex two-sidedness of resistance – the critique of what exists combined with the aspiration for something different – which manifested itself sometimes through marches of joy, sometimes through protests of rage. There was singing and kissing in the street, and there was cursing and window-smashing.

Yet for all the diversity of the protests, for the most part they were united by two major issues: *justice* – opposing the global division of wealth and power, and the resultant marginalization of Indigenous people, migrants, the poor, and the disabled – and *democracy* – opposing the rule of elites (be they G20 governments or multinational corporations) with calls for community control, direct democracy, and self-determination. Both of these currents of protest find their common purpose in their opposition to neo-liberal capitalism.

To a large degree, the protesters in Toronto manifested the anti-globalization wisdom of "thinking globally and acting locally." Defying the cliché of summit tourists who hop from protest to protest, the majority of the demonstrations were organized by local groups around local issues. Instead of focussing on what can seem like distant issues or institutions, such as globalization, the rainforests, the IMF, and the World Bank, protesters generally organized in such a way as to demonstrate the global dimensions of their local issues. A frequent activist organizing trope was the call to mobilize so that regular people could "see the G20 on their own block."

In the weeks leading up to the G20, it was common to hear activists warn that the G20 convergence, like all large anti-globalization convergences, would only be a moment. There is invariably an enormous amount of energy unleashed as well as media attention at these events, but equally invariably they soon end, and life returns to normal in the cities that host them. There is thus a widely recognized danger of focusing too much time and energy on such a moment, to the detriment of the ongoing grassroots work that requires attention day in and day out.

But Toronto activists also recognized that a global event like the G20 is a rare opportunity to show the world the problems, the inequalities, and the unfreedoms that characterize their home. It is a chance to leverage international attention in order to strengthen their demands. It is a chance for progressives to communicate with their allies across the world, to demonstrate the kinds of organizing they are doing, the successes they have had, and the obstacles they have encountered. *Whose Streets?* continues in this spirit – calling attention to the massive problems that neo-liberalism brings to our doorsteps, while simultaneously sharing stories and strategies of resistance, so that we, as part of the global social justice movement, can take stock, learn from one another, and make our collective movements ever stronger.

A Timeline of Events

Although the vast majority of media attention focused on the weekend of June 26 and 27, the first actions against the Toronto G20 took place a week earlier; all in all there were ten days of demonstrations, workshops, rallies, and more. Though it is impossible to adequately capture the excitement, fear, rage, and exhaustion that characterized the days of action against the G20 in Toronto, the following timeline of the main events will provide some context for the chapters that follow.[1]

Saturday, June 19, and Sunday, June 20, were days of the People's Summit, organized by an alliance of trade unions, environmental groups, and NGOs. The People's Summit consisted of over a hundred workshops on everything from "Economics of the Canada-EU Free Trade Agreement" to "Activism in the Attawapiskat Nation."

Monday, June 21, saw the first protest, organized predominantly by a group of antipoverty activists from southern Ontario. Several hundred protesters marched – radical, angry, and loud – and the police carried out a handful of targeted arrests. One well-known Indigenous activist was arrested for holding a unity flag, while a leading anti-G20 organizer was arrested for "breaking and entering" her own place of work, with her own key, simply because the building was near the protest.

The following day witnessed a series of demonstrations on gender justice and queer rights. The actions were creative and lively: famous statues of military men were dressed in pink feather boas, while a public downtown "kiss-in" saw hundreds of queer people and their allies reclaiming the usually homophobic streets and startling nearby bankers through open displays of affection.

Wednesday, June 23, saw the biggest demonstration of the week up to this point, focusing on environmental and climate justice. Called the "Toxic Tour of Toronto," the protest snaked through the streets with its participants jeering various corporations that contribute to climate change. Although surrounded by police, the demonstration was jubilant, filled with music, drums, dancing, and face paint, and infused with optimism.

On Thursday, June 24, was the march for Indigenous sovereignty, led by Indigenous organizers and called by the cross-country Indigenous network Defenders of the Land. This demonstration was bigger again than the one the day before, and the tone was solemn and dignified. The police kept their distance.

Friday, June 25, was the community-led day of action organized under the banner "Justice for Our Communities." Led by local social movements, several thousand people demanded citizenship status for all migrants, an increase in welfare rates, Indigenous sovereignty, and more. Loud and angry, but without physical confrontation with the police, the march proceeded through the downtown core, ending in a block party. In the evening the party transformed into an overnight tent city, which stood until the morning as a visible demand for an end to homelessness in Toronto.

Saturday, June 26, was the day that all hell broke loose. The previous week of protest culminated in a demonstration with an attendance estimated at anywhere from ten thousand (according to police) to forty thousand (according to organizers) – in either case a truly massive turnout for Toronto. The march was called by a coalition of unions and NGOs under the banner "People First!" Starting at the Ontario legislature building at Queen's Park, the march circled through downtown and then returned to the park. During the march, an anti-capitalist and anti-colonial contingent (including a black bloc) broke away from the larger march and headed towards the security perimeter (the guarded fence encircling the summit), becoming increasingly confrontational as it went.[2] As the media widely reported, the police let this group of protesters proceed unhindered into the financial district, where several police vehicles left unattended in the middle of the deserted streets were vandalized and set on fire. The contingent continued through the downtown core, as some in the black bloc smashed windows of banks and stores (mainly of multinational corporations like Starbucks and the Gap), before disbanding.

Later that day, long after police had permitted the black bloc to disperse unchallenged, the police retribution began. Security forces attacked and arrested large numbers of protesters in peaceful demonstrations at Queen's Park and outside the Novotel Hotel, several kilometres away. That night, police raided the University of Toronto's Graduate Student Union and arrested approximately seventy activists, then arrested dozens more outside the temporary detention centre that had been set up in a film studio.

On Sunday, June 27, the militarized occupation of the city and the police violence continued. Hundreds of protesters and bystanders were "kettled" – trapped on all four sides by riot police – for hours in the pouring rain before being arrested en masse. A large segment of the city's radical left was in jail. Police were stopping everyone on the street who looked like they might be a protester; they circled the alternative media center as well as the convergence space. A handful of activists still free tried to organize a response to the police actions but since meeting in any public place would surely have led to more arrests, a telephone conference call was all they could manage.

Despite the difficulties of organizing while under threat of arrest, on Monday the twenty-eighth, a solidarity demonstration thousands strong marched through the streets of downtown Toronto, demanding the release of the jailed and an immediate inquest into police brutality. It was an inspiring day as thousands of people – including many who were arrested over the weekend and had just been released from temporary detention – managed to conquer their fear and come onto the streets once again to insist that they would not be silenced.

The Fallout

The massive demonstrations against the G20 ended amidst unprecedented police force and staggering repression. Over eleven hundred people were arrested during the weekend of June 25–27. Though all were treated atrociously, most were released within a day or two, and the vast majority were never charged or have since had their charges (largely bogus to begin with) entirely dropped. How can we explain the rationale behind the police actions, severe and disproportionate as they were? Clearly the arrests were a straightforward mechanism for temporarily removing protesters from the streets. Images, which flashed around the world, of young people dressed in black setting fire to police vehicles provided police with an excuse to clean the streets and engage in widespread brutality and flagrant abuses of civil liberties (though, as chapter 9 discusses, illegal police activity and harassment were widespread before the protests had begun). But the purpose of the police oppression went deeper than this. Almost a billion dollars had been spent on G20 security – a truly astronomical sum given that (as Smith and Cowen note in chapter 17) the London G20 summit of 2009 cost only US$30 million, while the security portion of the Pittsburgh summit later the same year cost only US$12.2 million. Indeed, the budget for Toronto's two-day summit was almost as high as Canada's entire annual budget for the Afghanistan war.[3] A large portion of the G20 security budget was dedicated to contracting with police departments across the country to supply officers, thereby amounting to an enormous, covert increase in federal security funding.[4] The federal government could not commit such enormous financial resources to summit security without a justification, which massive police actions on the streets helped provide.

But beyond justifying the security budget, the extensive police actions had a more important and far-reaching goal: silencing dissent. In the dark morning hours of Saturday, June 26, before the weekend of large demonstrations had even begun, the police kicked down the doors and burst into the homes of a handful of activists and arrested them. More activists were subsequently arrested as the week went on, and in the end twenty people were indicted as the so-called "ring leaders" of the black bloc protests and charged with conspiracy to commit indictable mischief, property damage, and assault of police. They face up to ten years in prison. Their legal fees are set to run to over a million dollars.

The one billion dollars in security spending did not just purchase the largest mass arrest in Canadian history, but also a massive and unprecedented clampdown on organizers and activists of the left. The twenty charged with conspiracy are some of the most well-known, respected, long-time social justice organizers in the country. With these people under house arrest, forbidden to go to meetings because of broad "non-association" conditions, and unable to engage in political organizing, the left suffers a serious blow. All twenty, it is worth noting, are involved in Indigenous solidarity work – likely a potent source of fear for the Canadian state. The threat of urban activists linking up with Indigenous communities in struggles for sovereignty and self-determination calls into question the foundation – and indeed the very legitimacy – of the Canadian state. Incredibly, two of the arrestees – one from Vancouver and the other from Montreal – were charged despite having no involvement with organizing protests in far-off Toronto. But this fact was clearly less relevant for the authorities than their prominence as radical social justice activists, their identity as people of colour, and their politics of being allies of Indigenous movements.

This is one of the legacies, then, of the G20 protests: the ongoing collective trauma suffered by progressive communities in Toronto and southern Ontario. In order to silence dissent, the police traumatized hundreds of activists and protesters – by intimidating, hurting, beating, and jailing them. The result is that, in the time since the G20, much activist energy in Toronto has been focused on recovery: recovery in emotional and psychological terms, but also in pragmatic terms, in the sense of providing legal support for those still facing charges. So the silencing of dissent continues in an indirect fashion as activists find themselves having to devote much of their time and energy to legal support and fundraising for allies facing charges – to the detriment of other desperately needed grassroots organizing and the continuation of their social justice endeavours.

This is why it is vital to maintain the momentum unleashed from the G20 protests. The major issues that galvanized people to take to the streets in June 2010 are still very much alive. Inequality in Canada has not stopped growing, austerity continues to threaten needed public services, and Indigenous populations are still ignored and subjugated across the country. The state repression that was unleashed upon the G20 demonstrations was an attempt to set a new precedent for the use of force in Canadian society – it is vital that it not be a successful attempt. Because, above all, the repression aims to silence dissent, above all, the resistance must refuse to be silent.

Before, During, and After the G20

Whose Streets? is divided into three parts, representing the three main goals of the book: sharing the lessons social justice activists learned from organizing a massive protest summit that other global justice activists might find useful; providing a first-hand account of what transpired during the days of action, so that the inspiring protests and appalling police brutality are not forgotten; and strengthening our collective resistance to austerity and global neo-liberalism by deepening our analysis of both the G20 itself and the social justice movements that oppose it.

Although the book contains a wide range of authors, clearly not every perspective is represented. Any collection inevitably contains omissions. We have attempted to minimize such omissions as much as possible by striving to include voices that reflect the diversity of the opposition to the G20. Every author is progressive, and each one was directly involved with the protests as an organizer, participant, or bystander, yet that is the extent of the common ground. Political perspectives range from social democratic to anarchist to Marxist. This book does not claim to represent "the left" in any comprehensive sense. We have simply tried to bring different critical perspectives into dialogue so that we can reflect and learn together. To this end, we have clustered chapters that deal with similar themes from different perspectives.

Part One focuses on the lead-up to the G20 convergence, collecting the experiences of activists responsible for organizing many of the protests in Toronto. These authors are at the forefront of building progressive social movements in southern Ontario, and here they discuss the work they did to organize the demonstrations, the challenges they faced, the mistakes they made, and the things they learned.

In chapter 1, Tom Malleson describes the work of the Toronto Community Mobilization Network, the umbrella group responsible for preparing the infrastructure for the protests. In chapter 2, Mac Scott of the Ontario Coalition Against Poverty discusses the trepidation felt by community-based organizers at mobilizing against an international summit. In chapter 3, Syed Hussan, an organizer with No One Is Illegal–Toronto, describes the central role of migrant justice activism in anti-G20 work, and details the heightened police repression that migrant justice organizers contend with on an ongoing basis. In chapter 4, Lisa Currier provides an Indigenous perspective on the organizing of the Indigenous sovereignty march. In the next two chapters, Archana Rampure, a current member of the Canadian Union of Public Employees (CUPE), and Jeff Shantz, a former member, discuss, from contrasting perspectives, labour's involvement in the G20 mobilizations and in the larger progressive movement. In chapter 7, Dan Kellar from the Alternative Media Centre reports on the role of alternative media as a counterbalance to corporate media during the G20 summit. Finally, in chapter 8, Monique Woolnough recounts her experience providing crisis support for the trauma that would emerge from the police repression.

Part Two moves from the pre-summit organizing to the demonstrations themselves, collecting stories from a range of people who experienced police violence first-hand. The raw and often heart-wrenching accounts in these chapters lay bare the visceral experiences of activists and bystanders who were harassed, beaten, shot with plastic bullets, arbitrarily arrested, and systematically mistreated and tormented by police in the temporary detention center. They document the fearsome spectacle of power without accountability.

Chapter 9 is a detailed account by legal workers of the Movement Defence Committee of the police and security forces' systematic violations of civil, political, and human rights during and leading up to the G20 summit. In chapter 10, Nat Gray tells a powerful and distressing story of being shot twice by plastic bullets while attending a peaceful demonstration, and of the dehumanizing experience of arrest and detention. Chapter 11, a first-hand description of the "cages" in the temporary detention centre, was written by David Wachsmuth several days after the conclusion of the G20 summit. In chapter 12, Sarah Pruyn recounts her own arrest and detainment and that of her father, John Pruyn, an above-the-knee amputee. She paints a bleak picture of the pervasive ableism of the Canadian government and Canadian society more generally. In chapter 13, Shailagh Keaney describes the arrest and atrocious treatment of a number of women protesting the G20, and uses their stories to construct an insightful analysis of policing strategies and their relationship to gender oppression. In chapter 14, Nicole Tanguay, a mixed-race Cree two-spirit woman, a poet, and an activist, recounts her experience of G20 policing in powerful poetic form. In chapter 15, Swathi Sekhar reflects on three interrelated experiences with carceral spaces – her exposure to Canadian immigration detention, working with a prison population in Malawi, and her own detention during the G20 protests – to illustrate the interconnections of the prison-industrial complex. Chapter 16 is an account by Elroy Yau, a transit employee who was on his way to work in full uniform when he was violently set upon by police and arrested. He describes the lasting physical and mental health trauma he has suffered as a result of his arbitrary arrest and thirty-six-hour detention.

The final section of the book, Part Three, takes a step back from the fray of the G20 protests to build our collective analysis for the future. Written by activists as well as scholars, these chapters situate the G20 protests and the state response within a national and global political-economic context in order to take stock of the progressive movement and analyze its prospects in an age of austerity.

In chapter 17, Neil Smith and Deborah Cowen connect the G20 in Toronto to global trends of neo-liberal capitalism and urban securitization. They place the police riot against protesters in the proper context of state power and the state's claimed monopoly over legitimate violence. Chapters 18 and 19 discuss the controversial questions of diversity of tactics and the black bloc. First, Tammy Kovich, through the lens of her own experience marching with the bloc, analyzes what we mean when we talk about activist "violence." This chapter provides a fascinating contrast with the next, in which Clarice Kuhling critiques black bloc tactics for their inability to build mass movements of working-class resistance. In chapter 20, Lesley Wood and Glenn Stalker use a survey they conducted of hundreds of participants in Toronto's G20 protests to challenge common assumptions about who protests and why, and they discuss the implications of their findings for grassroots activism. In chapter 21, Clare O'Connor critiques the central role that the concept of "community" played for G20 activists, calling for a less divisive means of addressing questions of diversity and privilege in social justice organizing. Finally, in chapter 22, David McNally analyzes the prospects for social protest during a global "age of austerity." He describes the growing gaps between the rich and poor, the explosive outbreaks of social protest, and the ever more repressive forms of policing that characterize such an age, and he asks how the left might move beyond this age of austerity and indeed beyond neo-liberalism itself.

Together these chapters provide an extensive overview and analysis of the G20 protests in Toronto. They depict ferocious state repression, which never manages to overshadow the hope and resolve of thousands of activists and demonstrators to show that a better world is indeed possible. The dedication of the organizers, tenacity of the protesters, and courage of the jailed, which these chapters document, is proof of such determination.

Part One

Before the G20

Organizing a Protest Convergence

1

Building a Protest Convergence
The Toronto Community Mobilization Network

Tom Malleson

DURING THE FOURTH WEEK OF JUNE 2010, TENS OF THOUSANDS OF people descended on downtown Toronto to demonstrate against the policies and politics of the G20. None of us who were there will ever forget our experience. For many, these days of protest marked an important beginning. For some this was the first large-scale demonstration they had attended and perhaps the event that awakened their political consciousness. Many residents of the city had their first exposure to brutal police repression. For seasoned activists, the Toronto G20 was the first major protest against post-crisis austerity measures. Yet for organizers of the Toronto Community Mobilization Network (TCMN), the G20 protests felt in some ways less like a beginning than an end: an end to the months of planning and work and to the anticipation of seeing all the organizing finally come together.[1]

For our resistance movements, though, the protests marked neither a beginning nor an end but were rather a visible manifestation of the ongoing process of building broad social movements. For an increasing number of left activists, our understanding of the political purpose of protests has changed. Instead of seeing protests as the focal point for our work – the aim of all our organizing – many of us see them as simply moments when our movement-building process crescendoes and becomes especially palpable. Protests are mirrors by which we can judge our strength, see how far we have come, and see how much work still needs to be done to expand our numbers and deepen our analysis. Protests are important – but it is the building process, rather than the protest itself, that is the crucial purpose of our organizing.

The Toronto Community Mobilization Network and the G20

It is easy to take it for granted that when international politicians decide to meet for summits like the G20 the demonstrations will just somehow happen – that the routes will be planned for marches, the speakers chosen for rallies, and so on. It is easy to miss the months of hard work that create a largely invisible infrastructure to support the demonstrations: the transport and sleeping arrangements for out-of-towners, the provision of regular meals, the preparation of a convergence space, the coordination of media events and press releases, the organization of medical practitioners to help the injured and legal workers to help those arrested, not to mention the coordination of various activist groups into an overarching plan that strives to balance the groups' autonomy with the overall collective goals. It was the job of the Toronto Community Mobilization Network to provide this infrastructure. We sought to provide the scaffolding, as it were, on which the protesters could mobilize and the resistance could be built.

The TCMN was born about six months prior to the G20 summit – initially proposed by activists already involved in grassroots organizing in the city (particularly in anti-poverty and migrant justice groups) who were organizing what would become the Friday, June 25, community-led day of action.[2] At the time, the hope was that the TCMN would evolve into a large coordinating body that would attract new volunteers to do the bulk of the enormous logistical work in order that those people already doing grassroots work would be able to keep doing what they do best: outreach and organizing in their communities. This was the right idea, but it didn't quite work out. Unfortunately, most of the logistical work and the fundraising was left to those grassroots activists.

The main purpose of the TCMN was to provide the infrastructure for the week of protests – the "days of action" leading up to the G20 summit. This meant organizing logistics (such as food and places to sleep), producing communications materials (such as media releases), coordinating the various demonstrations that would take place, and providing general outreach and education. We were an umbrella group – we would help organizations with their actions, but we would not be involved in the actual planning of specific actions or events ourselves. We didn't have a formal basis of unity but our implicit understanding was that we wanted our work in the TCMN to last beyond the week of the summit itself. We saw the G20 not as a self-contained event, but as a catalyst for us to galvanize our various movements.

The TCMN didn't have a platform or a shared political program. It was open to all. But it is probably fair to say that the majority of people involved were those sympathetic to building social movements as opposed to political parties. The general political perspective was anti-capitalist and anti-colonial. The core organizers (the people doing a lot of the day-to-day work) were generally, though not exclusively, anarchist or anti-authoritarian in their politics; there was very little direct involvement from sectarian socialists. The participants were not as diverse as we would have liked; the majority were in their 20s or 30s, mostly able-bodied, formally educated, and white (as Wood and Stalker show in chapter 20, this was representative of the overall G20 protest demographics). Such lack of diversity was not unique to the TCMN but reflects a problematic reality of the broader activist milieu in Toronto.

The question of how politically broad and inclusive a network like the TCMN should be is an important one. On the one hand, a greater breadth leads to the involvement of more people. On the other hand, the broader the membership, the more fractious and fractured the network is likely to become. Once the gap between political philosophies gets too large, the inevitable result is deadlock. Organizing gets bogged down by incommensurable political difference, debate turns into acrimony, old antagonisms flare, personalities clash, nothing gets done, and new people go from being excited to bewildered to appalled and soon leave altogether.

Leading up to the Toronto G20, there was a split from the start between the radical network of the TCMN and the social-democratic network of the People's Summit, which was led by unions, NGOs, and mainstream environmental groups and focused on organizing a weekend of talks, conferences, and workshops in a style similar to the world social forums. This division worked out to be a pretty good remedy for avoiding ideological squabbles without becoming overly fractured. It meant that both umbrella groups were able to move forward with good will between them.

Building a Protest Convergence

Building the TCMN from within the Anti-globalization Movement

The political purpose and strategy of the TCMN did not come out of a vacuum. The recent historical experience of the anti-globalization movement shaped our goals and aspirations. Our understanding of what protest convergences are, and what they should be, stemmed from what we had learnt from participating in a wide range of prior convergences – in particular the 1999 World Trade Organization protests in Seattle and the 2001 Free Trade Area of the Americas protests in Quebec City.

Protests in Seattle and Quebec City had taught us the dangers of summit hopping. You don't build movements by concentrating all your resources and energy on one short-lived event, after which everyone goes home. Summit hopping is an ineffective way to build lasting movements. It is also an inherently privileged form of activism, since the people most directly affected by the structures and institutions that protesters target cannot easily take time off to travel to protest. In many ways summit hopping can prove detrimental to long-term movement building as it often leaves local organizers facing criminal charges (with the resultant non-association conditions that hamstring organizing efforts, as well as the massive cost of legal fees) and local hostility from neighbourhoods affected by the protests.

Previous anti-globalization demonstrations had also failed to attract poor communities, Indigenous communities, and communities of colour into their ranks – thus calling into question some of the basic goals of the organizing. So the TCMN was intent on using the G20 not as a venue for summit hopping, but as a springboard for widespread outreach and education throughout the city. We were determined to take direction from active social movements, and, as much as possible, from people directly affected by G20 policies.

Since accessibility is also a consistent weak point for many social justice movements, the TCMN aimed to help protest organizers improve access to their events by providing important resources such as ASL interpreters, childcare, peer support, and wheelchair-accessible spaces. We created clear policies about racism and sexual assault.

In addition to the lessons we learned from the Seattle and Quebec City convergences, were those learned from the more recent experiences of demonstrations against the North American security summit in Montebello in 2007, the G20 summit in Pittsburgh in 2009, and the Olympics in Vancouver in 2010. These mass protests led many of us to realize that in critiquing summit hopping we had swung too far in the other direction. People weren't coming out to demonstrations in the same numbers anymore. It had become fashionable for activists to disregard large summits and remain focused entirely on their own work in their own field. In some ways the movement had shot itself in the foot: many older activists who themselves were radicalized at summits were now dissuading younger activists from going. As a result, we now have a generation of young activists (who make up the majority of activists because we are a youthful movement) who have no summit protest experience to draw on. These activists have heard the arguments for eschewing large summits, but they've missed the many benefits that can come from mass protest experience.

Firstly, Canada is a huge land mass with a small population. Large summits allow rural activists, and others who feel isolated, to meet each other, work together on issues, and build relationships. Overcoming isolation is especially vital at a time when pessimism is so widespread in progressive circles. Secondly, being on the streets with huge numbers of like-minded people – a vitally radicalizing and empowering experience – is not generally possible in Canada without these kinds of summits. Witnessing first-hand this show of massive solidarity along with police repression is often a paradigm-shifting experience. It is a common phenomenon for young people to go to summits as social democrats only to be intimidated, harassed, pepper sprayed, and tear gassed by the police, and end up leaving as anti-capitalists. Finally, these summits are important because they remind us that the left is alive and vibrant. They solidify the left as a real political force – one that the media must recognize (even as it distorts) and that politicians must negotiate with. All of this is to say that social justice organizers should take a balanced view of summit hopping: instead of simply abandoning summits, we should build for them and, most importantly, use them as launch pads for further community organizing.

Nuts and Bolts

Anyone who has been involved with the organizing of a mass convergence or counter-summit can attest to the enormous amount of work that is required. Months of organizing, often with three meetings a day, culminate in twelve-hour working days before the protests even begin. And although the organizing takes months of effort, the summits themselves typically last only seventy-two hours – sometimes even less. This leaves many wondering if the effort is worthwhile. Are our movements stronger after the convergence is over? Overall, I believe that progressive movements in Toronto have been strengthened through organizing for the G20 summit – as some of the following chapters attest – though we are not left without bruises, or regrets about what we might have done better. A review of the TCMN's organizing work – both what we did well and what we did poorly – can perhaps offer some lessons for other activists.

Basic Structure

Most of the work and the decision-making of the TCMN was done through a group of committees (logistics, education-and-outreach, communications, fundraising, art, action), which were open to anyone to join. Monthly general network meetings, open to the public, provided information-sharing and feedback about what the committees were doing, however, these network meetings were not for decision-making. This structure was not perfect, but given our time frame and the coalition nature of the group, it worked quite well. All large groups with a commitment to radical politics have to figure out how to negotiate the tension between wanting maximum democracy, participation, and accountability, on the one hand, while recognizing, on the other hand, that it is practically impossible to make concrete decisions and allocate work in meetings with a hundred or more people. To actually get the organizing started we empowered committees to make decisions, reasoning that since committee membership was open this structure maintained an acceptable level of internal democratic participation.

In addition, two other levels of meetings developed: joint committee meetings to coordinate between committees, and teams for doing concrete jobs, for instance, postering in various neighbourhoods. The purpose of the teams was to provide an "in" for people who wanted to do some work but didn't want to be part of the organizing or go to all the meetings. Although summits in different cities will want to organize their structure slightly differently, in general it's a good principle to create different levels of possible involvement so that students, workers, parents, and others with difficult schedules can find a way to get involved. Outside the TCMN structure, but closely aligned, were three important additional groups: medics, alternative media, and legal support (see chapters 7–9 for more about organizing these groups).

TCMN Structure

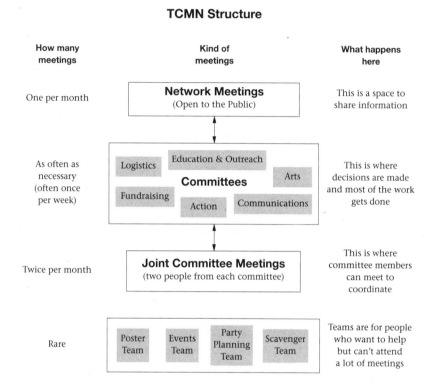

Lessons Learned

Many of the details of the TCMN's organizing were specific to the Toronto G20, but a number of general lessons that we learned might benefit other activists.

First, despite our original hopes, we learned that *organizing a convergence will inevitably drain energy away from ongoing grassroots organizing.* The last thing we wanted was the city's ongoing social movement organizers to have to stop their work and focus on planning events, finding hundreds of sleeping bags, cooking mass meals, organizing buses, and so on. The problem was that we could not simply will into existence a whole new group of activists to take on these logistical tasks. Most of the people who stepped up to do this work for the TCMN were the grassroots organizers themselves. As much as local grassroots organizations may want to avoid pouring their energy into summit infrastructure work, the reality is that when new organizing in a city needs to happen, nine out of ten times it will be accomplished by activists already engaged on the ground.

Second, *committees tend to ossify*, so organizers need to develop ways to move people power around. This is an important issue that we did not recognize at the beginning. The problem was that people initially joined whichever committee they were most interested in but, after going to meetings with the same people for a couple of months, relationships were formed, acquaintances became comrades, and people developed knowledge about their particular committee. This meant that when it became clear that some committees had too few members and others too many it was very hard to shift people around – the committees had ossified. This made us inflexible and created bottlenecks in our organizing because there were no established ways to shift resources around.

Third, *organizers should assume that police are everywhere*. As the dust settles in Toronto it is clear that we had police informants in many of the committees (and probably many more we don't know about). Some that we now know of were involved in activist circles for a year or more before the G20. They were skilled at manipulating our sensitivities. One informant's cover for not talking about her history was her claim that she had escaped an abusive male partner. Another informant – an older, racialized Muslim man – was unchallenged by younger activists who felt uncomfortable questioning his identity. Our movement is rightly respectful of different people's lived experiences, and the cops take advantage of this. There is probably little we can do about this trap, except to be aware that it happens and try to prevent our paranoia from undermining our democratic openness.

Fourth, *all work should, as much as possible, build beyond the summit*. Part of the inherent difficulty of organizing summit protests is that it takes enormous amounts of time and energy – often many meetings a day for weeks on end. This tends to create a tidal wave of pressure to just focus on the immediate tasks at hand. So although the organizing starts with noble declarations about building beyond the summit, in practice this can easily fall apart under the sheer weight of the immediate logistical tasks. This means that one needs to take special care to establish mechanisms to prevent people from losing sight of longer term goals, for instance, by insisting that committees frequently ask themselves, "how is this work going to last beyond the summit?"

Finally, *the most important way to build beyond the summit is to focus on education and outreach.* Summits of the world's elite do not come around very often, so they present a rare opportunity for activists to draw links between global structures of capitalism and local manifestations of power, privilege, and exclusion. They are unique consciousness-raising moments. Educating the public should always be where the bulk of our energy goes. This means organizing public forums and community discussions all over the city. If this means running the risk that some of the logistical work falls short, so be it. Making sure the organized protests go off successfully is important, but it should not be the ultimate goal. Every protest is like the tip of an iceberg – it looks impressive, but its real power comes from the weight and solidity under the surface, from the people who are knowledgeable and passionate about the issues, who constitute the movement itself.

Convergence Space

For many activists in Toronto, and nearly all of the out-of-towners, the TCMN convergence space served as a focal point for activists to come together and a home for much of the resistance. It was a fantastic space, and one of the most successful aspects of the summit. For two weeks, this rented building in Parkdale (a low-income, west Toronto neighbourhood) was transformed into the home, office, and nerve centre of the TCMN's organizing. The convergence space created an atmosphere of solidarity and camaraderie. It was an inspiring political space in its own right, hosting a community (albeit temporary) that acted as a microcosm of the just society we all long for. The space was autonomous, accessible, off limits to police and media, and run on principles of mutual aid and self-determination. People worked together, cleaned up after themselves, removed the gender-specific washrooms, cooked together, made art together, watched each other's backs, and in millions of tiny ways built solidarity in place of the usual antagonism and bitterness of everyday life.

Respect for a Diversity of Tactics

The well-known Monty Python skit showing a feud between the "People's Front of Judea" and the "Judean People's Front" is a funny way of making a serious point: political denunciations between progressive groups are as old as political life itself. Mindful of this, and recognizing that the TCMN existed to facilitate all kinds of actions, a couple of months before the protests we produced a statement of "solidarity and respect,"[3] which defined the TCMN as a network that recognized and respected a diversity of tactics. Respect for a diversity of tactics absolutely does not imply that all tactics are good tactics, or that more confrontational tactics are necessarily better than more peaceful ones, or that people should be in any way forbidden from debating which tactics are best. The point is only that certain tactics – particularly around questions of violence and property destruction – bring up fundamental disagreements within the left: disagreements that have existed for decades, if not centuries, and are not going away any time soon. Our position was that it is healthier to respect different positions on this issue, to debate the question of strategy and tactics amongst ourselves as vigorously as ever, but not to carry that debate over into the mainstream media or to the police, since the public airing of denunciations can only serve to weaken us.

Unfortunately, our statement of respect and solidarity led to controversy, anger, and infighting in the TCMN, particularly from a handful of committed and principled pacifists, who felt very strongly about their opposition to a diversity of tactics. Whether property destruction constitutes violence and should therefore be condemned is a fundamentally divisive question for the left (see chapters 18 and 19 for more discussion of this difficult question) and one that summit organizers must negotiate. I believe that organizers need to be realistic about how controversial a statement of solidarity and respect is, but they should nevertheless try to encourage the widest possible support for organizing within such a framework. For hundreds of years the left has been poisoned by a sense of absolute rightness, verging on ecclesiasticism, which says that I am absolutely right and you are therefore fundamentally wrong, deviant, or reactionary. Too much of our political history is a history of modernist certainty and dogmatism, of the belief that if only I can get you to read this chapter of Lenin, or that book by Gandhi, you will see the light and join my position. Our movements need to move beyond this stubbornness. We need to strive for political maturity: that means having the humility to acknowledge that we don't know everything, and that those we think are wrong are not therefore inferior or stupid, just different in their evaluation of the facts. We must learn to live with the pluralism and dissent that comes with this, and accept the inevitable messiness of building unity from this diversity.

Coordinating Days of Action

The TCMN did not organize any actions itself. Rather, we established a framework within which actions could be organized and coordinated and we provided some of the infrastructure. We helped to set themed days of action, and published information on what other groups were planning, thus allowing like-minded groups to cluster around issues. This transparency allowed for exciting cross-pollination between activist groups, as well as a respect for a diversity of tactics – the antic- ipated risk levels of different actions were made available, allowing individuals and groups to plan whether to take part or not, reducing the risk of anyone finding themselves in a situation that was much riskier than they had intended.

Building a Protest Convergence

Are Convergences Useful?

Now that some time has passed since the tumult of the protests, we have a little more perspective on the value of organizing the conver gence. We are able to consider whether or not building temporary networks such as the TCMN, oriented around short-lived summits such as the G20, is a useful endeavour for today's social justice move- ments. We can ask whether or not these experiences make us stronger.

In the end, I think that the movement in Toronto *is* stronger for having organized the G20 protests and that our work was worth the effort. One of the biggest rewards of organizing in this fashion is the relationships built in the process. Strangers become friends, and in politicized spaces, such as meetings, demos, or the convergence space, such friendship can bloom into comradeship – that wonderful sense of affinity fused with alliance that comes from working together with like-minded people in common purpose, which gives so much mean- ing to our struggles, indeed, to our lives. The months of intense coop- eration leading up to the G20 have produced a wave of activists with new skills, knowledge, and personal connections. There is no doubt that this kind of organizing swallows endless hours and energy, and thus activists risk burnout and distraction from day-to-day community organizing. That said, the TCMN managed to bring some new people into the local social justice movement, energize seasoned activists, radicalize people, foster networks, build alliances, increase our knowledge, improve our skills, and strengthen our resolve. All in all, we came out stronger.

It seems to me that the critical lesson from this experience is that there are two basic ways to approach organizing mass protest convergences. The usual approach is to organize actions for the summit itself. This takes a huge amount of energy and the results of the actions are forgotten soon after, leaving people burnt out and the movement no stronger. The better approach is to organize around pressing social justice issues and connect them to the summit – to use the summit as a springboard for advancing local struggles. If organizers expend the bulk of their energy this way, empowering people to connect the G20 to their own lives in their own neighbourhoods, such effort will undoubtedly pay off.

2

Community Organizing for a Global Protest

Mac Scott

WHEN WE FIRST HEARD THE NEWS THAT THE G20 SUMMIT WOULD BE held in Toronto in 2010, members of the Ontario Coalition Against Poverty (OCAP) saw potential. The G8 and G20 leaders meet to organize and enforce their austerity regime, pushing the cost of the economic collapse onto poor people, working people, and particularly people in the Global South. OCAP members organize to fight this austerity every day. We see austerity when people are told that they cannot have an extra $200 from social services to feed their children, when people are told that there are no more beds at a shelter, when a person is told that they cannot move out of a collapsing apartment owned by 'public' housing. With the upcoming G20 summit we saw a chance to give the issues we deal with locally a much bigger profile, but also, more importantly, to empower our constituency through mass militant mobilization.

The Ontario Coalition Against Poverty is a poor people's organization (though not all of us are poor), formed in 1990 after a caravan crossed Ontario to fight for poor people's rights. Originally a cross-Ontario coalition, we are now solidly Toronto-based, but unable to abandon our name. We are anti-capitalist and we organize using direct action, in particular direct action casework, to help people gain material benefits. (Once, twenty angry members went to a welfare office to demand that a member get her welfare cheque.) This model of organizing has become influential, and other "CAPs" have spread across the country and even further; there is now an LCAP in London, England, set up after one of our members visited a few years ago. Our main campaign around the time leading up to the G20 summit was one that focused on saving the Special Diet Allowance, a program which allows people an extra $200 to $300 on their welfare cheques if they can show they need it to meet their medical or health needs. OCAP members worked with another local group, Health Providers Against Poverty, to sign up tens of thousands of people for the program knowing that no one can live a healthy life on a welfare cheque in Toronto (cheques for single people are capped at $593, while renting an average bachelor apartment in the city costs around $700 a month).

So it made sense for OCAP members to see the G20 summit as an opportunity to link our local austerity problems to the global villains responsible. But at first we were apprehensive. More than a year before the Toronto G20 summit, local community activists called a meeting to start planning for the protests. The meetings were well attended, but the room was mostly white and mostly young, with fewer community organizers than we expected. Activists there were confused. We failed to reach conclusions. And the coalition to organize for the summit protests? Well, I hesitate to say it fell apart, but there were no more meetings for a while.

Some of the same debates I'd come across in my summit protest experiences a decade ago held us up again. The question of "diversity of tactics" was a sore spot for many, but the old "summit hopping" question was the big one for OCAP. It is funny how the same debates dog our movements time and time again. In some ways it's good; it means we're really trying to think about and deal with the hard questions. In some ways it's frustrating – it feels like we aren't moving forward.

Now, I'm an old man. I was already an old codger when the Free Trade Area of the Americas (FTAA) protests were organized in Quebec City in 2001 but I remember that the debate about summit hopping was already a contentious one at that time. At one point, Quebec organizers toured eastern Canada, telling people to organize at home rather than come en masse to Quebec City. People were concerned about the sapping of local campaigns and the drain on community organizations as their energy went into arranging accommodations for activists in town for the FTAA protests. Serious questions were raised about the racial and class makeup of the protests, and about issues of homophobia, sexism, and ableism in the organizing (not to mention the very real concerns about sexual harassment and assault at such large-scale gatherings).[1] Activists worried about the serious damage that the police would inflict on community organizations, organizers, and the movement in general during the protests and afterwards.

These were the same questions behind our trepidation leading up the G20 demonstrations in Toronto. OCAP members were worried because we had faced significant repression after we organized a large, militant demo against the neo-conservative provincial government in June 2000. Several of our organizers were charged and their legal battles went on for years; this took a lot out of the organization. We are not a huge organization and in the run-up to the G20 our campaign around welfare rates was taking a lot of our energy. We were hesitant to commit too much to a protest that we felt would not give back as much as it took out of us.

Other community organizations had similar concerns, as well as justifiable worries about what the messaging and politics of the mobilizations would be. These groups (including OCAP) wanted the mobilizations to be solidly anti-capitalist, anti-imperialist, anti-sexist, for queer rights and gender justice, for environmental justice, and against ableism. So we came together to build an organizing body that would be solidly community-based and the Toronto Community Mobilization Network (TCMN) was created. Apparently, it's now considered a criminal organization so we must've done something right.

Hesitantly at first, we sent reps (including myself) to the TCMN meetings to organize a community-based day during the summit. We joined with No One Is Illegal, DAMN 2025 (a direct action disability rights organization), a group of organizers who would later found Environmental Justice Toronto, Jane Finch Action Against Poverty (a community group based in a poor neighbourhood in Toronto that has been a historic target for racist policing), and many others. We agreed on a list of demands that were locally based, we linked them to the policies and structures of the G20, and we came up with demonstrations that hit local targets: police headquarters to protest racial profiling and police harassment in poor communities and communities of colour; a welfare office that dealt with people on the Ontario Disability Support Program; and an inaccessible transit station. We would end with a tent city in Allan Gardens, a park that has been a historic site of struggle for poor and homeless people. We did our best to make the demonstrations accessible (although we made mistakes); activists from DAMN led the organizing for the day, and we built great alliances with the gender justice activists who organized their own fantastic action on June 22.

As the summit date drew closer, and the police moved to socially cleanse Toronto in preparation for the arrival of the world's rich and powerful, OCAP members were barred from stores and quietly (though usually not gently) encouraged to leave town. We distributed a flyer explaining the links between welfare cuts, cuts to shelters, increased policing of poor communities, and the austerity agenda of the G20.

When the community day of action came on Friday, June 25, the demonstration was huge – much bigger than we expected. We had planned for approximately 1,500 people but four times that many came. We didn't have enough marshals. It was also horribly over-policed. Lines of riot squads met us every time the march tried to get closer to the summit site, which wasn't even in use yet. We disagreed about how militant our response should be. Many of the pre-planned targets were behind the police lines and had to be abandoned. A deaf member of the demonstration was surrounded and severely beaten (in typical police brilliance, even when they were told he was deaf, the police attacked him when he didn't hear their orders, and attempts made to defend and support him were met with violence). In the end, we pulled back and set up our tent city.

The tent city demonstration was a great success. It was much bigger than expected and many OCAP members and constituents played a central part. Later in the evening, activists who had attended speeches by Maude Barlow, Clayton Thomas-Muller, and Naomi Klein marched from the University of Toronto campus to join us. It was a beautiful moment of alliance building.

The next morning we woke up to the news of pre-emptive arrests for conspiracy charges, an early taste of a day that would be at times euphoric and sometimes terrifying. By the time forty-eight hours had passed, we had seen one of the largest militant mobilizations in Toronto's history, along with the largest mass arrest in Canadian history.

In the End

So, now that it's over we're left asking if the Toronto G20 summit protests were worthwhile for OCAP and other community activist groups. Have we solved the debate that pits summit hoppers against community organizers? I don't know, for the life of me – smarter people will have to figure that out.

I do know that some incredibly skilled and experienced organizers, including many who come from backgrounds of poverty, became new OCAP members.

I also know that in the aftermath of the summit, many of our constituents were targeted when the police picked up people for alleged property damage. The police held one of our members for months before they realized they had the wrong person. Though police did not press charges against any OCAP organizers, dozens of organizers in student groups, from union backgrounds, and from Indigenous solidarity groups face serious conspiracy charges and have only recently been allowed out of house arrest.

That said, the fragile little coalition that organized the community day of action has held. Together we have organized demonstrations against Toronto's new right-wing mayor, Rob Ford. Together we worked to organize a demonstration and march for the March 15 International Day Against Police Brutality. We fight; we disagree; but for the first time in the thirteen years I've been with OCAP, we are part of a diverse coalition with other groups with similar politics working on very different issues (I have never known us to work with environmental justice groups before). It's change. It's difficult. I don't know that the coalition will last. But I think this may be the most positive thing that can come out of these summits for community organizations – it has forced us to adapt, to work with new communities and new people. It has forced us to look at our tactics differently. It is uncomfortable. It is hard. At times it is frankly terrifying (particularly because of the state's response). But it is positive change. And that's what we're fighting for, isn't it?

No One Is Illegal demonstrator near King St. and Bay St., June 26, 2010. Photo by Don Toye.

3

Collective Movement, Collective Power
People of Colour, Migrant Justice, and the G20

Syed Hussan

A SON AND GRANDSON OF DISPLACED MIGRANTS, I'VE LIVED IN
Toronto on Turtle Island (the Anishinabe name for North America) for
four years – first on a work permit, and for the last year without immigration status. I am an organizer with the Toronto chapter of the
migrant justice group No One Is Illegal (NOII) and a supporter of
Indigenous sovereignty, anti-war, and environmental justice movements.[1]

On the morning of June 26, 2010, after helping pack up after the
Allan Gardens tent city protest, I climbed into a cab and headed for a
press conference. Suddenly, two unmarked vans pulled up on either
side of the cab. Eight or so men jumped out of the vans; a couple of
them pulled me out of the cab and hit me on the head before tossing
me into one of the vans. As I lay on the floor of the van, a burly man
sitting on top of me told me that I had been arrested. Meanwhile, as I
was on my way to the specially constructed detention centre, police
yanked another NOII organizer, Farrah Miranda, out of her cab, and
drove her around the city for forty-five minutes before dumping her
at the side of the road. That day police also arrested, harassed, and
abused NOII organizers from Montreal and Vancouver.[2] By the end of
the day, police had beaten seven other NOII organizers, leaving two of
them with serious concussions and one with a broken hand. Later, I
learned that this was part of a broader police attack in which over
eleven hundred people were arrested and thousands were arbitrarily
searched, beaten, harassed, or intimidated.

Since my release (charged with three counts of conspiracy and two
counts of counselling to commit an indictable offence), I've been subjected to ongoing police surveillance and harassment, sometimes bor-

dering on the absurd. On a warm day the following winter, I was walking with a friend when a police car drove by. The officer in the passenger seat flashed me a handwritten sign that read, "House Arrest" and they followed me for a block. A number of times, police officers have called my name as I walked down the street and, once, as I sat outside a café in Kensington market, two police officers rolled up on their bikes, pointed at me, and yelled, "G20!" These calculated attempts to scare me, like the bail conditions placed on me and other activists – stipulating house arrest, disallowing access to mobile communication devices, and prohibiting protest organizing and participation – are meant to intimidate activists and stifle political organizing.

Soon after my arrest, Citizenship and Immigration Canada rejected my work permit application and initiated deportation proceedings, which were later deemed illegal. An Access to Information request revealed that copies of *National Post* newspaper articles that describe my G20 protest participation had been added to my Immigration Enforcement file – a clear effort by the police or Crown attorneys to increase the likelihood of my deportation. Only immense public pressure forced the Canada Border Services Agency to delay the deportation proceedings and pushed immigration authorities to issue me a year-long study permit. If convicted on my G20 charges, however, I face deportation. I've spent the last year living in a state of fear, uncertain about my future, constantly looking over my shoulder.

But my experience of state repression is far from unique. The brutal behaviour of police during the G20 was not uncharacteristic – it was just more visible. Collusion between the police and Immigration Enforcement, along with police violence, is a part of the every day experience of residents of Jane and Finch, Rexdale, Davenport-Perth, Parkdale, Lawrence Heights, and other racialized and poor communities in Toronto. The police use the facade of migrant illegality to divide people by pitting citizens against so-called illegal immigrants: encouraging some to become informants, pressuring others to remain docile, and jailing many for trying to survive. Using sensational language, stereotypes, and the cooperation of the mainstream media, the police are able to create a sense of heightened insecurity in Toronto: they characterize particular neighbourhoods in the city as violent and follow up with immense repression. Police repression in these neighbourhoods, like the repression of activist communities, silences dissent.

Refusing to be Passive

No One Is Illegal–Toronto is part of a growing movement of migrant justice organizers who work directly with undocumented people and migrant workers and will not be silenced. Together, we refuse to allow the Canadian government – a colonial power – to continue its work unchallenged. We insist that a settler state has no moral authority to impose immigration restrictions. (For example, NOII–Toronto has worked closely with two undocumented men, Daniel Garcia and Alvaro Orozco, who police stopped on the street – in a clear case of racial profiling – and then handed over to Immigration Enforcement. Although mass mobilizations forced the release of Alvaro Orozco, who was then granted status, Daniel Garcia was deported.)

In stopping people's deportations, in fighting for access for migrants to basic services such as education and healthcare, we challenge the very notion of citizenship. In questioning Canada's role in displacement, and in asserting freedom of movement, we create a radical politics that has increasingly become a threat to the Canadian state and its bureaucrats. Part of our organizing model demands that people of colour – and especially women and trans folk of colour – are foregrounded as decision makers and spokespeople. We build alliances and coalitions with grassroots community organizations, believing that none of us can win until all of us win.

Our fight is based locally but it is a global struggle against imperialism, colonization, capitalism, racism, patriarchy, homophobia, transphobia, and ableism. As one part of this worldwide struggle for justice, the migrant justice movement claims for all people: freedom to move, freedom to return, and freedom to stay. To make these three freedoms possible, all the conditions that force people to move – wars, economic inequities, environmental catastrophe, patriarchy, gender violence, homo/transphobia, and ableism – must end. Exclusionary immigration systems must be dismantled. Everyone must have access to education, healthcare, food, livelihood, justice, and dignity. This is an ambitious agenda, and rarely are activists presented with the opportunity to bring all these issues to the public's attention. The G8 and G20 summits provided such an opportunity.

Decisions made by the G20 leaders and their corporate conspirators have a concrete impact on migrants in Canada. As a NOII statement put out before the G20 summit pointed out, "the G8 and G20 countries and their corporations make most of the weapons on the planet, profit from war, subsidize oil corporations and massive industrial projects, and are responsible for pushing millions out of their homes each year. Migrants arriving in G20 countries are treated as exploitable labour – fenced in to precarious work – and often living in fear of detention and deportation."[3] Migrants from around the world come to Canada vying for permanent status; many are denied. Over three hundred thousand migrants without full immigration status work as temporary workers. Nearly half a million live without any status at all – often invisible and without rights.

No Fences, No Borders: Migrant Justice at the G20

For a year and a half leading up to the summit, for long hours on Wednesday nights, dozens of NOII–Toronto organizers argued about what our part should be in the G20 protest convergence. Echoing discussions happening all over Toronto, we asked ourselves Elizabeth (Betita) Martinez's widely asked question, "Where was the colour in Seattle?"[4] We wondered if the Toronto summit protests would be different somehow or would reflect the same lack of diversity. We asked ourselves if it was possible to ensure that all movements could have equal power in the organizing. We worried that organizing for the summit protests would limit community organizing, and we questioned the real and symbolic impact our protest participation might have on our long-term political work.

Based on our organizing practices, and inspired by the Root Cause marches that took place before the 2003 FTAA Summit in Miami, we decided that for us the anti-G20 convergence would be not only about the G20 but also about building community power – it would be about movement building (one of the key principles of NOII organizing). It would be a chance to get as many of Toronto's progressive organizations as possible to work together, to create real alliances. Only through working together on real projects, we concluded, would we be able to truly build meaningful relations between activists in our city.

So NOII, along with members of the Ontario Coalition Against Poverty and Indigenous sovereignty activists, began to reach out to radical community organizations across the city, giving presentations, releasing statements, and asking people to attend meetings to help shape the mobilizations. This work brought migrant justice organizers into conversation with the anti-globalization, anti-capitalist, and anarchist activists who usually initiate calls for summit protests. Together with anti-poverty, environmental justice, trade union, and Indigenous sovereignty activists, we formed the Toronto Community Mobilization Network (TCMN). In breaking from past practice of anti-summit organizing, organizers established the TCMN as an infrastructure and logistics hub that was meant to leave community organizations free to continue doing the work that they do best – organizing in poor and racialized communities. This network of community organizations, affinity groups, and individual activists developed a story of the anti-G20 protests, as Lesley Wood puts it, that was about collective community organization.[5] Some community organizations that were involved in the initial, formative stage of the TCMN stepped out soon after – some because they became involved in organizing the demonstrations themselves, others because they felt that their ongoing local campaigns would be weakened by participation in the anti-G20 convergence. In February, in an attempt to broaden the participation of community organizations in the anti-G20 organizing, members of No One Is Illegal emailed thirty-five community organizations in Toronto, inviting them to join the organization efforts for the days of resistance (June 21–24) and the days of action (June 25–27). These groups had at some point been involved in discussions about the anti-G20 convergence but four months before the summit was set to begin many of them were absent. In our message we explained that we shared the concerns of many others:

> . . . there is little space for local communities of colour and Indigenous peoples, of poor and working people, of queer folk, of disabled people to exert power. Many are unsure that there is resonance against the G8/20 in the places we organize in. We at NOII share these same concerns. We know that each time there are large mobilizations anywhere in the world, they sidestep local demands and become about the 'big' things. We believe that if enough of us work together we can change that, this year, here in Toronto.[6]

In response to the email, a few new organizations took up organizing for specific days of action. Many did not, largely, I suspect, because the structure of channelling resource-intensive logistical work through the TCMN in order to leave community groups to focus on popular education and mobilizing their constituencies was something that had not been tried before.

Nevertheless, along with other community organizations in the city, dozens of members of NOII (myself included) were involved in organizing the legal support, the street medic response, and the logistics for the anti-G20 mobilization. NOII–Toronto organizers were also involved with the demonstration for queer liberation and gender justice. Our members were out in force for the Toxic Tour of Toronto, challenging Canadian complicity in environmental displacement. Along with thousands of others, we marched for Indigenous sovereignty under the banner "Canada Can't Hide Genocide." On June 25, NOII members joined over five thousand people who marched in a demonstration for "Justice for Our Communities," setting up a tent city to connect homelessness here with displacement the world over. The next day (as I sat in jail), NOII activists marched with the "People First!" labour demonstration, and then, along with hundreds of other protesters, we were part of three different break-offs to push towards the summit security perimeter and through the banking district. On Sunday, June 27, amidst massive police crackdowns and rumours of snatch squads and police raids flying through the city, many people went into hiding. At around 3:00 a.m., community organizers put out a call for an anti-police demonstration and by noon over three thousand people, including NOII members, had gathered outside the Toronto Police Headquarters to protest against police brutality and repression.

Where Was the Colour in Toronto?

Despite our earlier concerns about the diversity of the convergence protests, as the anti-G20 demonstrations hit the city, migrants, people of colour, Indigenous people, and many Toronto residents took to the streets collectively. Though the mainstream media completely whitewashed the anti-G20 convergence (note, for example, the February 2011 CBC *Fifth Estate* documentary on the G20 protests, "You Should Have Stayed At Home," in which four white men and a white woman are the only people interviewed), the Toronto mobilizations were organized on anti-colonial, anti-racist principles with people of colour and Indigenous people in decision-making roles and thousands of people of colour participating in the demonstrations.

Across the city, activists and community members, including many poor people and people of colour, responded to the violence and intimidation of the police with acts of resistance, solidarity, and autonomy. Though much of the public discussion about the Toronto G20 protests has been about police repression, stories about how people from diverse communities stood up to this brutal expression of state power are rarely told. Though the early morning police raid at the University of Toronto's Graduate Student Union building and the arrest there of seventy sleepy Quebec activists made headlines in the mainstream media, few heard the story of the foiled police attempt to raid a Regent Park community centre, where, as activists slept, volunteers and staff barred police from entering. When police raided the convergence centre, a community worker offered shelter in her workplace to targeted activists. When police tried to snatch organizers and activists off the streets, groups of demonstrators, some dressed in black and others not, de-arrested people, pulling them out of police clutches. The Toronto street medics treated hundreds of people for injuries ranging from broken bones to cracked heads to eyes filled with pepper spray. Immigrant women and children (some with precarious status) refused to be intimidated, showing their solidarity with detainees in the temporary detention centre by coming en masse to jail solidarity rallies and staying despite rubber bullets and tear gas. A week after the summit ended, Mayor David Miller watched from the audience, embarrassed and unsure of how to respond, while a youth theatre troupe – composed entirely of youth of colour from Jane and Finch – denounced his brazen support of the violence perpetrated by the Toronto police.

After the summit protests ended, in many circles, organizing turned to agitation for a public inquiry into police abuse. For the most part, this work – much of it done by people who were not involved in the pre-summit organizing – lacks an anti-colonial, anti-racist analysis and presents police violence as an aberration rather than the norm. Such storytelling disrespects the communities of colour for whom police repression is familiar and the violence inflicted by G20 policies is a daily reality.

What's more, the participation of people of colour, Indigenous people, and marginalized communities in summit organizing and street demonstrations is clearly not enough to change the perception of who activists are. Though most video footage and photos of the protests show diverse community participation, the mainstream media's rhetoric of the demonstrations as a show of force by "good, middle-class, white kids" serves to delegitimize and silence the voices of grassroots people of colour.

Nevertheless, in neighbourhoods across Toronto, people have not forgotten the brutal police violence or the undeniable state repression that they saw during the G20. Many residents have made the connections between the G20 and their own communities and now see the urgent need for transformative social and political change. This opportunity will not be squandered. A new wave of anti-austerity organizing in the city (like that being done by the Toronto Stop the Cuts Network) has already begun the fight against policies concocted at the G20 summit. In this struggle and others, people of colour continue to lead and support collective movements to create collective power.

4

"Canada Can't Hide Genocide"

Marching for Indigenous Rights

Lisa Currier

ON JUNE 24, 2010, AS POLICE FORTIFIED THE CITY FOR THE UPCOM-
ing G20 summit, three thousand Native rights activists took over the
streets of downtown Toronto and marched in the Indigenous Day of
Action – the largest Indigenous rights protest in Canadian history. We
marched to tell the world that Indigenous peoples in Canada continue to suffer, that living conditions have not improved in recent
years, and that funding for Aboriginal communities continues to
shrink as government austerity measures target Canada's most
marginalized group. We marched because, while Canada consistently
ranks in the top ten countries on the UN's Human Development
Index, if Canada's First Nations communities were ranked on this
index their deplorable living conditions would place them closer to
forty-fifth worldwide.[1] In response to the repression and brutality of
the world's most powerful nations, we marched to claim the inherent
rights of our own sovereign and distinct Indigenous nations.

Indigenous resistance during the summit protests focused on the
impact of G20 economic, social, political, and environmental policies
on Indigenous people. We spoke up about the racist legislation and
systemic oppression rooted in the Indian Act.[2] We spoke up about the
indifference of most Canadians to Indigenous land claims, treaty
rights, and the exploitation of Aboriginal land by uranium and oil
mining companies. We spoke up against the Alberta tar sands. We
spoke up for missing and murdered Indigenous women, and for the
rights of Indigenous children. We demanded that Canada sign and
implement the United Nations Declaration on the Rights of Indigenous People (which it finally did in November 2010). We told the
world that Indigenous rights affect us all.

Months earlier, I had joined a coalition of grassroots organizations to organize for the Indigenous Day of Action. I was grateful to find a group of people who would soon become close friends and adopted family, who were ready to take action for Indigenous rights, and who understood the historic racism and oppression of Indigenous people in Canada.

Grassroots Indigenous groups led the organization of the march and were responsible for major decisions. We decided not to request a city permit for our march; instead, we asked for and received a letter of permission from the last tribe of traditional landowners of Toronto, the Mississaugas of the New Credit First Nation. We wanted to represent the "peace first" protocol of our ancestors, who stood up for our people before us – since our elders, youth, and children would take part in the march, we organized for peaceful, non-violent action. Our meetings followed an Indigenous circle protocol. Every meeting was opened and closed with traditional smudge and prayers; this kept us grounded and gave us a sense of safety despite the growing police presence in downtown Toronto.

Non-Indigenous solidarity groups respectfully took direction from Indigenous people and actively supported our organizing efforts. As the day approached, solidarity groups helped out by providing non-violent direct action training, street medics, legal observers, and legal representation. While the media and the G20 security and intelligence services portrayed peaceful organizers and actions as criminal, militant, or violent, the Toronto activist community came together to support one another, creating a sense of security for protesters as we prepared to meet the thousands of police who were armed and waiting for us in the streets.

Members of our coalition worried about police violence, CSIS (Canadian Security Intelligence Service) visits, infiltration, provocateurs, arrests, and the criminalization of activists. Their level of concern was new to me, and admittedly intimidated me. My mind was filled with thoughts of police repression and the police state that was forming around us. One day, while on a break from our coalition meeting, outside smoking and socializing, we saw more than twenty police minivans drive past. With the vans' sliding doors ajar, we could see they were packed full of uniformed and armed police officers. It was obvious we caught their attention as each of the vans drove by. I was speechless and could only stand there overwhelmed by the reality of their billion-dollar security budget. I had to confront my fear that we might face arrest or criminalization for standing up for the rights of Indigenous people.

Our march was one of the first major actions during the summit, so we could only base our expectations on past G20 news reports and video footage. Knowing that the media and police often characterize our demonstrations as militant and violent, we asked marchers not to wear bandanas or camouflage, in order to show the real human beings affected by these issues. We chose a police liaison organizing member and a peacekeeping force that had the responsibility of guiding the marchers to ensure a peaceful and safe action and to act as a buffer between marchers and police.

We met at Queen's Park, the site of the Ontario legislature, and marched through downtown Toronto, stopping at significant points such as the child welfare offices (a 2011 study found that "aboriginal people make up about two per cent of the population, but between 10 to 20 per cent of the children in care"[3]), the American embassy (to show solidarity for jailed activist Leonard Peltier), police stations, justice buildings, and the offices of corporations that continue to trample on the land and the health of Indigenous people. As the Canadian state prepared for violent police repression and the largest mass arrest in Canadian history, we proudly displayed banners proclaiming: "Canada Can't Hide Genocide," "Native Rights Are Human Rights," "Our Children Are Not For Sale," and "Native Land Rights Now!" We loudly chanted "Whose water? Our water! Whose land? Our land!" "No G20 on stolen native land!" and "Justice, freedom, self-determination! Canada is an illegal nation!" The march ended at Allan Gardens, peacefully and with no arrests.

It took courage to confront the truth, to speak out, to advocate, to organize, and to take action against diminishing Indigenous rights, the exploitation of traditional territories, and impoverished communities. Organizers for the Indigenous Day of Action drew on the principles and values of Indigenous culture and spirituality handed down to us for generations. We found a sense of security in the traditional medicines we used, the spiritual protocols we followed, and the level of support we received from the broader activist community in Toronto. We look forward to strengthening our new and meaningful relationships with Indigenous solidarity groups. Standing up for Indigenous rights, history, and culture, we will match the resilience of our ancestors, who paved the way for our activism today.

Indigenous Day of Action, June 24, 2010. Photo by Gerardo Correa.

5

Labour's Role in Opposing the G20
Building Resistance to Austerity

Archana Rampure

This Moment in Time

In retrospect, the June 2010 mobilizations against the Toronto G20 summit were not just another anti-globalization protest but also the beginning of a North American movement to resist the new austerity regime. Since the assembly of G20 nations, led by Canadian Prime Minister Stephen Harper, announced that the global recession was over and that it was time to turn from stimulus spending to austerity measures, we've seen far too many examples of those measures put into practice.[1]

In the United States, Republicans have targeted public sector workers and public sector unions; the most egregious example, in Wisconsin, includes draconian legislation that strips almost all rights from public sector unions. But it isn't just happening in Wisconsin. As Jane McAlevey notes, "the threat to unionized workers is playing out in all fifty states, to the drumbeat in the media about states going broke because of government workers' wages, pensions and benefits. By late January . . . hundreds of bills had been introduced seeking to hem in unions if not ban them altogether."[2] And some of these bills have been passed. Often, as in Wisconsin, they are passed in the face of great anger from unionists and the public, but nevertheless their passing codifies into law some of the most virulent attacks on the union movement in recent history.

In the United Kingdom, a Conservative-led coalition has instituted massive cuts to public services and ensured that over half a million public sector workers will lose their jobs. The cuts focus on services to seniors, social services, and health care, and include major hikes to tuition fees and other user fees. As in the United States, the 2011 UK budget also includes corporate tax cuts, meaning even less government revenue available for public spending.

Here in Canada, we face our own austerity agenda. Both provincial and federal governments have been racing to reduce corporate tax rates, thereby reducing state fiscal capacity. Public services at all levels have been attacked because of the fiscal deficit created by these low corporate tax rates. And it is public sector workers and their unions who are directly in the line of fire. Across the country, governments have coerced or forced wage freezes, sometimes with back-to-work legislation like that brought against postal workers after two weeks of strikes and lockouts. The Conservative government has made massive cuts to the federal budget. The Ontario government tried to roll out a "compensation restraint policy," which would have seen all public sector workers voluntarily agree to a two-year wage freeze. At the municipal level, Toronto's new right-wing mayor, millionaire Rob Ford, is trying to break the city workers' unions; he has already convinced the province to take away the right to strike from workers in Toronto's public transit system.

An attack on public sector unions is also a proxy attack on public services themselves. Public services are one of the few remaining bridges across the ever-widening gap between the rich and poor; they are the core of the twentieth-century compromise between labour and capital that we call the welfare state. But the welfare state has been under attack almost since its inception and across the Global North it has been weakened considerably since the 1980s.

Creeping privatization and increasing user fees make public services such as recreational programs unaffordable for many. Core social services such as health care and post-secondary education are under immense pressure: hospitals are closing acute care beds and discharging patients without adequate supports; qualified applicants are unable to access university education because of spiralling tuition fees. The poor and the vulnerable are hit much harder by service cuts than the privileged; they also benefit far less from tax cuts. Public sector unions – partly out of self-interest but mostly out of a strong, member-led commitment to universal and accessible public services – have been at the forefront of fights against cuts. Union members are fighting hard against the global austerity agenda of privatization, deregulation, and corporate globalization.

So it is no surprise that neo-liberal governments and their corporate donors are concerned when public service workers and those who rely on public services make common cause. The hundreds of thousands who gathered in Wisconsin to protest the Republican assault on public sector unions carried out exactly the kind of mobilization that frightens right-wing politicians and their funders. During the Wisconsin protests, nation-wide polls in the United States showed that, by a margin of two to one, Americans don't approve of the attacks on public sector unions and don't believe that slashing public sector compensation will salvage their faltering economy.

In Canada, as in the United States, public sector unions are at the centre of this struggle precisely because they are a bastion of strength for the labour movement. And the labour movement is the bedrock of progressive politics in this country. Without a strong, organized labour movement that can afford to contribute resources from members' dues – in cash and kind – to other social movements, we will all be weaker. No other social movement can muster the numbers that the labour movement can: the large mobilization we saw in Toronto on Saturday, June 26, 2010, owed a lot to the thousands of union activists bussed in from around Ontario. But the labour movement offers more than its ability to turn out a few thousand activists (although the power of its workers is the core of its strength); its size and structure allows it to lobby and organize campaigns and resource them on a scale that other Canadian progressive organizations cannot.

Trade unions represent a vast cross-section of working people; from auto workers to academics, from nurses to nuclear power plant workers, and from transit workers to tradespeople, the more than three million people represented by organized labour in Canada cross all demographic groups. When workers are attacked and their already stagnant wages fall behind inflation, everyone suffers. Depressing the wages of unionized workers depresses the wages of non-union workers. So what seems like a narrow attack on unionized workers is really an attack on all workers – even if politicians are able to attract some working-class support for such an attack by fostering the myth of overly compensated public sector workers.[3]

The G20's communiqué from Toronto, announcing a return to austerity, was by no means a narrow attack. The agenda of the G7, G8, and now the G20 has always been to limit government spending, which in turn limits public services and creates markets for those services to be privatized and sold to transnational corporations. In

Canada, public services like health care, water and wastewater services, garbage collection and recycling, energy generation and distribution, public transit, and road and highway maintenance are at risk. Major transnational corporations are eyeing these services – where public monopolies often exist, where assets belong to governments – as the next layer of lucrative business opportunities to be exploited and "monetized." Public sector unions have long resisted privatization; as part of public interest groups such as the Canadian Health Coalition, People for Public Education, Water Watch, and the Trade Justice Network, unions have contributed to public interest research, to litigation, and to educating the public about the negative impact of corporate control of public services.

Labour's Role in the Run-up to the G8 and G20 Summits

The mobilization we saw in Toronto in the run-up to the G20 is the kind of coalition building we're going to need more of in order to fight the austerity agenda. The Canadian Labour Congress (the umbrella organization for the Canadian labour movement) began working with civil society organizations in 2009 to formulate an organized opposition to the official summits. National unions such as the Canadian Union of Public Employees (CUPE), the Communications, Energy and Paperworkers Union of Canada (CEP), the United Steelworkers, and the Canadian Union of Postal Workers (CUPW) chose their own levels of involvement. Many union locals, especially those in Toronto, were directly involved with planning events. And many individuals involved in protest planning were union members, some explicitly participating in their role as union members and others not. This kind of deep union involvement was one of the reasons why the G20 mobilization was as successful as it was. The use of the Cecil Street Steelworkers Hall, in the heart of downtown Toronto, for public meetings and for steering committee sessions, is just one example of the kind of invisible union support that supported the mobilizations.

Labour was involved in planning much more than Saturday's "People First!" rally. We were an integral part of other mobilizations around the city that week. I'm proud to have been involved in the People's Summit, a weekend of popular education held June 18–20. The Canadian Labour Congress and some of its affiliate unions played a significant role in organizing and promoting the more than one hundred workshop sessions that were on offer that weekend. The Toronto Community Mobilization Network – though it might not have had official labour delegates – included many trade union activists.

It should go without saying that any year-long process of organizing will have its tensions and clashes. During the Toronto G20, the major clash for many labour activists was about "diversity of tactics," and what that meant to the various groups involved in the mobilization. One reason for this clash, it seems to me, is the tension between the hierarchical structure of the labour movement and the more organic structure of many other groups. Labour will never be one large affinity group. Unions cannot move or make decisions in the way that smaller, voluntary groupings of like-minded individuals can; they are formal, hierarchical organizations and their elected leaders must answer not just to a circle of activists but also to a broad cross-section of society. This is both the strength and the weakness of the union structure.

Some other progressives blame so-called union bureaucrats for the rank and file's disinterest in politics and protests. But the truth is that union leaders are generally more progressive than their membership; and the small band of rank-and-file activists who are truly radical often push leaders further left. Anyone who has tried to get ordinary union members – not leaders or activists – to meetings, rallies, or protests, or to volunteer their time will know that many of our members are not as invested in the movement as some of us would like them to be. My former CUPE local, with over five thousand members, would count it as a good night when fifty members attended a meeting. Of the almost two hundred and fifty thousand CUPE members in Ontario, we were only able to mobilize a few thousand to take to the streets during the G8 and G20. Getting our few thousand members out was a signal success, but it is a fraction of our membership. I don't think the majority of them stayed home because labour's planned activities were not militant enough. And if they did, they have every opportunity to elect more radical leaders. Rightly or wrongly, the structure of the labour movement leads to moderation, not militancy. But if the result of moderation is that we are able to create mass mobilizations, then it appears to me to be a trade-off worth making. Moreover, we all work in the hope of radicalizing more people over time, as members learn more about political issues and expand their own comfort zones. Without going through what from the outside can look like an agonizingly slow process of radicalization through education, there is no hope that we can ever have a militant working class mobilizing on the streets of our nation.

There will always be tension between labour's reliance on a hierarchical structure of elected leaders who make decisions on behalf of the membership and the insistence on direct democracy by some social movement activists. In organizing for the G20 mobilization, we went some of the way toward establishing a process for membership and community consultation that both social movement organizations and the labour movement were willing to live with – but we didn't get all the way. The fallout from the black bloc tactics employed by a few dozen protesters at the end of Saturday's march demonstrates that there is a lot of alliance building still to be done. I understand why organized labour's quick response of distancing itself from such tactics angered some community organizers. That said, while I'm a supporter of a diversity of tactics (though there are tactics that I would not personally engage in), I feel betrayed by the actions of those who chose to use black bloc tactics in the midst of what was planned as a non-confrontational, family-friendly march. Too often, the phrase "respect for diversity of tactics" is invoked as a way of silencing criticism from those who do not agree with confrontational tactics.

My hope was that those who wanted to engage in more disruptive activities would not participate in Saturday's "People First!" rally. As it happened, some people did not respect this wish: they used the rally as a cover within which to hide, and I think it's entirely understandable that trade union members were infuriated by this. The tactic of a non-confrontational, peaceful demonstration was chosen for the decidedly practical reason that this would get out the largest number of our members. Disregarding or disrespecting peaceful tactics does not radicalize the labour movement, as some have suggested; instead, it further limits labour's ability to take on social-movement work. It only serves to strengthen the voice of those within our own membership who would like to see unions focus more on the nuts and bolts of collective bargaining and to abandon social justice activism.

The threat to progressives of all stripes is from the right; it is not from the perceived flaws of the labour movement. It's time for us all to unite against the neo-liberal agenda rather than fight amongst ourselves. We need to develop a new partnership between the labour movement and the social movements. The old model had labour handing over cash to community activists without being part of their planning process. It's not a model that works for me personally, and I don't think it's done a great deal for either the unions or for social movements. There's no doubt that both sides have often been satisfied with this process – for labour it meant participating in social movements without the messiness of direct involvement, and for some of the movements it was a way of accessing resources without really having to account for them. But this kind of detachment on labour's part has left some union members feeling that social movements are a distraction for union staff and activists. We need to find a way to share both resources *and* decision making. A promising example of this is the Greater Toronto Workers' Assembly, which began to take shape in 2010 and which brings together activists from unions and social movements.

A minor protest that took place Monday, June 21, illustrates the importance of labour and social movement collaboration. The demonstration included a brief confrontation between some activists and a handful of front-line social services staff about an announcement from the Integrated Security Unit that the four Children's Aid Societies (CAS) in Toronto would work with police during the G20. Front-line social service providers do not make major policy decisions. If those activists who decided to confront CAS workers had consulted with the unions representing those workers, we could have – together – planned a larger event, perhaps at the office of the elected Minister responsible for the CAS. Directly confronting front-line workers over policies that they have no control over simply makes it harder for those of us who want to build bridges with social movements to encourage union members to walk over those bridges.

Uniting to Fight Austerity

The evening of June 26 was chaotic: it was no coincidence that it wasn't until after labour's chartered buses departed the main rally site at Queen's Park that police attacked protesters still gathered in the so-called free speech zone. Even in the moment, this seemed like a calculated attempt to escalate tensions between labour and other protesters, tensions that were already inflamed. The police – and their puppet masters – were clever to exploit the labour movement's anger at having Saturday's peaceful demonstration hijacked. Not all labour protesters agreed on tactics but the CLC had worked with locals to fill buses from across Ontario with rank-and-file members and they'd made a firm commitment to their members, based on months of negotiations with partners in the mobilization, to organize a family-friendly peaceful action. At the same time, a smaller group of more radicalized labour activists were intent on peacefully "confronting" the outer rings of the police cordon by walking south from the agreed-upon march route.

But it was the actions of the tiny minority who decided to take their anger about the inequalities of the system out on Yonge Street shop windows that enabled police and politicians to separate "good" protesters (labour) from the rest of the demonstrators. The divide is spurious and does not help the movement but it will persist as long as we do not learn to respect each other's diversity of tactics. This time around, this divide made it possible for the police to attack those still on the streets of Toronto after the property destruction had ended. Union members were among those who were intimidated, attacked, and arrested indiscriminately over those forty-eight hours, along with other protesters and even random members of the public.

Many will argue that the unions overreacted to the breaking of a few windows when they denounced these actions as violence. Equally, many within the union movement will point to these actions as evidence for why unions should stay away from social movement activism all together. Believe me, I have heard from both sides on this issue! The union movement is under threat – under the hostile political conditions detailed above, unions are desperately looking for public support and they will not take positions that reinforce the erroneous but popular public perception of them as greedy and extremist. They will not be moved from this defensive position until and unless public opinion moves – and nothing in the aftermath of the G20 suggests that "radical" tactics will radicalize the population at large.

The real problem that activists from both the union movement and social movements face is how to persuade more people to become part of the fight against the austerity measures. How do we convince people that unions are not fighting merely for their members' jobs and pensions but also for public services and for the public good?

How can the left mobilize more people who live on the margins of society? It's not enough to blame the mainstream media's biased coverage of protests for our failings in this regard. We need to consider whether we're making common cause through our actions or alienating would-be allies.

Back to the Future

Labour's role in the G20 protests didn't end with the "People First!" rally on June 26. Over a thousand people were arrested on the streets of Toronto during that week, and so in some ways the mobilization that led up to the rally was only the beginning of our summit struggle. Over the next few weeks, during the many demonstrations against police brutality, we saw the results of the radicalization of many of the people of Toronto – labour was a visible part of this continued fight.

We can all learn from examples like the rally against police brutality on the afternoon of Monday, June 28. What began as an expression of anger and disbelief by a couple of dozen people quickly became a gathering of a few thousand people. The sheer number of people who showed up at this demonstration, having heard about it from friends and allies, was proof that the politics of dividing protesters was not going to work.

Since the G20, there have been numerous rallies pressing for a full public inquiry and unions have consistently backed this call. The National Union of Public and General Employees worked with the Canadian Civil Liberties Association (CCLA) to hold public hearings in November 2010 and produced a report – "Breach of the Peace" – on the widespread violations of civil liberties at the G20.[4] Its production – and pressure from other unions including CUPE and the Canadian Auto Workers (CAW) – was what led some federal Members of Parliament to appear at a press conference with the CCLA to demand a full public inquiry. Union pressure also pushed the Ontario New Democratic Party to call for a public inquiry as soon as the summits were over. CUPE, the CAW, and many individual union members have supported the Legal Defence Fund set up to help those who were arrested at the G20.

Activists are still feeling the impact of the G20 protests. One of the most serious consequences of the G20 protests is that all of us who were on the streets of Toronto were sent a message about how the state would deal with democratic dissent. The austerity agenda will be rolled out ruthlessly; we have seen in police actions since the G20 that we've entered a new era of authoritarianism with brutal treatment for those who seek to register their discontent with the system. A rally on March 15, 2011, to mark the International Day against Police Brutality drew a few hundred participants but far more police officers on bikes and horses and in minivans lined up around the corner. We cannot let the fear of this increasing intimidation stop us from mobilizing again and again against austerity measures. We must organize now in our union locals and in our communities against the coming onslaught of cuts to public services and the pressure to privatize, monetize, and deregulate.

We can't afford these austerity measures. They will be devastating for individual union members whose jobs are on the line, but more broadly they will gut our public services, which are one of the last remaining equalizers in a society that is increasingly polarized between the wealthy and everyone else. So we have to revisit the successful models of coordination, cooperation, and consensus building that we developed in the year-long preparations to confront the G20 in Toronto. We all need to push back against the attacks on public services and public sector workers. Nearly a thousand people came out to workshops and educational sessions during the People's Summit. Tens of thousands of people marched in the streets of Toronto over the course of the week of the G20. We got some of the mobilization right; we need to do it again and we need to do it better. The G20 met for three days; the battle against the austerity agenda will last for years.

6

Unions, Direct Action, and the G20 Protests

Obstacles and Opportunities

Jeff Shantz

THE CRUCIAL CHALLENGES FACING MOVEMENTS FOR POSITIVE SOCIAL change, like the broad mobilizations opposing the G20 meetings in Toronto, involve the relationship between unions and community-based social movements. The form taken by alliances, coalitions, and organizations involving unions and community-based groups (anti-poverty activists, no-borders activists, and anarchists, for example) will determine the scope of opposition to states and capital and the real potential of mobilizing opposition to neo-liberal politics. A key point on which this challenge pivots is the question of direct action and civil disobedience – the relationship of social movements to property destruction and violations of law. This is a question of strategy and tactics to be sure, but, even more, it is a question of how we understand the character of the state within capitalist societies like Canada. This question has been ongoing, intensifying in the period of neo-liberal globalization and with the emergence of alternative globalization movements and demonstrations against institutions of global state capitalism, such as the G8 and G20.

These issues can be difficult to address honestly; they tend to elicit strong emotional responses from participants on both union and social movement sides. Critics can be too readily dismissed as "outsiders" who don't appreciate the way things are done in the movement or group in question. I am perhaps particularly well situated to address this tension; I am a long-time union member who has served as a representative on local executives and as a delegate to provincial labour federations in Ontario, and I am also a long-time community activist, involved with groups that regularly engage in direct action. I have participated in various demonstrations as a rank-and-file unionist and as a member of black blocs. I have rallied anarchists to join picket lines during strikes and mobilized fellow workers to take part in direct actions in defence of poor and homeless people.

In light of the G20 protests and the fallout since, I see problems but also possibilities for developing resistance movements against neo-liberal capitalism in Ontario. To move forward, it is important to examine union responses to direct actions during the G20 and contextualize them within ongoing practices and perspectives on organizing. This can help us to transcend the divide between labour/community organizing and mass/direct action, which has contributed to something of an impasse in political mobilizing in Ontario and elsewhere.

Which Side Are You on Again?

Exceptional events like the G20 protests and state clampdown provide real opportunities for understanding that are not always available when the left is going about "business as usual." The numerous calls for repression of the black bloc and support for the state capitalist rule of law by would-be spokespeople of the labour movement in Canada offer a case in point. One of the most striking examples is an astonishing statement from the Ontario wing of the Canadian Union of Public Employees (CUPE Ontario), my former union federation:

> Property was damaged, publicly owned police vehicles were burned, and innocent people were attacked and detained as a result of taking part in protests. All of this is wrong. What we have witnessed is nothing short of the abandonment of the rule of law, both by a small group who took part in the protests, and by a massive and heavily armed police force who were charged with overseeing them.[1]

Having equated the black bloc with the police in their scorn, the statement goes on to say:

> And it's a sad day when some of those, who feel powerless to change the direction of their elected leaders, find in that feeling of powerlessness an excuse to break the law and vandalize the property of their fellow citizens and who, in so doing, silence the legitimate voices of so many others whose commitment to protest and dissent is matched by their rejection of violence and vandalism.

Suggesting that the black bloc is an expression of powerlessness rather than confidence is one thing, but suggesting that breaking the law renders any activists or organizers illegitimate, as the statement does, should make jaws drop. It is the logic of the bosses and the state (who set the property laws and benefit from them in the first place). And why should we view capital as our "fellow citizens" anyway?

The CUPE Ontario denunciation of direct action was just one example among many, and it was echoed by the officialdom of the Ontario Federation of Labour (OFL), the provincial union federation. OFL President Sid Ryan boasted that OFL leadership "liaised with the Toronto Police and cooperated at every turn"[2] during the large June 26 protest. He then went further, denouncing other activists, organizers, and indeed union members who participated in direct actions. The Canadian Labour Congress (CLC), the national union federation, felt the need to add its voice to the chorus attacking activists. They also drew attention to their collaboration with police: "We cooperated with police in choosing the route and had hundreds of parade marshals to maintain order."[3] In both cases, the leadership made a public commitment to state capitalist order, the restricted terrain of capitalist legality that serves such an important role in the neo-liberal legitimation of anti-working-class policies (which are nothing if not legal).

How such assertions are helpful in building movements that might actually halt neo-liberal capitalist regimes is not clear. What is clear is that many rank-and-file union members were troubled by these public displays of deference to the very authorities who were still holding in prison many activists and organizers, including union members. That the CUPE Ontario and OFL pronouncements did not express a consensus view among union members is reflected in a rank-and-file statement letter to the CLC, released on July 5, 2010. The more than 250 unionists who signed the letter included members of CUPE, the Public Service Alliance of Canada, the British Columbia Government and Service Employees' Union, the United Steelworkers, the Canadian Union of Postal Workers, the Ontario Secondary School Teachers Association, the Ontario Public Service Employees Union, and the Canadian Auto Workers. The statement outlined the problems created by open appeals to state authority and criminalization of activists by union leadership:

The focus on vandalism and attacks on private property espoused by the CLC statement and some mainstream media outlets, expels from the debate the legitimate concerns and lived injustices of many within the labour movement who turned out to protest the G8/G20. By commission or omission this limited focus legitimizes the suspension of rights and liberties in this city, including the right to assembly and the right to political protest.[4]

In conclusion, the rank-and-file members pointed ahead to the many tasks facing working-class movements more broadly: "We will not and cannot win the struggle we face against the violent onslaught of neo-liberalism by abandoning our allies and our communities in the wake of a massive crackdown on dissent."

There is nothing new about such rank-and-file militancy; labour history is rife with examples of workers using direct action to demand justice. More recently, during protests such as the riot at Queen's Park in 2000 and the 2001 Quebec City protests against the Free Trade Area of the Americas, many rank-and-file union members chose to go to the front to challenge the police lines, fences, and weapons, which are the material expressions of the rule of law. They refused simply to march, to hear empty speeches, or to uphold the fetishization of "peaceful protest" regardless of its actual effectiveness. After Quebec City, in fact, rank-and-file unionists, angry about the defeatist call of leadership to march away from the fences and into an empty field miles away from the meeting site, demanded direct action training in their locals when they returned home. Many of those who called for or led direct action workshops were CUPE members. Indeed, in 2001 CUPE National president Judy Darcy urged delegates at the CUPE Ontario convention to raise levels of militancy within the labour movement, defend community struggles, notably anti-poverty struggles, and develop rank-and-file organizations. That convention adopted a proposal to push for a general strike in Ontario and Darcy's words were met with chants of "Strike! Strike! Strike!"[5]

Limiting Structures

The recent tensions around anti-G20 mobilizations are best understood with some context. Within the labour movement in Canada, negotiation is presented as the most reasonable and effective way to address inequality. Officials strive to get the best possible deal for their members rather than to attack the overall system of exploitation. Emphasis is placed on bargaining power within the capitalist labour market. Over the past few decades, working-class opposition in North America has been contained largely within official, legalistic channels. Most common among these tactics are established bargaining and grievance procedures negotiated by union representatives over predominantly economic matters. This has been accompanied by a containment of political action within the official channels of party politics and elections. Undeniably, the separation between economic and political spheres (and the relegation of unions to the limited terrain of economic management) is a reflection, and result, of the collapse of infrastructures of resistance that expressed the connections, even unity, of economic and political action. Activities such as occupations, blockades, wildcat strikes, and sabotage have been diminished or dismissed within unionized workplaces in which unions act as a means of surveillance and regulation of workers, attempting to contain their actions within the framework of contracts with employers.

Indeed, the main role of the unions has become supervision of contracts in the periods between legal bargaining rounds and symbolic mobilization to support official union negotiations during the bargaining process. Rank-and-file militants have faced lack of support, disciplinary actions, or outright shunning by union officials. Some contracts include provisions that prohibit wildcat actions.

In Canada, the institutionalization of unions as economic managers has been accompanied by the institutionalization of working-class politics within electoral politics through the social-democratic New Democratic Party (NDP). Politics has been reduced to party campaigns and lobbying for legislative reform as proposed and channelled through NDP caucuses.[6] In moments of upsurge in struggle, the tensions in this arrangement become apparent. During the Days of Action (city-by-city strikes organized against the ironically named Progressive Conservative government in Ontario in the mid-1990s), for example, cracks emerged between those who wanted to organize a real movement for change to drive the government from power and those who saw the Days of Action in primarily symbolic terms. While members of the Ontario Federation of Labour voted in favour of proceeding with a general strike, the initiative was cancelled in an underhanded manner by moderate union officials tied to the NDP. Fearful that the Days would hurt the NDP's future electoral prospects, leadership worked to withdraw resources and slowly wind the movements down. When anarchists tried to take over the stock exchange and invade the Tory policy convention, union marshals pushed people to march on to the empty legislature building to listen to Billy Bragg. Marshals acted to police militants, including rank-and-file workers. Some openly questioned the participation of anarchists in the Days.

At a meeting I helped organize to discuss alliance building during the Days of Action, then-OFL-President Wayne Samuelson proclaimed that there are labour issues and social movement issues, and unions should stick to labour issues. Social movements, he suggested, could stick to the rest. This is, unfortunately, a view that still governs thinking among many union leaders. Ever since the collapse of the Days of Action and the failure to follow through on a province-wide general strike in 1997, the resistance to neo-liberal governments in Ontario has been fractured and confused.

Currently, these institutional pressures and habits continue to constrain working-class responses to structural transformations of neo-liberalism and economic crisis. Unions seek to limit losses rather than make gains. Their main approach has been to negotiate severance deals that limit the harm done to former employees (and members) rather than contest the rights of employers and governments to determine the future of workplaces and workers' livelihoods.

These arrangements have also engendered a certain reliance upon prevailing social relations among the working classes. Rather than seeking new relations or a new society, the institutions of the working class repeat the message that working-class desires and needs not only can be met within capitalist society, but, even more, *depend* upon capitalism for their realization. Such a notion plays into the "trickle down" fantasies of neo-liberal Reaganomics, which insists that policies and practices that benefit business will see some of the gains made by capital eventually find their way to the working class and the poor. Such was the justification for the massive multi-million dollar bailouts handed to corporations during the economic crisis of 2008–2009.

This fatal position is reflected in the CLC statement on the G20 protests: "We were exercising a democratic right to tell G20 leaders that there can be no recovery from the economic crisis unless they place a priority on the creation of good jobs."[7] The demonstrations are posed as simply a request that capital try to keep workers in mind. There is no analysis here of exploitation and no recognition that neo-liberal advances for capital have been underlined by lousy jobs. Even more troubling is this passage: "We are urging the leaders not to move too quickly to austerity measures and warning them not to chop public services."[8] Urging political and economic leaders *not to move too quickly to austerity measures*? The problem is not austerity, but the timeline in which it is imposed? No sign of fight-back, resistance, or alternatives?

The problem is not simply one of the unions, however. Community organizers have too often avoided real engagement with labour institutions or have avoided forums in which they might meet and discuss matters with rank-and-file union members. Sometimes younger activists have little sense of the tenor and rhythm of workplace organizing. While I was involved in anti-poverty organizing I helped to establish a phone tree for members interesting in doing worker solidarity. A crew of younger members came forward to say that they did not know what "rank and file" meant.

Too often the measure of labour involvement in coalitions in Ontario has been the amount of money given to a campaign, the forcefulness of rhetoric from high-profile leaders, or the winning of a motion at this or that convention. The only way that any sort of credible resistance movement will be forged in Ontario, however, is through a redoubling of efforts to make connections between grass-roots community groups and rank-and-file workers – the same workers who, in the Canadian Auto Workers, for example, openly condemned their leadership for not going to the fence in Quebec City, and demanded direct action training after they returned home. Indeed, direct action workshops are something anarchist activists can and should offer. They should also be ready to help build flying squads or mobilize industrial unions among unorganized workers, as the Industrial Workers of the World (IWW) have done among squeegee workers in Vancouver. Community activists should attend labour council meetings and make themselves familiar to union activists. They should join picket lines and organize support for striking workers.

Promising Developments

In order to move beyond the union/community activist, direct action/ mass action dichotomies, it is important to learn from real efforts by union members to develop militant action in solidarity with community organizers. Happily, there have been important developments in working-class political practice in Ontario over the last few years. Unfortunately, these developments have been overlooked and too little remarked upon in recent debates and discussions over the G20 protests. These encouraging projects include flying squads and the Greater Toronto Workers' Assembly.

The flying squad is a rapid-response group of union members who are ready to mobilize on short notice to provide direct support for pickets or actions. It may or may not be a recognized body of the local. The structure may consist of little more than phone lists and meetings but, significantly, should maintain its autonomy from the local and national union executives. Generally, flying squads should be open only to rank-and-file members since they must be free to initiate and take actions that the leadership may not approve of. Some flying squads refuse even a budget line item so that they are in no way dependent upon leadership. In Canada, flying squads have offered crucial support to direct actions around immigration defence, tenant protection, squatters' rights, and welfare support by mobilizing sizeable numbers of unionists who are prepared for actions without regard to legality. Flying squads take direct action to interfere with bosses' abilities to make profits. Not limited in their scope of action by specific collective agreements or workplaces, flying squads mobilize for community as well as workplace defence.

Not coincidentally, the contemporary flying squads active in Ontario made their reappearance in several CAW locals in Windsor during the mid-1990s as a mobilization force for actions against the neo-liberal provincial government. The network within the CAW spread during the Days of Action. In the midst of a lengthy strike against Falconbridge mining in 2001, during which picketers were subjected to ongoing violence by company goons and security thugs, members of CAW Local 598 initiated a regional Northern Flying Squad to reinforce and defend the lines and step up the struggle against the company. They helped to organize a solidarity weekend that brought flying squads from across Ontario for militant actions against Falconbridge, actions that many consider to have been the high point of the strike.

My union in Toronto, CUPE 3903, inspired by the CAW flying squads and the direct action movements against capitalist globalization, formed a flying squad to support the Ontario Coalition Against Poverty (OCAP) in direct action casework around immigration defence and welfare support, to provide strike solidarity for other workers, and to organize direct actions within mass anti-capitalist demonstrations. At its height the flying squad had more than eighty members ready to mobilize on short notice to provide direct support for pickets or actions. Significantly, the flying squad maintained its autonomy from the union executive, refusing a budget line item. In response to concerns raised by rank-and-file union members that their unions were not doing enough to prepare members for direct actions during alternative globalization protests, members of the local provided other union activists with direct action training and workshops on forming and developing flying squads.

The presence of union flying squads has been crucial in the success of various community-based actions, particularly around social assistance and immigrant defence. Government officials, security, and cops respond differently to a room packed with workers holding union flags and banners than when confronted with a smaller group that they dismiss as simply activists. Through such actions, the flying squad demonstrates how organizations of rank-and-file workers can step out of traditional concerns of the workplace to act in a broadened defence of working-class interests. Flying squads can offer opportunities for building bridges between workers, across unions and industries, and between union and community groups. With their autonomy from traditional union structures and commitment to militant non-hierarchical practices, rank-and-file working groups and flying squads can also provide real opposition to conservatism within the unions. They provide a better approach than the more common model of the "left caucus," which tries to reform union policy, usually through resolutions at conventions.[9] Flying squads are inspiring examples of labour's vital involvement in direct action.

One of the most interesting union-community-bridging developments to emerge in Toronto, and one that has increased its profile since the G20 protests, is the Greater Toronto Workers' Assembly (GTWA). Initiated partly in response to the economic crisis, the Assembly has become a venue for participants to address the constraints of existing movements, including the labour movement, and to bridge

Unions, Direct Action, and the G20 Protests

the gaps that keep activists divided along lines of race, class, gender, and sexuality, but also job sector, workplace, employment, and citizenship status. The Assembly's aim is solidarity among the working class defined in the broadest possible terms. Members are involved in many of the community groups that helped organize the militant G20 opposition, including OCAP and No One Is Illegal. As well, union members who have contributed to direct actions have been active members of the GTWA. The Assembly provides an organizational space to overcome the gap between broad anti-capitalist politics and the very specific, particular focus of many community-based groups and unions.[10]

In the lead-up to the G20, ahead of the Fourth Assembly, the GTWA joined a range of community advocacy groups to host several events to mobilize opposition to the G20. The GTWA stressed the need to build for the protests with an eye toward longer-term organizing that might challenge political and economic elites on a more durable basis. GTWA members stated their goals as follows:

> To bring together activists within the broad working-class movement, to explore the experiences and approaches to struggle that both unite and divide us as a starting point for overcoming divisions and building greater collaboration, exchange, strategic discussion and action amongst us.
>
> To share our understanding of the problems created by capitalism and the current economic crisis and the need to develop alternative visions that challenge the logic and power of private corporations, and the states that back them, over our lives.
>
> To identify and develop concrete strategies and organizational forms of struggle which defend working-class people's immediate needs and lay the groundwork for an equitable and democratic alternative to our present economic and political system.[11]

The GTWA currently has over 250 members and almost 300 supporters (who maintain varying levels of activity). Members come from about forty community organizing groups and approximately twenty unions or locals. The early goals have been regular city-wide assemblies and shared resources such as publications, a website, and eventually a space. The GTWA organizes educational forums and a discussion series on a range of topics, including movement publishing and analysis of the economic crisis.

Participants in the GTWA have been clear from the outset that contemporary movements in Canada, both labour and otherwise, pose an inadequate challenge to state capitalist political, economic, and social systems. While these movements have been inspiring, their capacities for struggle have come up short against powerful opponents. The GTWA stands as one attempt to address those shortcomings. It makes an appeal for a new politics, with new organizational structures and infrastructures. As Herman Rosenfeld and Carlo Fanelli explain:

> Seeking to move beyond coalition and network politics, the Assembly is an organization that individuals belong to without giving up their membership and allegiances to community organizations, unions and left groups. We are committed to developing our understanding of what we're up against, who our potential allies are, and to organize and act in new ways that will take us from a politics of resistance to emancipatory alternatives.[12]

The GTWA attempts to transcend the divide between mass action and direct action, between labour movements and militancy. Members seek a renewed labour movement that is democratic and participatory and which does not eschew practices that challenge state capitalist terms of legitimacy and illegitimacy. Still, the usual challenge remains: "If the assembly process is to give birth to an organizational force capable of challenging the hegemony of capital, . . . it must surmount the impasse of the old politics of networks and coalitions, as well as business-as-usual unionism."[13] Interestingly, the GTWA has seen labour activists working alongside and in productive harmony with direct-action anarchists, including groups like Common Cause, which have long supported direct actions during alternative globalization protests. Here is an example of labour and anarchism complementing each other rather than occupying opposite ends of a stark dichotomy. Significantly, the politics and practices of the GTWA have resonated powerfully with working-class activists elsewhere in Canada, notably Vancouver, Ottawa, Montreal, and London.

The capitalist offensives of the last decade have broken down working-class organization and resistance in Ontario. Dismantling employment standards, freezing the minimum wage, eliminating rent controls, and deepening cuts to social assistance for unemployed workers has made life more precarious for broadening sections of the working class.

> This situation is not just a matter for deep humanitarian concern but a serious warning to the Workers' Movement. If the working class is reaching such a level of polarization and a section of it is experiencing such misery and privation, we are in a profoundly dangerous situation.[14]

Many workers are tired of engaging in struggle only to find themselves under attack, not only by politicians and corporations, but also by the officials of their own unions. The questionable positions taken publicly by union spokespeople have convinced some grassroots activists and rank-and-file workers alike of the need to make end runs around union officialdom and develop alternative projects directly. For activists, this means meeting with rank-and-file workers and having serious discussions about what sort of assistance anti-capitalist movements can offer to workers' struggles against conservative leadership, policies, and structures in their own unions.

Moving Forward Together

If alliances, coalitions, and organizations are to develop and thrive on a more resilient basis it is important not to paper over differences and divergences. We need an honest, open, and critical analysis of challenges and obstacles to building movements that might be capable, not of criticizing or complaining about neo-liberal regimes, but of stopping them.

When union leadership expresses fidelity to the "rule of law," what it really affirms is fidelity to the state and to the bosses. For much of its history, the union movement has been "against the law," its actions criminalized, its organizers arrested and worse. Would CUPE Ontario have sided with the rule of law against the sit-down strikers of the 1930s, against the Windsor strikers of 1945, the Mine Mill strikers of 2000–2001, or against the various general strikes? What about recent factory occupations? Siding with the rule of law really does make clear "which side you are on," to answer one of labour's ancient questions. Unions that uphold the rule of law – in the face of employers who steadfastly and routinely do not

– are accepting conditions of capitulation and defeat. Nothing less.

Indeed, it was through the UAW's 1945 strike against Ford that unions won what would become crucial features of collective bargaining in Canada, including the closed shop and dues check-off. The strike against Ford climaxed with a direct action in which workers surrounded the plant with vehicles, creating a barricade of the facility several cars deep, which prevented any attempt by the company to access the plant and its materials while preventing the police from reaching workers. This was a show of creative militancy (in which union flying squads played a significant part) that remains a compelling testimony to struggles beyond the confines of legal bargaining.

Mass actions of the kinds that unions excel at organizing are desirable and necessary. Unfortunately organizers in mainstream unions often draw a false dichotomy between mass action and direct action. What is necessary is mass direct action. And, while numbers are important, they are not sufficient. We should be sceptical of large-scale rallies that do little to challenge the economic and political power of elites. At some point economic and political disruption, imposing a real cost on the elites who would impose harmful policies upon us, is required. The history of the labour movement and strike action teaches us this. So the question is really about how to show the *social power* of the working class, not simply its numerical strength. Even large-scale protests can be ignored if they do not demonstrate a real capacity to effect social change, as many demonstrations against neo-liberal governments in Ontario and elsewhere have shown. This is a lesson that should certainly have been learned by the long-time organizers who crafted the CUPE Ontario statement.

More importantly, union organizers are wrong to assume that rank-and-file members will not engage in direct action. The frustration expressed by members after demonstrations from Quebec City to Toronto over the lack of preparation for more militant action – and the calls for greater preparation next time – offer ongoing testimony to this fact.

Mounted police charge journalists at the Queen's Park "designated speech area,"
June 26, 2010. Photo by Vincenzo D'Alto.

7

Presenting the Movement's Narratives
Organizing Alternative Media

Dan Kellar

AT 1:00 A.M. ON THE NIGHT OF SATURDAY, JUNE 26, WE FOUND OUR-
selves outside the Eastern Avenue detention centre dancing away in
front of a giant reproduction of Erik Drooker's painting "People vs.
Military" to intermittent blasts from a 3000-watt stereo system built
into the back of a rented cargo van. With hundreds already arrested,
including many of the event's organizers, the Saturday Night Fever
all-night anarchist street party was transformed into a jail solidarity
party. As the police started to close their kettle, and the messages and
music of resistance broadcast by campus radio station CKLN were cut
off, one organizer shouted, "Just keep fucking dancing!" and the
rhythms of a radical marching band took over. As the two hundred
dancing activists considered their options, an ominous warning
blasted over a police loudspeaker telling people they were breaking
the law and must disperse or face arrest. Over two hundred police
blocked the exits, and with nowhere to go and over three hundred
people watching the demo live via a Twitter-enabled Ustream feed
broadcast from a smartphone, this dance party became the second
police "kettle" of the Toronto G20.

By 2:00 a.m., through negotiations that were livecast on the web,
the police agreed that if the dancing and the noise stopped, the kettle
would open and people would be allowed to leave without arrest or
harassment. Camera in hand, I asked a cop, "Are we just going to be
arrested when we get a hundred metres down the road?" He assured
us we would be free to go home, so, after a quick consensus-seeking
discussion, people started to filter through the police line, on our way
to supposed "freedom." However, as the final twenty-five people
walked away from the demo site, the cops re-formed their kettle and

arrested everyone inside it, including organizers, street medics, and safe-space facilitators, the people serving food, legal observers, and four members of the Toronto G20 Alternative Media Centre (AMC), myself included. This was the end of my visible participation in Toronto G20 protests but not the end of my coverage of the event for the AMC.

The Toronto G20 Alternative Media Centre

In the weeks leading up to the summit over seventy radical media activists and critical journalists from across the Americas arrived in Toronto for the G20 protests, joining the ten or so local activists who had worked to set up a safe media space in the storage garage of linux-caffe (a popular open source meeting spot in Toronto) and had been taking on most of the organizing for the AMC. Our task was to produce investigative news reports on the impact of the G20 summit and convergence protests in Toronto and a critical analysis of the impact of G20 policies in Canada and around the world. At the same time, we needed to remain accountable to our own communities and to the social and ecological justice movements we are part of.

A central goal of the AMC was to tell the stories and broadcast the voices of those who had come to Toronto to show their distaste for the G20 governments responsible for oppressive austerity measures and other neo-colonial economic misadventures. The Toronto AMC built on the lessons and the successes of the VancouverAMC (active during the convergence against the Vancouver 2010 Winter Olympics), and operated with a modified (loose) consensus model for decision making, with anti-oppressive and radical ideals.

For both of these convergences, the pre-existing local media co-op facilitated the space, provided staff and equipment, and lent editorial support to help the AMC reach its goals: providing narratives of the movement and only producing content that respected a diversity of tactics (as was explicitly supported by organizers of both convergences). In Vancouver, engagement in the AMC solidified the Vancouver Media Co-op's position as a bastion of critical local news with radical narratives, while the Toronto Media Co-op successfully utilized the G20 convergence as an opportunity to build its position as a new and important radical player in Canada's largest city and media market.

The Canadian Mainstream Media and the G20 Protests

The ability of the mainstream press to determine the tone and scope of protest coverage, and thus shape public discussion, is an indisputable fact. In Canada, six companies own about 90 per cent of print (magazines, daily pay/free papers), TV, satellite, and radio media; very few independent Canadian voices are available. Two of the Canadian media giants also own and control the majority of Internet bandwidth available to the public. Mainstream media outlets must respond not only to their corporate owners, but also to their corporate advertisers, who fund day-to-day operations. It is no surprise, then, that to satisfy their stakeholders and customers, the press covers anti-corporate and anti-capitalist activities in a biased fashion. One important example is the mainstream media's distinction between "good" and "bad" protesters. Mainstream outlets praise the "good" protesters, the "law abiding" groups who walk in circles and listen to speeches; at the same time, they work to discredit direct action and militant resistance to the hierarchical and oppressive status quo. They denigrate such activism as the work of so-called violent anarchists, terrorists, and thugs.

Before the G20, the national newspapers in Canada used their front pages to demonize protest organizers; after the G20 they became sounding boards for state operations to criminalize dissent (by publishing "most wanted" pictures of alleged vandals, for example). Prior to the protests, the Canadian Broadcasting Corporation (CBC) – Canada's publicly owned television and radio broadcasting service – ran pieces that briefly outlined the concerns of protesters and even introduced a basic understanding of anarchism. This seemed to be an attempt to present a more balanced view of the upcoming convergence. But by the time the protesters were actually in the streets, the tone had shifted to parrot the corporate media outlets. Another national TV news broadcast featured Treasury Board President Stockwell Day (a minister in the Conservative government) suggesting that a US travel advisory issued for Toronto came as a response to the power of "a small group of thugs . . . the anarchists and the violent groups,"[1] who were only attending the protests to cause trouble. This statement was met without critical response, an early indication of the tone of mainstream coverage for the rest of the week.

During the G20 protests, the right-leaning bias of the mainstream media was obvious, with little critical news published or broadcast.

Presenting the Movement's Narratives

For the first five days of protests, the mainstream media provided short pieces with thin analysis of the reasons people were in the streets. Most coverage focused on altercations between police and protesters.[2] The fifteen thousand people who came out to show their opposition to G20 policies were largely ignored. It was obvious that the mainstream press was only interested in showing images and telling stories of property destruction and protester "violence." After the major demonstrations on June 26, which saw tens of thousands of people mobilizing on the streets as well as targeted attacks on police cars and buildings, banks, and other symbols of global capitalism, the corporate media responded with a repetitive chorus of words from police representatives, pro-authoritarian pundits, and irresponsible mainstream activists, and images showing nothing but "meaningless vandalism" undertaken by "dangerous hooligans."

Canadian Alternative and Independent Media and the G20 Protests

Thankfully, it is certainly not all bad news when it comes to media in Canada. There are still some independent and non-commercial voices on campus and community radio stations; in print through zines, journals, and broadsheets; and on the Internet with interactive websites, podcasts, and video clips.

Rabble.ca offers one source of left-of-centre news. They host radical media, but the majority of their podcasts, written work, video broadcasts, and forum discussions are non-revolutionary and often reformist. *Rabble* was an important outlet for information in the lead-up to the G20, on-the-ground reporting during the G20, and continuing coverage and engagement after the G20. During the convergence, several *rabble*-affiliated journalists, myself included, posted news and updates on both the local media co-op's website and on *rabble*. However, some of the pieces posted by *rabble* in the lead-up to the convergence and in the immediate aftermath attacked the more militant elements of the protests, and in particular the idea of respect for a diversity of tactics, which (as Tom Malleson explains in chapter 1) was articulated by the Toronto Community Mobilization Network (TCMN) and other protest organizers.

Following successful engagement at the 2001 Free Trade Area of the Americas convergence in Quebec City, activists in Quebec developed an Indymedia network, reporting on local events and news. Since the August 2007 protests against the Security and Prosperity Partnership in Montebello, Quebec, Indymedia has become a model for alternative media in Canada. Because of this history of alternative news engagement, there was a strong involvement of Quebec journalists in the Toronto AMC.

The Toronto-based quarterly journal *Upping the Anti* has printed critical reflections on G20 organizing, as have independent publications *Briarpatch Magazine*, the *Molotov Rag*, and the *Dominion. Submedia.tv* has been producing constant updates on the post-G20 legal fallout, as have the *rabble* podcast network, *RedEye Radio* in Vancouver, *AW@L Radio* in Kitchener-Waterloo, Toronto-based *The Real G8/G20*, the cross-continent *Real News Network*, and the Canada-wide network of media co-ops, with local chapters in Toronto, Halifax, Vancouver, and Montreal. This network of media co-ops has been steadily growing and gaining respect as a trusted source of news and information and as an important new model for organizing community-based media.[3]

The principles of the media co-op network include support for and solidarity with the grassroots, which were at the base of anti-G20 organizing.[4] The Toronto AMC tracked and released information about the G20 protests – in real time with Twitter, mobile Internet, and cell-phone-based reporting software – through a portal on the website 2010.mediacoop.ca. This interactive and accessible webpage, which was online until hacked in early 2011, was created using Crows, an open source website platform for real-time reporting and communication, which was also used in the G20 protests in Pittsburgh in 2009 (leading to several arrests), and the 2010 anti-Olympics convergence in Vancouver (among others). The Toronto Media Co-op hosted the majority of the content produced by the AMC – the same arrangement the AMC had had with the Vancouver Media Co-op (VMC) during the anti-Olympics protests earlier in the year. However, while the VMC was militant in upholding respect for diversity of tactics, the Toronto AMC did host several posts that attacked tactical decisions of protest organizers and participants, feeding into the mainstream narrative of "good" versus "bad" protesters.

Presenting the Movement's Narratives

What the AMC Did in Toronto

As the G20 convergence commenced, AMC journalists arrived in Toronto and the AMC space was immediately used to host orientation meetings and press conferences alongside the print, audio, and video editing stations. Even before the space was fully organized, the AMC produced news from the pre-convergence educational People's Summit. As pre-registered and pre-screened journalists arrived, they were given AMC press passes, and a tour of the space. Those who hadn't pre-registered could still be a part of the AMC after a screening process in which known activists could vouch for less well-known colleagues, in an effort to keep out state infiltrators. (As I will explain later, these efforts were not entirely successful.) On several occasions during the convergence and the immediate aftermath, mainstream Canadian and international media attended press conferences outside the AMC space, and this helped to quickly satisfy our goal of creating dialogue and media narratives to counter the hegemony of the corporate media.[5] The AMC space was staffed around the clock and reached its carrying capacity on the fifth day of the street protests, as the G20 summit commenced.

To ensure that the narratives of the movement and the specific themed days of protest were properly represented, the AMC remained in constant contact with protest organizers; in some cases, media activists organizing specific actions were directly affiliated with the AMC. Twitter, phone, and radio reports, and smart phone video streaming were used to feed real-time information to the journalists at the AMC space, who quickly updated the AMC website. This live information was complemented on the website by other, slower reports and dispatches.

Social media websites became important sites for information dissemination when the #g20report, #g20, and #toronto hashtags quickly started spreading on Twitter, Flickr, and other social media as corporate journalists, bystanders, unaffiliated citizen-journalists, and protesters joined the dozen AMC journalists who were reporting real-time from the protests and press conferences. In what one AMC journalist called "a real-time media war," AMC journalists continually promoted the direct voices of the movement while countering misleading, untruthful, or divisive news narratives through a ceaseless barrage of blog posts and news updates, comments and corrections on mainstream media websites, updates on Facebook and Twitter networks, interactions with other social media, and press conferences and direct contact with mainstream reporters.

When inaccurate reports of a raid of the media centre started to circulate, they were quickly countered and corrected on Twitter and Facebook, and when accurate reports of raids, arrests, police buildups, and ad hoc street actions were released, the use of hashtags and social media allowed the news to be quickly spread to those who needed it (and were equipped to access it with smartphones, phone/text-trees, or computers). The Toronto G20 protests demonstrated that hashtags can be a useful tool in spreading news quickly and effectively. They can also be hijacked by state or corporate propagandists, although this was only a minor problem during the Toronto G20 and was combated through discrediting the agents of misinformation on the same networks on which they were operating. The police attempted to enter the AMC's online space but were stopped at the securely gated entrance.[6]

In addition to the Internet-based reporting undertaken by the AMC, independent journalists produced a daily broadsheet called the *Spoke*, modelled on the *Balaclava*, the daily from the Vancouver Olympics convergence. Both of these broadsheets are still published sporadically. During the summit protest week, the *Spoke* was distributed across the city each morning, appearing at the convergence space, at cafés, at university buildings, in the main public squares, and at each day's protest actions. The broadsheet contained stories and images from the day, information about upcoming events, and links directing readers towards more information by, for example, following the protests on the AMC websites or on Twitter through hashtags and user accounts. After each day's general meeting (which included debriefs from the current day, discussion on the coverage plan for the next day, and space for discussing other issues), those interested in working on the *Spoke* got together and started working. There was a core group of AMC members who nightly ensured the broadsheet was finished (usually by 4:00 or 5:00 a.m.), but each day different people took on the tasks of writing articles, designing layout, editing copy, printing the paper, and delivering the *Spoke* across town. All of the broadsheets are still available online.

Finally, the AMC was also connected to local radio stations, producing daily updates and other collaborative reports from the protests. While the AMC did not achieve total dominance of the media spectrum, the confluence of all the diverse media used – and the participation and dedication of dozens of media activists – allowed the Toronto G20 AMC to spread breaking news faster than mainstream media outlets and to ensure the stories of the movement were presented responsibly, truthfully, and accessibly to a broad audience.

The Impact of Our Work

By the third day of the protests, the mainstream media was following Twitter feeds and the AMC websites for breaking news and contacting the AMC for leads, but were never prepared to assist in alleviating the financial constraints non-corporate media face. Besides producing widely-accessed stories from the perspective of social justice movements (and occasionally becoming the focus of the narrative), AMC journalists were also embedded in protest marches, self-tasked with identifying and exposing plainclothes police officers and agents provocateurs, and reporting on police movements.

Indeed, the effectiveness of the AMC and affiliated journalists may have led to targeting, harassment, and abuse by G20 police forces. Several AMC members were assaulted by police – one person was hospitalized due to tasering; at least one was sexually assaulted by police while in detention; several had their equipment stolen or destroyed, or had their footage erased; and over a dozen were rounded up and jailed alongside eleven hundred other people in the temporary detention centre.[7] By the end of the week of protests, there were incidents of police targeting mainstream reporters and photographers for harassment, detainment, and assault. TVOntario host Steve Paikin tweeted from inside a police kettle (before he was allowed to leave) and again as he saw police beat and arrest *Guardian*-affiliated AMC journalist Jesse Rosenfeld.[8] At the same time, mainstream news outlets failed to critically report on many of the attacks on alternative journalists; indeed, a column in the national daily the *Globe and Mail* directly questioned the legitimacy of movement journalists and the AMC.[9]

Still, reports about the attacks on journalists opened space for a discussion that does not usually take place in Canada. Rather than being a distraction from the issues of protesters, the attacks on AMC journalists and others media-makers worked to illustrate the daily realities faced by those most targeted by the violent programs and oppressive policies of G20 states, and the lengths those states are willing to go to stop the documentation and exposure of their vicious nature.

The AMC and Toronto Media Co-op websites received more than 10,000 unique visitors on June 26, and traffic levels have remained high ever since. *Rabble* reported similar spikes in traffic, has seen increased visits to its podcast, blog, and discussion networks, and has since developed an active video section of its website. This has all resulted in a substantial increase in long-term capacity for alternative media in Toronto with the media co-op and other independent media outlets still producing content on a regular basis.

For the most part, AMC journalists managed to accomplish the important goal of "not doing the state's work," by using careful camera work and non-divisive language in producing content. However, there were several major security breaches. Acting on trusted information, one police infiltrator was identified during the convergence; she disappeared without attempting to return to the media centre or produce content. A second police infiltrator has since been identified and the work to inform affected communities and to learn from these violations is still underway.

Thinking it Over and Moving Forward

Among media activists and in other activist communities, the general sentiment is that the G20 AMC undertook important work and greatly contributed to documenting and disseminating stories from the movement that the mainstream media glossed over, misrepresented, or wholly ignored. Through the combination of real-time social media engagement, use of specialized reporting software, traditional web and print reporting, a dedicated local organizing core, and the commitment of dozens of alternative media activists and journalists, the Toronto G20 AMC was able to meet and exceed its stated goals while satisfying its stated principles.

Since the G20, both independent and mainstream media have reported on the legal proceedings against activists arrested during G20 protests, the continued targeting of communities of resistance, and the fallout from investigations into police behaviour during the week of the convergence. While independent media have consistently told these stories from a critical perspective, the emerging role of independent journalists and amateur video in bringing to public attention a plethora of evidence showing violent and illegal acts by G20 police has been in large part driven by the liberal newspaper the *Toronto Star* and CBC-affiliated documentary film makers. Both of these mainstream media sources have responded to pressure from the public and have worked to reveal the names of officers who concealed their identity by taking off their name tags, hiding their ID numbers, or obscuring their faces with masks and riot gear. These actions do not indicate a wholesale shift in the perspective of these media giants, nor do they excuse media collaboration in police investigations, but they do suggest that when public pressure is brought to bear critical work is possible from mainstream sources.

The prominent role for "citizen journalists" and media activists was one of the success stories of the Toronto anti-G20 organizing. The more accessible and non-hierarchal structure of the AMC underscores the fact that the mainstream media in Canada is ill-situated, ill-prepared, and ill-equipped to adequately report the reality of protest and dissent. The increasing affordability of web accessible cellphones, smartphones, and other media hardware, and the relative ease of use of the associated software, means that independent and alternative media is in a strong position to seriously challenge the dominant narratives presented by corporate media. All of this ensured that many heard the messages of the social and ecological justice movement. Perhaps most important of all was the close relationship that the AMC was able to maintain with protest organizers – seeing ourselves as a part of the movement we are responsible to. The media activists and movement journalists affiliated with the AMC represent a strong base on which to continue building media and communication structures that support the efforts of communities working everyday against G20-style austerity and imperialist capitalism.

8

Got Your Back!

Building Radical Crisis Support into the G20 Convergence

Monique Woolnough

I am proposing that we create a world where so many people are walking around with the skills and knowledge to support someone that there is no longer a need for anonymous hotlines. . . . I am proposing that we create a society where community members care enough to hold each other accountable so that a survivor does not have to flee their home. I am proposing that all the folks that have been disappointed by systems work together to create alternative systems. I am proposing that we organize.

— Rebecca Farr, Communities Against Rape and Abuse

ON SATURDAY, JUNE 18, 2010, I ATTENDED A THREE-HOUR SKILLS-SHARE for the G20 peer-to-peer crisis support team at Ryerson University. This was seven days before the events that the mainstream media have chosen to remember as "what happened at the G20" in Toronto. As I biked to Ryerson that night, I noticed that the fifteen thousand police officers brought to Toronto from Calgary, Durham, York, Montreal, even the United States, had started to arrive. There were dozens of police officers on bikes on what seemed like every corner. Sitting in the meeting with about twenty other people, envisioning how we were going to deal with the violence the police would bring to our communities, I couldn't shake the weight of the police presence from my chest.

A few weeks earlier, about ten people had come together to talk about making the Toronto Community Mobilization Network's sexual assault policy more than just words on paper. We were nurses, psychotherapists, shelter workers, students, medics, and community members. We had years or even decades of experience in DIY volunteer, professional, and intimate crisis and trauma support work. Our first meeting was on a sunny rooftop patio near downtown Toronto. I was involved in organizing the queer liberation action, was signed up to cook for the convergence space, and planned to help set up the thirty-foot by twenty-foot "Native Land Rights Now" banner that would be dragged along Toronto's streets during the "Canada Can't Hide Genocide" action. Thinking about the months of police surveillance and CSIS visits (later we would find out this had been going on for years) had my stomach in knots. I was consumed with imagining arrests, pre-emptive or otherwise, and I laughed nervously about how I would probably be the one needing crisis support.

We organized the skills-share for members of the crisis support team, street medics, and people who knew they'd be supporting their friends, their affinity groups, and people they met that week. We knew that police violence would reopen old wounds and create new ones. With limited resources and capacity, we liaised with various organizers, groups, and coalitions who had taken up the work of creating safe(r) spaces in the lead-up to the G20. As is so often the case, sometimes conflicts about sexual assault and community accountability found us, in disastrous and slightly less disastrous ways. We set up a twenty-four-hour phone line for the week and found a place to conduct crisis support. Our teams went to demonstrations to talk to people about what we were doing and what kinds of support we could provide.

I was humbled by the incredible process of sharing resources and skills as this team came together. We had honest dialogue about our limitations. Whatever support we provided would be short-term, because many of the organizers were from out-of-town or had pre-existing commitments to other organizing and support work. Conflicts about sexual assault and community accountability are raw, complicated, and so alive in our communities. People with experience dealing with trauma at previous mass mobilizations shared invaluable knowledge. We connected with people around the world who had organized similar support structures for large demonstrations. We struggled with the meaning of confidentiality when we were embedded in the communities we would be supporting. We had a hell of a time finding anything like safe space in what had become a huge militarized zone downtown. We tried to imagine how people could get around the city to us and avoid the police on the way. Most spaces offered to us were smack in the middle of checkpoints.

Yet as our friends, loved ones, and perfect strangers started coming out of the Eastern Avenue detention centre on Sunday, June 27 and telling their stories, the peer-to-peer crisis support team grew four times bigger. People from all over the city started offering their skills and services in various healing modalities for free, on a pay-what-you-can or sliding scale basis, or on payment plans. In Montreal, people who had not been in Toronto, but had watched in anxious horror as the weekend unfolded, set up healing and crisis support resources for people coming home. We provided resources and contacts across the country to people who had been affected by early morning raids, police kettling, sexual assaults, threats of gang rape, homophobic, ableist, racist, and transphobic taunting, denial of medical care, and witnessing police violence in its myriad forms. I cried a lot when I learned a few months later that my boxing coach, who runs the only women and trans-positive boxing gym in Canada, walked up and down the street on Eastern Avenue handing out tampons to people who needed them as they came out of the detention centre. The smallest expressions of support mean so much in times of crisis.

We all had buddies to make sure that we weren't walking around alone, vulnerable to being snatched by police and arrested. For all the violence the police inflicted on us during the G20, it is striking that it was the first time in my life that I never had to wonder about my safety plans for getting home.

If mass mobilizations provide us with a moment to build possible alternatives, then I hope that building capacity to support each other can become more central to movements and communities that have marginalized the knowledge and experience of Indigenous, feminist, queer, and anti-ableist organizers. Healing and support are crucial forms of resistance. The crisis support work at the G20 drew needed attention to the invisible and undervalued support work that anchors our communities every day. In September 2010, for example, community organizers in Montreal hosted a two day forum on building radical crisis support into communities of resistance. This support work is more important than ever, as neo-liberal attacks on the meagre support structures that already exist continue to escalate, with cuts to immigration settlement agencies, Indigenous organizations, faith-based organizations, and sexual health centres.

Now, as I unravel my own trauma from police surveillance, non-association bail conditions between my friends and loved ones, and hearing state prosecutors (colonially known as "Crowns") steal our stories and dreams and paint them as sinister extremist acts, I hold our collective strength and power so much deeper in me. The G20 protests forced some of us to get better at building structures that allow us to rely on each other, instead of the state, for our basic needs, healing, and well-being. In some communities, this invisible work was brought out of the shadows. I hope it will stay out. In this age of austerity, we are all going to need each other's support.

Part Two
During the G20

Documenting Resistance and Repression

9

Police Violence and State Repression at the Toronto G20
The Facts

The Movement Defence Committee

ONTARIO SAW TWO LARGE PROTESTS IN THE SUMMER OF 2010. ACCORD-
ing to police estimates, each protest was attended by upwards of ten
thousand people. Both protests were called to oppose government policy and both protests gathered in public places, including on the lawns
of legislative buildings. The city that played host to the first protest, in
May, saw no significant change to the ordinary policing of the city and
no incidents of police violence or misconduct were reported. To prepare for the June protest in the second city, police had a budget of over
a billion dollars: to pay for extra weapons and staffing to deal with the
protest; to conduct surveillance of the organizers of the protest; to
erect miles of barricades; and to set up a temporary jail to hold people.
In total, nineteen thousand officers were deployed to police the second
protest. The May protest was a right-wing, anti-choice, anti-abortion
rally held on Parliament Hill in Ottawa. The June protest was a
response to the arrival of the G20 in Toronto.

Many have characterized the security and police response to protesters at the Toronto G20 summit as restrained during the week of
protests leading up to the summit, negligent during the black bloc
action, and disproportionate during the remainder of the summit.
Based on our frontline experience, we believe this is an inaccurate
description. Widening our focus beyond the events of June 26 and 27
and looking at the months and weeks before and after the G20 summit in Toronto, we find that rampant violations of civil, political, and
human rights by police and security agents during the G20 represent
not a misstep by police in handling large protests, but a systematic
targeting and repression of social movements on the left, including
those who oppose the policies of the Harper government.

Who We Are

The Movement Defence Committee (MDC) – an autonomous working group of the Law Union of Ontario made up of legal workers, law students, activists, and lawyers – provides legal support to progressive organizations and social justice activists in Toronto. We believe that positive and lasting social change will only come from action taken outside the legal system and we are therefore committed to supporting organizations that aim to bring about such change and are criminalized for their attempts.

In 2010, the MDC offered legal support for people involved in the community-led demonstrations against the G20 in Toronto. The MDC's Summit Legal Support Project (SLSP) led "Know Your Rights" workshops for activists in Toronto and other nearby cities to review the constitutional rights and protections afforded to individuals by law. We trained and fielded almost seventy legal observers to document police action during the summit and we organized a group of over twenty-five volunteer criminal defence lawyers to provide *pro bono* legal representation for G20 arrestees at bail hearings and at the temporary detention centre on Eastern Avenue. We staffed a legal support line from June 18 to June 30 and received calls from hundreds of people who had been harassed, detained, searched, arrested, or brutalized by the police.

The MDC was the first non-police point of contact for many people who had been arrested and detained. In addition to facilitating access to *pro bono* legal representation by experienced defence counsel, we supported detainees by making phone calls to their families or workplaces and contacting potential sureties for bail, by ensuring that their dependents and pets were cared for in the interim, and by advocating on behalf of detainees who required special accommodations (such as prescription medicines, assistive devices, or ASL interpretation).

Our direct experience of the G20 protests gives us a unique perspective on the policing of the Toronto G20. We hope that the facts documented here help contextualize the individual testimonials in the other chapters of this book, and help underscore the serious questions that remain unanswered about events around the G20.

Police Harassment and Illegal Detentions and Searches

In the months before the protests, police visited the homes and work-places of people they perceived to be organizing protests and resistance to the G20 and showed up at their meetings. The MDC received reports of twenty-nine incidents of this type of systematic harassment. In the weeks leading up to the G20 summit and during the summit weekend itself, the police also conducted a systematic campaign of illegally detaining and searching pedestrians. Between Monday, June 21, and Saturday, June 26, the MDC received reports of over eighty people being harassed, detained, and searched by the police. We believe that many more people were similarly detained but did not report this harassment. Notably, these detentions generally involved pedestrians who were young and who were targeted for their appearance. They were conducted by police without reasonable grounds; they often involved groups of armed police officers surrounding pedestrians; they invariably included illegal searches of bags and pockets without any caution to the pedestrians that they had a right not to be searched; and they involved the illegal seizure of personal belongings, including leftist political literature.

On many occasions the police claimed increased and fictitious powers to detain and search pedestrians who were kilometres away from the security fence. People entering Allan Gardens on June 25, 2010, for example, were told they could not enter the public park without having their bags searched, pursuant to the Trespass to Property Act. Police stopped another group of pedestrians on University Avenue, telling them that they had the power to search their bags under the Public Works Protection Act (PWPA). Others reported that the police claimed search powers under the PWPA in or near the Toronto subway system. It turns out that there was indeed a regulation passed in secret by the Ontario cabinet under the World War II–era PWPA. However, this regulation only gave police enhanced powers *within* the fenced-off areas that surrounded the conference site itself. These incidents show a blatant pattern of bad faith searches on the part of the police and a pattern of proactive targeting of activists on the political left, which began well before Saturday, June 26.

Police Militarization: Queen's Park, Saturday, June 26, 2010

The police tactics employed at Queen's Park on Saturday, June 26, can only be described as a concerted effort to terrorize demonstrators protesting on the lawn of the legislature building. Riot police employed corralling or "kettling" tactics: officers in riot gear formed lines around the crowd, blocking paths of exit from the kettle; these lines of police then marched toward the crowd, forcing them into the shields of opposing riot police, making the kettle space smaller and smaller. The police marched repeatedly, relentlessly, circling in on the crowd, while individual officers broke through, arbitrarily tackling and dragging protesters behind police lines, where they were handcuffed.

Police used horses to intimidate people, charging at very close range in groups of four to six mounted riot police, and they fired tear gas canisters and rubber bullets at the crowd assembled on the Queen's Park lawn. Riot police charged and arrested groups of protesters participating in sit-ins. Legal observers witnessed police use their clubs, bikes, fists, or the heels of their boots to assault protesters who were sitting on the lawn or the street. Police sprayed other people in the face with chemical weapons such as pepper spray. Legal observers present heard no announcements by police asking the crowd to disperse.

Rampant and Illegal Use of Preventative Arrest and Detention

The police deployed large-scale preventative detention strategies over the G20 weekend, arresting 740 people for "breach of the peace," a power that authorizes police to temporarily detain people who are acting or are likely to act in a way that will "result in actual or threatened harm to someone," without laying any criminal charges.[1] "Breach of the peace" is not a criminal offence; rather it gives the police power to arrest and remove an individual. Because the power may be used in a preventive manner, in circumstances in which no criminal offence has taken place, it is a power that must be used carefully in order to ensure that liberty rights are not abused without cause. However, at the G20 demonstrations, police used this breach of the peace power unlawfully and with unprecedented abandon. With no claims that these 740 people arrested were involved in any criminal activity, police detained them for extended periods of time in abominable conditions and then released them without charge. Contrary to statutory and constitutional requirements, many of these detainees were held without charge for over twenty-four hours.

The police also illegally used the "Riot Act" to arrest groups of people. The "Riot Act" gives police the power to declare a gathering illegal and require participants to disperse within thirty minutes. Legal observers witnessed the police read the "Riot Act" to a group of demonstrators outside the temporary detention centre and then prevent them from dispersing. When the police finally let the demonstrators leave, the police then arrested some of them for not moving "fast enough." These tactics were used at several G20 protest sites.

These examples reveal organized efforts on the part of police to suppress public protest by categorizing the protests as "breaches of the peace" or "riots." The broadening of these legal terms to include any form of demonstration during the G20 shows a systematic misuse of police powers, specifically targeting the left, with the intention to stifle dissent against both the substance and the management of the G20 summit.

Violations of Procedural Rights

People who are arrested or detained by police are entitled to procedural protections enshrined in the Canadian Charter of Rights and Freedoms. However, during the weekend of the G20 in Toronto, the MDC received reports that suggest a pattern of procedural Charter rights violations. For example, police neglected to inform many detainees of the reasons for their arrest and failed to provide translation of the reasons for arrest to French and ASL speakers. At the detention centre, police delayed detainees' access to counsel over the telephone or denied it altogether. Additionally, police delayed or denied access to the free duty counsel available at the detention centre (apparently failing to advise detainees that lawyers were stationed there) and flouted the law that requires arrestees be brought before a justice for a bail hearing within twenty-four-hours. In violation of the Identification of Criminals Act, police used facial recognition software to photograph people held under breach of the peace. When finally released from custody, people were often subject to unreasonable terms of release prohibiting them from attending demonstrations and in some cases prohibiting them from being in downtown Toronto at all. This included people released without charge, who were led to believe that they were subject to release conditions that did not in fact exist.

Inhuman Conditions at the Temporary Detention Centre

Between Saturday, June 26 and Monday, June 27, the MDC received over two hundred phone calls from detainees held at the temporary detention centre on Eastern Avenue. The majority of callers were emotionally distressed, exhausted, and on the verge of tears. Many were outraged at their treatment and informed us that they were being "treated like animals." We received numerous reports of inhuman conditions and treatment during arrest and detainment. People told us that during arrests police had punched and kicked detainees in the legs, ribs, and head while shouting, "stop assaulting police" or "stop resisting arrest." Others told us that police continued to physically assault detainees who were already restrained. In the detention centre the abuse continued: for twelve or more hours, police provided little or no food or water to detainees and no blankets or socks for protection from cold temperatures; bright lights overhead made it impossible for detainees to sleep; police taunted detainees with racist, sexist, and homophobic slurs, and made threats of physical violence and gang rape; and police watched detainees as they used the toilets. Police caged detained youths with adult prisoners and did not allow them to call their parents.

Many detainees reported that that police denied them appropriate medical treatment. Legal observers in custody at the temporary detention centre witnessed police neglect to help one man who, due to a prior medical condition, was bleeding from his fingernails. Another man in the cells, after having been kicked in the face by riot police during his arrest, slipped in and out of consciousness without medical attention. Police taunted these detainees when they asked for medical assistance. Other detainees, unattended to by the guards, shivered from the cold and from shock, their lips turning blue.

Many who called the MDC from the detention centre reported that the guards used a number of tactics that had detrimental psychological effects on detainees desperate to be released. Some reported that, for no obvious purpose, detainees were repeatedly told to line up and provide their names and prisoner identification numbers. Guards walked by the same cages over and over again, calling out the same names even when it was obvious that those people were not in the cages. Others described how, instead of dividing detainees evenly among the cages, police filled some cages until they were overcrowded – some with more than two dozen people crammed in – while keeping only a handful of detainees in the adjacent cage, even when all the detainees had been arrested at the same time on the same charges. This had the effect of making those in the overcrowded cage extraordinarily uncomfortable while those next to them were terrified that police had isolated them from the others for some special reason. Some detainees reported that, in front of others in the cell, police told detainees that they were being released from the detention centre – hinting that everyone would be released soon – but then simply moved the prisoners to another cage. Many detainees were told by police that all the phones were in use and were sometimes made to wait more than twenty-four hours to make a call. Once at the telephones, however, detainees could see that many phones were available. Detainees who were given access to a phone were given insufficient time to speak with counsel. Psychological tactics like these served to further terrorize and disorient the detainees.

On Sunday morning, police representatives advised the MDC that no officers were available to make decisions respecting releases. This apparent bureaucratic confusion seemed to fade away as soon as Sunday evening rolled around. The processing delays vanished and the majority of detainees were released en masse.

Mass Violations of the Canadian Human Rights Act and the Ontario Human Rights Code

Before, during, and after the G20 weekend, police – municipal officers, provincial officers, and their agents – harassed and intimidated protesters and, in a manner that contravened the Canadian Human Rights Act and the Ontario Human Rights Code, suppressed their legitimate expression of political dissent. Indeed, the discrimination and harassment experienced by women, persons with disabilities, people of colour, Aboriginal activists, and lesbian, gay, bisexual, transgendered, and queer (LGBTQ) youth confirms the urgency of many issues highlighted by protesters, such as violence against women, Indigenous sovereignty, and immigrant rights.

Women reported to the MDC that while they were in the tempo-

Police Violence and State Repression at the Toronto G20

rary detention centre police sexually harassed and assaulted them, subjected them to sexual taunts or sexual touching, and sexually propositioned them. Male police officers performed strip searches – including cavity searches – on female detainees. In full view of male guards, women were forced to use washrooms without doors.

At the detention centre (and at other stages of the criminal justice process), police refused persons with disabilities the accommodations of their disability-related needs guaranteed to them by human rights legislation. For instance, after arresting a deaf man for not complying with police officers' verbal orders, police refused him ASL interpretation in the detention centre. He was accused of "faking" his disability. At follow-up court dates, no ASL interpretation was provided.

Police refused other people at the temporary detention centre access to necessary medication, even when they provided medical notes or prescriptions. Police confiscated people's personal aid and mobility devices upon arrest and refused detainees access to those necessary assistive devices while in detention. Later, people were released without their assistive devices, including wheelchairs, prosthetic legs, and glasses.

Police discriminated against young members of the LGBTQ community in detention, because of their sexual orientation. The MDC received reports that police used homophobic slurs and segregated LGBTQ-identified youth in solitary cages. After this degrading and humiliating treatment, most were released without charges. Police officers and their agents also targeted racialized activists with racist comments and Aboriginal arrestees with serious verbal harassment and physical violence.

Criminalization of Political Dissent

In addition to searches and seizures and mass arrests of protesters, well before the G20 summit began, police employed many other tactics aimed at the criminalization of political dissent. A few examples of these tactics provide a chilling glimpse of a broader pattern of state repression.

First, *the criminalization of political thought and expression* was rampant throughout the weeks leading up to the summit and those following. Two weeks before the summit even began, police held a pair of young political activists in custody overnight, charging them with seven counts of mischief for putting up posters with political content related to the G20. Media reports were replete with references to "alleged anarchists," as though holding a political belief had become a criminal act. During bail hearings, crown prosecutors used wearing black clothing and espousing anarchist political beliefs as evidence of a crime. Leftist literature was part of Toronto Police Chief Bill Blair's display of weaponry at a press conference on June 29, 2010. These weapons, according to Chief Blair, demonstrated "the criminal intent" of some of the protesters who were arrested.[2]

Second, *the criminalization of community organizers* was apparent as the police targeted and intimidated long-time community activists – committed advocates for social justice. Several community organizers reported being harassed and followed by police or visited by CSIS (Canadian Security Intelligence Service) at their homes or workplaces in the months leading up to the G20 summit. Many organizers were isolated and silenced, charged with serious crimes and placed on extraordinarily restrictive bail conditions, including terms of non-association with grassroots social justice organizations and bans on attending public demonstrations or expressing political views in public. This criminalization of dissent through the treatment of community organizers as dangerous criminals has alarming repercussions for non-profit community organizations working for positive social change.

Next, police furthered *the criminalization of "knowing your rights."* This was evident when officers targeted protesters with the MDC legal support phone number written on their arms. According to police rationale, law-abiding citizens do not need legal support and therefore possession of a lawyer's phone number is evidence of criminal intent. The MDC's "Know Your Rights" flyer – a quarter-page informational primer on constitutional rights for individuals who are searched, detained, and arrested – was included in Chief Blair's display of so-called weaponry at his June 29 press conference.[3] These examples demonstrate efforts by police to criminalize even the knowledge of (never mind the exercise of) constitutionally protected rights, including the right to counsel.

Finally, the G20 demonstrations made apparent *the criminalization of the protester.* Police seized items commonly used during public demonstrations, including bamboo sticks used for placards or flags, equipment used for protection against police chemical weapons (including goggles, kerchiefs, vinegar, and water bottles), as well as other innocuous items such as contact lens cleaner and bike helmets. These items also formed the basis of "intent to cause mischief" or "weapons" charges. The Crown later dropped most of those charges.

The Consequences of the G20 Security Strategy

The MDC believes that what happened in Toronto in the summer of 2010 – the repression of dissent and the massive and systemic violations of rights by police; the arrest and detention, in appalling conditions, of eleven hundred people, the majority of them not even charged; and the failure of any level of government to hold top civilian and police leaders accountable for allowing and facilitating such wanton disregard for people's rights – was not a random blip in our country's otherwise solid record of respecting the rights of its citizens and residents. Rather, by looking at who has benefited and who has suffered in the aftermath of the summit, the G20 security strategy can be viewed as the most obvious and recent example of a long tradition of state repression against social justice activists critical of government policies.

The police have clearly benefitted; the G20 security strategy provided them with new crowd control weapons and new surveillance equipment. The criminalization of dissent has allowed police to keep their jobs, despite their blatant disregard for the law. The federal government – and any future government that wants to stifle opposition to its policies – has benefitted as well. The security policies during the summit created a climate of fear – fear that speaking out will mean that you will be labelled a criminal thug and face police violence and arrest.

Those who have suffered most directly are those people in Canada who believe in standing up to injustice, who actively oppose government policies that further entrench social and environmental injustice. Ultimately, however, it is all of us who will suffer from the erosion of hard-won rights and political freedoms.

10

They Sought to Terrify Us out of the Streets

Nat Gray

July 17, 2010

A MONTH AGO, I TRAVELLED FROM MONTREAL TO TORONTO TO march in opposition to the G20. On Sunday, June 27, I joined a police-sanctioned jail solidarity demonstration in support of friends who had been surrounded and arrested the day before at the "designated protest zone" in Queen's Park. We were gathered around outside the detention centre when a line of riot police moved towards us without warning. As I tried to get away, police shot me twice with rubber bullets, then arrested me and incarcerated me for thirty hours. They charged me with obstruction of a "peace officer." I have never been more terrified, more dehumanized, or more in pain than I was that day. I wish my story were unique.[1]

That week, at the end of June, twenty thousand police officers – paid for with over a billion dollars of public money – arrested, incarcerated, and abused a thousand demonstrators, journalists, and passersby. As demonstrators, we were in the streets to protest the systemic and violent oppression caused here and around the world by the capitalist, corporate strategies agreed upon and celebrated by the leaders of the G20. We got a concentrated taste that week of the everyday human rights abuses we were there to oppose.

Outside the jail that Sunday around noon, a police line formed between our peaceful protest and the detention centre. Two unmarked minivans suddenly screeched to a stop behind the police line. Plainclothes police stormed through the line and into the crowd, violently pushed two people to the ground, dragged them along the pavement, and threw them into the vans, which then drove off. To the remaining demonstrators, this appeared to be a strategically orchestrated kidnapping. The small woman who was snatched would later become my cellmate. She told me that two large men sat on her and choked her until she was almost unconscious. A third man pulled her hair and all three verbally abused her, referring to her as "cunt," "bitch," "whore," and "street trash" on the way to the detention centre. All three officers refused to identify themselves.

As the vans drove away, we sat down, clapped our hands, and chanted, "We are peaceful, how about you?" Officers donning helmets, body armour, and gas masks joined the line in front of us and took out weapons. Several minutes later, again without warning, the police line moved quickly toward us. As officers yelled, "Get back!" we stood up and moved backwards. The police line parted to let through an officer who was wielding a large, intimidating weapon.

Being asthmatic, I had bought a painter's respirator from a hardware store to protect myself from chemical weapons. Not knowing what the weapon behind us was, I put the mask on as a precaution, and backed away from the police. It was then that police shot me in the sternum. As I turned away they shot me again in the elbow, and I immediately hit the ground, falling into the fetal position. I remember hoping that someone was on the way to help me. I knew I couldn't get up by myself.

Another demonstrator ran back for me and tried to help me to my feet but the riot line caught up to us and several police shoved me back to the pavement, face first. They yelled at me to stop resisting and kneeled on top of me. I was terrified, and lost control of my bladder. I remember begging them to be gentle because I was hurt. They dragged me to my feet and walked me to a nearby cruiser, the officer on my left insisting on gripping my arm over the bullet wound.

I spent the first half-hour of my incarceration lying in the fetal position in the cruiser or being moved around the compound by police. They didn't seem to know what to do with me, although I asked every officer I saw for medical attention. The first sergeant I was taken to see was told I was asking to see a doctor. He said "too bad." When I repeated my request, I was told to "suck it up." About thirty minutes after my arrest, a doctor was finally allowed to check my vitals and give me acetaminophen. (All that the detention centre doctors had to offer was acetaminophen or ibuprofen.) Then they put me on a stretcher and loaded me into an ambulance. This was when I overheard officers saying why they had targeted me: I had put the respirator on my face.

An hour later, I arrived at the hospital, where I was checked for internal bleeding and broken bones. Thankfully, I suffered neither; an hour and a half of internal bleeding might have left me dead. I was then taken back to the detention centre and put in a solitary cell. The detention centre consisted of rows of wire cages in several large, cold, concrete rooms. In a row against one wall were the solitary cells, which were much smaller and had sheet metal blocking the view on three sides. I would spend most of my time in solitary cells due to my injuries. I was soon taken to a makeshift office where three male officers interrogated me. After I told them my name one officer referred to me as "sir," and asked if I preferred to be called "Natalie" or "Gray," implying that my physical appearance didn't represent my sex (perceived gender).[2]

All the other G20 prisoners I've since spoken to experienced verbal abuse from the guards. The officers categorized and harassed people according to race, gender, sexual orientation, ability, gender expression and/or identity, presumed income, HIV status, or whatever else came to their minds. One officer told a person in a cell next to mine to, "Stop crying, faggot." A second said to a racialized detainee, "We let you into this country and this is what you do?" Another officer told a woman that she would be repeatedly raped while she was in jail. The scope and consistency of the verbal abuse in the detention centre is difficult to articulate.

After my interrogation was over, police took me to a small, wooden room to strip-search me. After I repeated several times that I wanted to speak to a lawyer before being strip-searched, I was surrounded by about eight officers. One of the male officers, referring to the men in his group, said, "I know she'll behave because if she doesn't, she knows *we'll* be coming in." I was strip-searched by four female officers. My experience was mild compared to another woman – she was strip-searched by several male officers, one of whom put his finger inside her.

Back in my cell, I knew that the acetaminophen would wear off soon and I'd be in severe pain again. I also needed to take my asthma medication. I started asking officers to see a doctor. I was finally taken to a doctor about an hour and a half after I started asking. Each time that I knew that my pain medication would soon wear off, I would tell the officers twenty minutes in advance. Each time, they would wait until the pain was unbearable before taking me to the doctor.

Guards occasionally gave us buns with a slice of processed cheese in the middle and small foam cups of water. The bathroom stalls, which faced the officers, had no doors. The solitary cells didn't have bathrooms at all. The floors and benches were concrete and puddles were common. The officers refused us blankets and warm clothing. I was refused a fresh pair of pants, and spent all thirty hours there in the pants I had urinated in. The fluorescent lights were left on non-stop, day and night. Around midnight, I huddled up in a corner of the cage and dozed off for a couple of minutes. But, like many other prisoners, I was too hungry, cold, and injured to sleep that night. Every four hours that night I asked to see the doctor, and every four hours it would be an ordeal – they consistently waited until I was hunched over, shaking, clutching my arm to my front, and crying.

The next morning, the police took several of us to the courthouse. One of the other detainees, a Black man, told me that he had been walking through Queen's Park when a police officer called him over. Fifteen officers then surrounded him and beat him. They kicked him and stomped on his face. When he put his hands over his face, they yelled at him to "stop resisting." Police broke his jaw and cracked several of his ribs. He was charged with resisting arrest.

I was one of the lucky people released on bail on Monday. It felt weird to leave my cellmates behind, but they reassured me and hugged me, and asked me to call their families for them once I was outside. Most people had been denied their right to a phone call. I stepped out into the sun and immediately burst into tears.

I sat on the ground outside the courthouse with some wonderful people who were waiting there to meet us with real food, medical supplies, and emotional support. While I waited for my friends to arrive, ten police officers surrounded the six of us and told us to get off the property. They followed us onto the sidewalk and harassed us until we were too far away to meet the newly released detainees. A person offering court support gave me a ride to my friend's place where I was staying. As one of my bail conditions I was restricted to that apartment, and I spent a week in there, constantly fearing a knock at the door, terrified of being taken back into police custody.

As I write this, most of the one thousand arrestees have been released, though twelve people remain incarcerated. These twelve have been charged with conspiracy, with bail set upwards of $85,000. They have been strategically targeted in an attempt to discredit and undermine our grassroots organizations. They are our friends and our comrades. The brutal police abuse of a thousand people that weekend leaves no question who truly committed injustice.

The police sought to crush our democratic rights to freedom of assembly and freedom of speech. They sought to terrify us out of the streets. They sought to silence our dissent. And they hoped no one would notice. They underestimated us.

We are hurt. We are sad. We are angry. We are also as passionate, as adaptable, and as determined as ever before. This tragedy has enraged us, inspired us, and united us.

State-sanctioned police brutality is a daily reality for so many people and communities within Canada's borders. What makes the weekend's violence significant is not so much its intensity, but the media coverage and the public outcry. We must start to talk about the institutionalized, everyday nature of police brutality, the majority of which is not caught on tape and will never be covered by corporate news. We must confront this and other forms of institutionalized violence, from immigration policy to austerity measures. We must escalate our presence on the streets to express our outrage.

Furthermore, we must insist on our right to flood the streets in solidarity with others around the world – those whose struggle for clean water, clean air, clean land, self-determination, and peace is a way of life – those whose daily realities are a direct result of the illegitimate, criminal choices made by Stephen Harper and the rest of the G8 and G20 thugs.

We stand together. We're here. We're strong. We resist.

March 16, 2011: Postscript

Months after my arrest, the footage of Toronto Police Chief Bill Blair denying that rubber bullets were used that day still played on the news. It was only once lawyer Clayton Ruby announced he would take my case that the Toronto Police admitted to shooting me. On August 23, after I travelled back to Toronto from Vancouver to appear in court, the charge against me was dropped. We filed a lawsuit against the police at the end of August, and seven months later the

Toronto Police Department launched a criminal investigation of the officers involved.

While I was in the detention centre, it was hard to imagine that sitting on the concrete floor that weekend would change my life so much. I didn't know I'd get an infection in my arm, leaving it useless for months. I didn't know that in July, a couple of days after I gave a speech about my detention, I would suffer my first acute episode of post-traumatic stress, or that for six months afterwards I would struggle to perform day-to-day tasks, to feel safe, and to believe that life was worth living. I didn't know that this episode of my life would trigger my depression, and I didn't know it would take me a long time to work my way out of that. I didn't know that this trauma would always be a part of me.

What I did know was that they weren't going to get inside my head; that my physical and emotional injuries were obstacles I would overcome; that our social justice movements are so much stronger than brute force; that we'd come out the other side of this scarred, but ready to finish what we've started.

They will never jail our hearts, and they will never jail our fighting spirit.

11

One Day in a Cage

Notes on the Temporary Detention Centre

David Wachsmuth

LAST WEEKEND I WAS IN TORONTO DEMONSTRATING AGAINST THE G20 meeting taking place there. At 2:45 a.m. on Saturday night, police arrested me for a "breach of the peace." The nineteen hours that followed were probably the most infuriating, frustrating, and frightening ones of my life. Unfortunately, it seems my experience was very similar to that of many of the eleven hundred people arrested that weekend. So, my story, despite being intensely personal, probably speaks for many others, at least in part.

The Protest

In preparation for a huge number of arrests the police set up an ad hoc detention centre at an old film studio in the east end of Toronto. On Saturday night, along with a close friend who had been a legal observer at the demonstrations, I joined a midnight jail solidarity action outside the detention centre. We were there to support people who had been picked up by police earlier that day in a series of arbitrary and violent arrests. Many of those arrested had not been protesting at all but had simply been in the wrong place at the wrong time. Shortly before 2:00 a.m., after a few hours of peaceful and spirited demonstration (featuring an excellent marching band), the police ordered us to disperse. At the same time this command was issued, dozens of cops in full riot gear moved in to surround us.[1] The 150 of us there were outnumbered at least two to one. For a minute or so we discussed staying despite the order to disperse, but soon everyone was moving in the direction the cops had told us to, filing between the ranks of riot police. A few minutes after we started to leave, and with no warning whatsoever, riot cops cut through the column of protesters and sealed off the two dozen of us at the back of the group. When we asked to leave, we were told that we'd had our chance to leave already and hadn't taken it – odd, since we were walking away when they sealed us in. All of us trapped there were arrested.

The Arrest

My arrest took about forty minutes and was relatively uneventful. It did make me realize how uncomfortable and difficult it is to hold your hands on your head for that amount of time. Since I was one of the last to be handcuffed, there was a lot of time for this to sink in. Next, police handcuffed my hands behind my back – this was much more uncomfortable, but I had expected that. The cop who dealt with me took me off to the side, asked me various questions, searched me, and so on. After a minute or two, I realized there was quite a lot of light on me – it turned out that he was processing me right in front of a television crew making a report. I asked to be moved to somewhere a little less intrusive, but the reporter apparently had the footage she was looking for, since various people (including my mother) later told me they'd seen me on the news. At least this meant my loved ones knew where I was – I was not allowed to make a phone call (or to talk to a lawyer) in the nineteen hours I was detained.

Police slowly loaded us into police vans to take us to the detention centre. After various delays, they stuffed us into little miniature jail cells inside the vans (in my van there were four cells, each of which held two of us) and off we went. After the minute or two it took to get inside the detention centre, we spent the next thirty minutes or so sitting in these tiny little van-jails. We couldn't see anything out the van's very small grated windows, but it sounded like we were parked in a big room with a lot of prisoners in it. The best part of the wait was the spontaneous round of mass meowing we heard from the prisoners outside; the cages really did feel like animal pens. The worst part was the increasing pain in my left arm, which was held awkwardly behind my back with plastic cable-tie handcuffs.

The Detention Centre

Police next unloaded us from the vans into a set of gender-segregated cages. I spent time in three of these, all the same. They were twenty feet by ten feet, with a four-by-four foot washroom inside. The washroom had no door and no toilet paper (some previous inhabitant had stashed a little in our first cage, but it was quickly used up). There were usually about twenty-five people in each cage; we had about seven square feet of space each. For the entire time we were imprisoned, we had to rotate between standing, sitting, and lying down, since there wasn't enough room for all of us to sit or lie down at the same time. Lying down didn't actually mean sleeping; the combination of the cold temperature and bright lights (plus the steady ruckus) ruled that out.

The way we were treated in those cages was blatant harassment and probably illegal. The list of offences I witnessed is fairly long. First, the cops didn't allow any of us – even one minor – to make a phone call or speak with a lawyer, despite telling us during arrest that we had the right to do so (some people were never even read their rights or informed of their charges). Second, the cops kept us in handcuffs the entire time we were detained. Third, the cops gave us very little to eat or drink; in my nineteen hours in the jail we were given two tiny little "sandwiches" (a single slice of soy cheese and a bit of margarine on a dinner roll) and four or five small foam cups of water. It was difficult to eat and drink in handcuffs, but for most of the time I didn't have much appetite anyway. Fourth, I saw the cops deny medical attention to two people with serious medical problems – it took us something like forty minutes to get a medic for one of my cellmates who was bleeding from under his fingernails and on the verge of collapsing. Last, the guards alternatively taunted us, threatened us, lied to us, or ignored us. Once, after we had been calling for food for some time, a guard deliberately sat down in front of our cell and ate his lunch.

Even if we had been a bunch of hardened criminals the guards' behaviour would have been completely inexcusable, but in fact not a single one of us had been arrested for anything that resembled just cause. Almost half of the people I was caged with had been at the jail solidarity demonstration with me and almost half had been at a peaceful demonstration outside the Novatel hotel when police surrounded them, beat them, and then arrested them en masse. The rest of the people I met in the detention centre were passersby. The most egregious example of this ridiculous police seizure of bystanders was the arrest of Elroy Yau, a TTC employee in full uniform – riot cops jumped him as he arrived for his shift at Queen's Park subway station, and he spent thirty-six hours in custody with no phone call, lawyer, or charges (see chapter 16 for his story). A few other people were arrested for the previously unknown crime of dressing in black and going to punk rock shows. One of these detainees was from out of town, and didn't even know what the G20 was. I spoke with two women in an adjacent cage who had been trampled by police horses and then charged with obstruction of police – the encounter left one of the women with a broken arm.

The detention centre guards used calculated harassment to create feelings of uncertainty and fear amongst detainees. The guards would move prisoners from one cage to another, keeping them disoriented and preventing them from getting to know their cage-mates, and keeping the rest of us uncertain about whether the individual had been released or just shuffled. On a number of occasions police told us that we were about to be released, only to then ignore us for hours and hours. Police asked us again and again to identify ourselves – twice guards took an inventory of everyone's name and ID number. When they tried a third time we refused to cooperate.

While I was in the detention centre I was inclined to chalk these things up to incompetence and confusion on behalf of the police. More than a thousand people were arrested, and the centre was clearly swamped. But after getting out, talking to others who were imprisoned, and thinking more about it, I now find it hard to avoid the conclusion that this confusion and uncertainty was deliberate. Too many times to count the guards told us they were working as fast as they could to process us but the paperwork needed for our release was taking a long time. When they actually did release us, this laborious paperwork never materialized – they simply walked us fifty feet to the exit and handed us our possessions. Many of the detainees were held for eighteen to twenty-three hours (just under the legal maximum), and it seems clear to me that those endless promises of impending release were deliberate lies – perhaps to disorient us, torment us, or punish us.

Many of the individual guards chose to taunt, harass, and abuse us. I'm sure many guards thought that we deserved it, and the others found it easier to just let it happen. The abuse was worse because it was completely arbitrary. Sometimes if we asked for a medic, guards would show up quickly and take our ill cage-mate to a medic. Sometimes guards would show up quickly but do nothing. Sometimes guards would not show up at all. The result of all this was that we were constantly on edge. We were alternately furious, frightened, depressed, and manic. At times we all banged on the cage and screamed at the top of our lungs. At other times we brooded silently. One detainee went into shock. By the time we were released, the detained passersby sounded just as radically anti-authoritarian as the protesters. Police had arrested us for different reasons, but they treated us all appallingly, and this united us in our outrage.

Looking Back

I'm acutely aware of how lucky I was relative to so many of the other innocent people who were arrested over the weekend. For one, I wasn't assaulted by the police before being taken into custody. But more than that, as an educated, well-off, straight white male I avoided much of the abuse and harassment that police used to target others. I'm sure it wasn't a coincidence that the person in my cage held longest was an Indigenous man. Police segregated queer people in separate cages, threatened women with rape, and subjected them to invasive strip searches.[2]

I'm now back in New York City, where I live, so I haven't been able to participate directly in the growing collective efforts to seek justice for all the injustice that occurred in Toronto over that weekend. I wish I could be part of this response. Being on the receiving end of police brutality hasn't changed my politics: it's confirmed them, and made me angrier. At the same time, while I am optimistic that forthcoming investigations and inquiries will condemn some of the police tactics, I don't think that the fallout from the G20 protests will be a setback for the cops and their enablers in government. I think the police and government strategy for getting away with tactics like these is to kick the ball forward as far as they can – public outrage and judicial action may subsequently kick the ball back a certain distance, but as long as the ball ends up further upfield than it was before, they can claim a victory of sorts. So, in general, I am pessimistic about how much good can come directly out of all this.

I do think, however, that there is reason to hope that this outrage will bring more people together and raise awareness of the fundamental injustices that underpin our society – injustices that we must expose before we can confront, and which are now harder to ignore after over one thousand peaceful protesters and bystanders have been arbitrarily beaten, jailed, or both.

June 30, 2010

12

"Hop!"

A First-Hand Account of Police Abuse at the G20

Sarah Pruyn

EARLY IN THE EVENING ON JUNE 26, MY FATHER AND I WALKED BACK to Queen's Park to look for my mother. We had been separated from her during the "People First!" march, which had started there that afternoon. My father, an above-the-knee amputee, was wearing an artificial leg, and all this walking wasn't easy for him. Hundreds of riot police surrounded the roadways leading to the lawn of the provincial legislature, but we managed to find an unguarded path in through the University of Toronto campus. As we searched for my mother, a line of riot police began walking toward us, ordering my father and I, along with hundreds of other protesters, to move.

My father refused to move – we were on public property and had a right to be there. The police pushed him and still he would not move. About five metres to the left, officers shot tear gas cartridges to force protesters to move. My father backed away from the police line. The line advanced a few metres and stopped.

We joined a group of protesters on University Avenue, and sat down beside two young men. They offered us water and we chatted about the police pushing people out of Queen's Park – the site of the Ontario government and a spot that had been designated an official demonstration area. Since the police had been firing tear gas, I wet my bandana with apple cider vinegar and kept it ready to protect myself.

Five minutes later we were suddenly attacked; the riot cop line pressed forward while shooting more tear gas. Officers from behind the line ran toward us. They slammed into us and hit us. Police lines surrounded us in front and on either side. Activists who had been behind us started to retreat. With the two men we'd just met, I tried to help my father move, but the crowded space impeded our efforts.

"These four!" one officer shouted, indicating to the others that he wanted us arrested. Someone ordered my father to stand but his artificial leg made it difficult for him to get up. Police kicked and bashed my father. They grabbed my left arm and twisted it behind my back. The two protesters who had offered us water tried to help my father up, telling the police again and again that my father only had one leg. As I yelled at them, "Let my father stand!" the officer clutching my arm grabbed a fistful of my hair with his other hand and dragged me to the other side of the riot line, pulling out a chunk of my hair on the way. After being forced along for a while, I managed to stand up and walk with the officer.

Next to a police van, the officer bound my wrists with plastic zipcuffs and searched my backpack, where he found my ID. As he completed a form, the officer told me that I had been arrested for "obstruction of justice." Next, my possessions were put into bags, my zipcuffs were removed and replaced with metal handcuffs, and I was locked in a cell of the van. I'm not sure how long I was in there for. Through a tiny window I could see officers in plainclothes running back and forth through the riot lines, arresting protesters. After at least thirty minutes, I was taken from the vehicle, shackled, and ordered onto a police bus. From the window of the bus, I saw a group of officers kicking protesters who were lying in submission on the ground.

After waiting a little while longer, we were driven to the temporary detention centre on Eastern Avenue. One at a time, we were forced off the bus. As I walked down the stairs of the bus an officer smirked, "Don't forget to tip the driver."

As soon as I got off the bus, police officers told me to kneel on a chair, which had been placed against a wall. They removed my legcuffs and handcuffs and then put a new pair of cuffs on my wrists. They brought me, along with eight other women, to a cage near the back of an enormous studio room. It was the first of five cells that held me during my twenty-seven hour stay in jail.

Before long, I was removed from the cell for processing. This took about an hour: police took my picture, confiscated my shoes, and searched me twice more. A sergeant asked me questions such as, "Why did you decide to get arrested today?" I refused to answer anything other than questions about my identity without first speaking with a lawyer. The sergeant told me that I had been arrested for "breach of peace." I don't know what happened to my "obstruction of justice" charge.

"What does 'breach of peace' mean?" I asked.

"That you disrupted the general harmony of Toronto," he replied.

Next, police took me to a cell in the detainment zone. On my way there, the officer holding me told me that I could make a phone call. At about 11:00 p.m. I was escorted to a phone booth where I contacted the TCMN legal support line run by the Movement Defence Committee. I was lucky; others were in jail for more than twenty-four hours and were never allowed to use a phone. Many never saw duty counsel. Most were never charged. Worst of all, some, such as a cellmate of mine with a bloody forehead, were refused badly needed medical attention for hours. When we asked the police why they were mistreating us some of them said that it was because we were criminals and others claimed it was due to organizational problems.

At 1:00 a.m. I was moved to another cell, about six feet by ten feet in size. Throughout the night, the police brought more women to the cell and by the late morning there were ten of us inside. At around 2:00 p.m. I was allowed to make another phone call. This was strange to me; some people had been there longer than me and hadn't been allowed a single call. I called the TCMN legal support line again. No one picked up. Later, I found out that many volunteer lawyers and others from the convergence centre had been arrested.

Without a link to outside legal help, I asked to speak to duty counsel. I am still bewildered as to why I got to see a lawyer while others did not. Poor bureaucratic organization? Were they playing "good cop" with me? Did they want things to seem chaotic so they would have an excuse for neglecting people's needs?

When we asked for food or water, the police told us that we could "have some shortly," but we usually waited an hour or two. Some people were in jail for eight to ten hours before getting any water at all. About four times while I was there, we were offered sandwiches made of white bread with butter and processed cheese. Since I am vegan, I could not eat the sandwiches. At 6:00 p.m. on Sunday I begged an officer for food that I could actually eat. About an hour later, he brought me to a cell out of sight of the other prisoners and gave me an apple and some orange juice. I was grateful for the food.

Since some of us had been in custody for more than twenty-four hours, we asked the cops who walked by our cells why they weren't releasing us. Some officers ignored us and others told us, "we are just too overworked to have time to release you," or, "I don't know, I just do what I'm ordered," or, "we are going to, very soon." Still others swore, "there are protesters outside and they are dangerous. We can't let you go until they go."

At around 4:00 p.m. my cellmates and I were moved to a slightly larger cell. About four hours after that some officers took me and another woman to a tiny cage in a room separate from the detainment area we'd been in for so long. Here, we were told that we were being let go, that charges against us would be dropped, but that there were conditions for our release, one of which was that we could not take part in any further G20 protests in Toronto. Our belongings were returned to us. We asked if we could have a copy of our charges and release conditions. We were ignored. The cops snapped another picture of each of us. Before we even had time to put our shoes on, we were shoved out a door into the pouring rain.

My Father's Story

After meeting up with friends and finding my parents, I learned that my father's experience had been far worse than mine. While police were dragging me away from Queen's Park, my father, unable to get up quickly because of his disability and the police pushing him, was accused of "resisting arrest." While he was still on the ground the police took away his walking sticks, ripped off his prosthetic leg, and then ordered him to hop towards a police van. He told the police that it was impossible for him to hop so they dragged him across the pavement to the vehicle. They took his glasses and his wallet, including $33. Though the police accused him of resisting arrest they never actually informed my father that he was under arrest or explained what offence he had committed.

At the detention centre, police locked my father in a cage outside of the processing area and kept him there for twenty-six hours. During this time, the police refused to remove his handcuffs even once. No one read my father his rights or allowed him to make a phone call. When he asked why he was not being processed like other prisoners, police told my father that his paperwork had been misplaced. When he and some others in his cage asked for water, several hours passed before police brought it. When my father was finally released, a court officer informed him that he should not have been kept in the cage for so long. He was given his driver's licence and artificial leg back, but police claimed that they had lost his glasses, whistle, money, and walking sticks, which have still not been returned. My father left the detention centre humiliated, with severe bruising and a head injury.

During the first few days after the G20, some protesters did not see the point of speaking out about how the police had behaved. Police brutality is nothing new to those who are familiar with struggles against oppression so there didn't seem to be any point in criticizing what had happened as if the conduct of officers was a surprise, particularly in the face of the media's pro-police spin. But as more protesters told their stories about police abuse it became harder for the rest of us to stay silent. What's more, proving that the police were systematically violent during and leading up to the G20 became necessary to get hundreds of people's charges dropped and many community organizers out of jail.

In July, my father and I filed separate complaints with the Office of the Independent Police Review Director. We have since withdrawn them because the complaint process might complicate our participation in other, possibly more effective, methods of legal action. As I write, my father is involved with a human rights complaint and I plan to take part in a class action lawsuit.

My father was not the only G20 arrestee with a disability who was abused by police. Police ignored the pleas of my father's cellmate – paralyzed on one side of his body – for help to go to the bathroom, so he ended up wetting his pants. Though the man only had the use of one hand and could not walk, police refused to remove his handcuffs until he was released.

Many people supported my father after the G20 through letters, blog posts, and articles. However, some who heard his story claimed that he should not have been in Toronto during the G20, that he should have known that his disability would put him at great risk. Others argued that my father was planning to use his disability to get away with mischief – that he thought the police would not dare touch him due to his prosthetic leg. These extremely troubling views demonstrate how "freedom of speech" is more accessible to able-bodied people than to people with disabilities. According to these views, people with disabilities should stay away from protests. My father prepares himself expertly for the possible physical difficulties he may face each day, but he cannot foresee or plan for them all, nor should he be expected to. He should not have been punished for thinking that he would be safe at the G20.

Justice for Our Communities demonstration, June 25, 2010, at College St. and Elizabeth St. Photo by Wesley Fok.

13

Women Resist, Police Repress
Gendered Police Violence at the Toronto G20

Shailagh Keaney

THE G20 DESCENDED ON TORONTO IN JUNE 2010, ACCOMPANIED BY a police occupation of the city's downtown core, ostensibly for the purpose of keeping world leaders safe. Having first used a small fraction of the $1.2 billion they were allotted for summit security to temporarily convert an old movie studio on Eastern Avenue into a jail, the police proceeded to search, raid, and arrest activists in tactical operations that saw over a thousand people detained – the largest mass arrest in Canadian history. Common experiences of police harassment, pre-dawn raids, targeted and arbitrary arrests, harsh detentions, and strip searches weave their way through the stories of everyone who was arrested that week. An examination of the Toronto G20 experience shows a pattern of police repression familiar from other recent large-scale summit protests – the so-called "Miami Model" of policing tactics. The police violence that resulted from the implementation of the Miami Model in Toronto was compounded by gendered violence against women.

According to human rights experts, the experience of political repression is different for women than men: "women experience the same violence men encounter, but also suffer additional torment in the form of sexual violence. While such violence is not exclusively the fate of women, it is overwhelmingly so."[1] Here the concept of the "continuum of violence against women"[2] proves useful. This idea acknowledges that "violence against women is not the result of random, individual acts of misconduct, but rather is deeply rooted in structural relationships of inequality between women and men."[3] Seemingly minor instances of sexist verbal harassment, then, emerge as symptomatic of a sexist society, and are historically and contextually connected to other, more acute forms of sexual harassment and violence. The pervasiveness of gendered harassment in society reflects the underlying, entrenched assumptions, attitudes, and social realities that lead to more acute expressions of violence. Racism and racial violence work in much the same way.[4] The gendered aspects of the policing strategy at the Toronto G20 emerged when women and queer-gendered demonstrators experienced harassment, degrading treatment, denial of sanitary devices, and threats of rape at the hands of police.

Realizing that the arrests and treatment by police in Toronto had taken on gendered dimensions, I interviewed people who identify as women, female-bodied, or queer-gendered to ensure that their responses to the G20 police violence they experienced would be heard. Listening to voices of those who experienced this repression first-hand can help us to better understand the policing methods applied at the Toronto G20 and prepare us to resist them in the future.

Models of Repression

Regardless of individual state propensities towards repression and everyday violence, summit protest policing has taken on a transnational scope through the widespread adoption of a form of militarized crowd control tactics known as the Miami Model. The major tenets of the Miami Model are information warfare, the surveillance of protest organizers, pre-emptive and mass arrests, the use of militarized force (usually bolstered by the purchase of new weapons and equipment), the prevention and denial of public assembly (often enforced through new temporary municipal laws), and police brutality.[5]

Drawing on the Miami Model, G20 security forces in Toronto initiated a propaganda campaign prior to the summit to intimidate would-be demonstrators and encourage the general public to identify more closely with police than with demonstrators. A police public relations campaign showcased newly acquired equipment and weapons – most infamously the cutting edge sound cannons – with which police planned to bolster G20 "security." This media campaign aided police efforts to create an environment in which police could repress and intimidate demonstrators.[6]

Leading up to the G20 demonstrations, police became ubiquitous in Toronto's downtown, using public training drills and mass shows of force to aggressively assert their presence. "It went from being regular beat cops in groups of two," remembered one activist, "to being . . . eight or ten cops wearing helmets, with a lot more, and a lot bigger, more militarized gear, and in much larger groups, and they would be marching." The police "paraded all of the weaponry and crowd-control devices that they were going to be using. And there were all these cops on motorcycles and horses and [they demonstrated] their sound cannons. It was really an aggressive, performative show of force that really just felt intentionally provocative."[7] Unbeknownst to most demonstrators, police had also been preparing in other, less readily observable ways. As early as a year before the G20 meetings, the police had embedded undercover agents in various social justice groups, contributing to the information warfare tactic of the Miami Model.

Prior to the summit, a coalition of police and armed forces – the Integrated Security Unit (ISU) – was formed to oversee policing of both the Huntsville G8 and Toronto G20 summits. This complex command structure meant that "the RCMP was responsible for controlling the area within the summit fence. The Toronto Police Service, assisted by officers from twenty-one provincial police detachments, was left with the rest of the city. The division of responsibilities was so unclear that as the summit began, even the head of the police board was confused about exactly where the ISU's job ended and the TPS's began."[8] This confusion left lines of police accountability unclear and made room for increased police brutality.

Arrest Narratives

The pre-emptive and mass arrest of activists that took place in Toronto during the G20 – classic characteristics of the Miami Model of summit policing – were often made more grievous for women and queer-gendered demonstrators through the police use of sexual harassment and humiliation, threats of rape, and sexual assault. Within this context, police treated women's bodies as less violent but more easily violated than men's bodies. As one activist explained, "the police understand that because so many people have experienced gender violence in their life that it's a tool that the police can tactically tap into at anytime to do very little and re-stimulate very much."

During the early morning hours of Saturday, June 26, police forcibly entered a number of Toronto residences and arrested people who had been sleeping inside. At one house, police first found a woman who was asleep on the front porch:

> Early, early morning of that day, before the sun even rose ... I was awakened by getting kicked in the stomach and surrounded by police, and I was like, "what are you guys doing here? ... I'm not wearing pants!" We were just sleeping, and they came into the house without a warrant and took my friend.

Despite the fact that she had no pants on, police forced the woman to stand on the porch at gunpoint. This was accompanied by a veiled threat:

> The female police officer who was standing outside with me was standing on top of the G20 childcare banner that was drying on the porch, and she was like stomping on it and she said, "Well I wonder who's gonna take care of the kids now, eh?" and chuckled and said, "Well I guess we'll have to."

Another woman was forced to stand topless and at gunpoint in front of a male cop. She repeated the mantra, "I do not consent to this." Afterwards she commented that the circumstances were "depressingly ironic," given that she had originally opted not to attend the Toronto G20 demonstrations because she was still processing her own experiences as a survivor of sexual assault.

The number of arrests swelled following the Saturday afternoon demonstration (which included significant property destruction) and by the end of the weekend police had arrested more than a thousand people. On Sunday, after leaving Allan Gardens, a group of women was followed by police for several blocks before they were arrested; they later recalled a number of disturbing incidents of sexual harassment and even sexual assault by police. Police officers hurled gendered insults at the women as they arrested them, calling them "hairy dykes" and "dirty cunts." When one woman argued with police about an officer's use of the word "cunt," a female officer responded, "I don't mind, it's fine." Officers were heard encouraging bystanders to take pictures of the arrests, saying, "shoot the dogs," and "they love it." Although arrestees told the gathering crowd that they did not consent to having their pictures taken, their requests were for the most part ignored. Later, photos of the arrests ended up online, and some were even posted to an erotic bondage website, only increasing the feeling of violation for the women arrested.

Searches carried out by male police officers as part of the arrest process were often difficult for women. One woman arrested Saturday night recounted that when the arresting officer took her belt off she found it "so violating. Especially having been there at the protest to protest the system's inability to provide justice for sexual assault, and feeling like that was exactly what was happening, ugh, it was such a representation of just everything that makes me want to throw up." Another woman described an incident of police sexual assault during her arrest:

> [My friend] actually began to yell at [Officer P], because he said he wanted to beat me right there, but he said, you know, "don't worry, it will happen when we get to jail." . . . [Officer P] wasn't the only one who was available to do a search, there were female officers certainly readily available, but I had to stand up and get my handcuffs moved from back to front handcuffs and . . . get my search done, and it was him [Officer P] who did the search. And it wasn't like, "okay, I'm going to search you now," it was "stand up" and then he started touching my body and it was a really quick, from head to toe, not even really searching for something, but touching, very much just touching and then, didn't bother with my left leg at all, but [my] right leg – hand up the thigh and then a really firm and intentional and obvious right-ass grab. That was my "search." . . . He got out his knife without telling me what he was going to do and then thrust his knife at my abdomen and cut off my waist-wallet, without sort of telling me, "this is what I'm doing with a knife at your abdomen" and I was really afraid and shaken up and pissed off.

Detention Centre

After their arrest, people were brought to the makeshift detention centre, which had been temporarily converted from a film studio into an elaborate holding area complete with cages. Once in the detention centre, people were denied access to water, food, toilet paper, and sanitary napkins. One woman recounted the horrible conditions that many detainees encountered:

Goddamn, it was horrible. I had never felt like I was treated like such an animal until I was there . . . it was freezing cold . . . we have our hands zip-tied together so tightly that you know, we can't even rub our arms or anything like that. . . . Food was revolting and not [offered] very often. . . . I remember at one point, I yelled out that we needed water, especially this one girl who was really freaking out and needed water, and I yelled that we need water, and a cop yelled back, "There's water in the porta-john."

When I asked women and queer-gendered detainees to describe their detention centre experiences, they told me stories that made it clear that the police used tactics of oppression common to mainstream, everyday gendered violence. This sexual harassment and abuse further victimized detainees and compounded the horror of their experience.[9]

The "porta-johns" were the site of some of the sexual harassment by police. Most of the cages housed one of these portable toilet units with its door removed. In order to protect themselves from police voyeurism, "people would sort of buddy-up and stand in front of the washrooms because the male officers would walk by as you were going to the washroom." One woman recalled a young woman who, because she was a minor, was isolated in the next cell:

There was nobody there to block her when she was going to the bathroom, whereas in our cell, because there were multiple people, we formed a human wall for whoever had to go to the bathroom, so that the people and the police officers walking by wouldn't be able to see us. But for her, because she was all by herself, everybody could see, all the police officers walking by. And there were times when police officers were walking by and they would stop, and they would watch her go to the bathroom, and comment on her and her gender. . . . [They would say] things like, just how young she was, and kind of like making me think, it was almost kind· of like a perverted attitude. And specifically how she was going to the bathroom, or like, if, like she was taking a shit, they would say, "she's taking a crap" or something, like they'd comment, like really casually on little things. . . . It was obnoxious.

In response, some of the women demanded that police move the teen into their cell "because she was all by herself and she was so young, we were yelling at the guards, demanding that she get put in the cell with us, and then they kept saying that was against the law. [*Laughs sarcastically.*] So, all of a sudden, they were respecting the law."

Basic sanitary conditions in the temporary detention centre were subpar at best, and sanitary napkins were not made readily available. One detainee recalled that a woman in her cell who was menstruating was only given one pad during her entire time in the detention centre. During her strip search, her underwear was "thrown on the ground, pad side down, and then she had to pick the underwear up and put it back on, next to her body, with all the really disgusting shit, because I don't know if you've heard about the floor of that place, but it was like paint chips and old pepper spray, [and] because it was built out of particle board, there was sawdust."

Within this punitive environment, strip searches were among the most traumatic experiences. One detainee, who could see from her cage people being taken for strip searches, described the helplessness she felt at seeing other women suffer:

> I remember seeing people being taken out and then people being brought back in, just crying, and bawling their eyes out. And there were a few women that just sort of collapsed onto the ground and were very clearly in a state of heightened trauma and were exhibiting extremely obvious signs of panic attacks and were in a crisis moment, and there was no one there to ask what they needed or what they wanted, and just being contained in that cage, that was really hard to watch too, but we would just sort of shout out, "Hey, we love you, it's going to be okay."

Some people were transferred to a nearby prison, where they endured yet another strip search. For one person, this was especially difficult "because a lot of people had [already] experienced really, really, really, really nasty strip searches, and . . . there were men [police] walking [down the hall] and pointing, laughing, rating."

For some the experience of forced strip searches recalled past experiences of more aggravated forms of sexual assault. One woman who didn't "have a history of really serious boundary violations the way that other people do," recognized that others were experiencing "triggering" feelings that called up previous sexual assaults. Another detainee struggled to avoid reliving past experiences:

While I was having my strip search . . . I heard a woman in the next box over just whimpering and whimpering and saying the word "why" over and over again. I myself, like many, many women have my own history of, you know, sexual assault survival and so when in a situation of sort of sexualized subjugation like being forced to bend over naked in front of complete strangers in a box, it's easy enough for old shit to get re-stimulated, so I definitely had to struggle with myself, less so for the experience that I was having than the sound-track of this woman screaming "why, why, why," in the box next to me and wondering what the hell was happening to her.

. . . so many people were being re-stimulated from old violences . . . particularly people who have experienced violence through their sexuality, their gender, their race. . . . The individual experiences [of the detention centre] were compounded by a reality that these are the violences that people experience every single day . . . the brilliance of an oppressive force is that the oppressor has to do very little other than remind the oppressed that they've been oppressed in the past, and [then]stick them [back] there.

Police also took it upon themselves to literally "police" gender. They segregated detainees they perceived as gay, lesbian, or queer from those they perceived as straight and they made "inappropriate comments instead of asking clear questions" about people's personal gender identification. This translated into harassment of queer-gendered folks. One detainee recalled:

There was someone who (I'm making the assumption) would identify as gender-queer, or perhaps . . . might identify as being a trans-person. Constantly seeing this person being switched between cells, over and over . . . the officers would chortle and laugh and say something like, "throw him over here" and be like "ha-ha . . . she . . . it," and it was so degrading, and I don't know, it was really obnoxious. It really reminded me [of] the behaviours of a team of frat boys just hazing and initiating young students.

Within this otherwise brutal setting, however, partly as a function of their dependency on one another, detainees felt solidarity, love, and respect for each other. One woman explained that with every-one's hands cuffed behind their backs the solidarity was not only necessary, but also "instant" – " 'I need you to pull my pants down [so that I can use the toilet], complete stranger, and then I'll do the same for you,' you know? It's a lot of trust, and it's different and harder for different people for different reasons." One woman experienced a "small empowering moment" when "the woman who had been strip-searched before me came out and she asked if I was okay, and told me that it would be alright, and just checked in." This helped her to cope with her own strip search, during which female officers ridiculed her because of her body hair. Another detainee emphasized the importance of solidarity at these moments:

> The one thing that I can say . . . is that there was this incredibly clear atmosphere of threat and intimidation around sexualized violence and around gender, but there was also this inherent, beautiful solidarity among people who are complete strangers and kind of checking in with each other and lending support to each other.

Power, Healing, and Protest

As we strive to enact positive change in this world and come up against forces that would rather preserve the status quo, our awareness of the methods used to suppress dissent, including the tactics of the Miami Model and the gendered violence that supports them, will help us to understand, predict, and combat the effects of such police repression on our communities. As one woman who was detained said:

> It kind of ripples out that when one person feels empowered and solid . . . that can be transferrable, [and] you can share that empowerment with others [and] share that within a broader setting . . . It's just like, being oppressed by this police officer really isn't a lot different from being oppressed by someone whose actions are inconsiderate, or abusive, or negligent of the needs of those around them. And I feel like that realization and . . . being able to visually see [and] relate with it so closely is a form of empowerment, you know – I can't look back on the whole thing really and say, "pfft, forget that." . . . Hopefully that's something that the community has taken from this as well, that it's not just an isolated experience that I'm having. Maybe I can help share that too.

These unsettling stories from the Toronto G20 protest – which make very clear that the goals of feminist and queer movements overlap with the goals of others who oppose state violence – should motivate us all to stop police violence and repression.

14

A Wall of Brick and Rage

Nicole Tanguay

They stood shoulder to shoulder,
tight together like a wall
A wall of uniform,
a wall of brutality
As they beat their shields in
unison my world changed forever.

They stood shoulder to shoulder,
in brick enclosed
No way out back alley
bang, bang, bang,
Get out of the way
move, move, move,
They screamed
like gun shots through my soul.

They stood shoulder to shoulder,
dressed in black
Shielded from head to foot,
armed with guns, batons, and rage
Moving like tin soldiers,
movements stiff,
a wall of brutality.

They stood shoulder to shoulder,
blocking both ends of freedom
Move, they screamed over and over.

To my right, a tall gate hiding my freedom,
hiding my heart.

To the left,
a brick wall.

To the north of me,
a wall of thunder and bullets.

To the south of me,
a wall of thunder and bullets.

To the right of me, visitors
deciding my life
While my heart is on the other side of the gate,
locked away maybe forever
Humanity lost for a second,
long enough to set panic and terror
through this part of the walls of rage and bullets.

Move, again they yelled,
beating their shields
Dressed in black metal
with shields from head to foot.

Move, move, move,
thundering shatters forever
The innocent sound of silence
Shattering what was once,
something that was never.

15

Connecting Carceral Spaces
Reflecting on Summit Detention

Swathi Sekhar

I HATE HOW MUCH I DREAM ABOUT COPS. THESE DREAMS ARE NOT all nightmares, but police presence has become a pervasive force in my subconscious. This, after a mere twenty-two hours spent at the G20 detention centre – an experience that was barely a taste of the horror that is correctional and policing culture in Canada and worldwide. Police arrested me on the night of June 26, 2010, with a group of about thirty people, just outside of the detention centre at Eastern and Pape. As a legal observer at the protests, I'd witnessed several brutal arrests and incidents of serious police violence over the weekend and felt compelled to join the small prison solidarity action that night. Soon after I arrived, riot police penned us in on all sides and then arrested us; it is clear to me now that once we got there, they had never intended to let us leave.

Inside the Eastern Avenue detention centre (which was housed in an old movie studio) we were kept in wire cages and it was freezing cold. The food was barely edible and we had little water. Few of us were given access to phone calls or counsel. People were denied medical care, and everyone faced a barrage of threats, insults, intimidation, and open antagonism from the authorities.

As a law student, and someone who has worked with people who are incarcerated, I'd been exposed to the prison industrial complex before my arrest at the G20. While I was detained, I was acutely aware that these conditions reflect the realities of incarceration everywhere. Yet writing this chapter has been a difficult exercise; I have battled with feeling that my relative privilege makes my experiences as a detainee invalid or illegitimate. Recognizing the interconnectedness of the various struggles that I have been a part of has been crucial to my personal understanding of how to harness this G20 experience and channel it into action. I hope such reflection will resonate with others as well.

Why Was I Surprised?

I was born in Canada but my parents came from India, where we would often return to visit my family. From a young age I was exposed to the harsh realities of daily life in one of the poorest parts of the world. I saw other children my age on the streets of South Indian cities and compared their existence with my own, knowing I had done nothing in particular to deserve the privileges I had. These experiences shaped my belief that there is very little justice in this world. But until recently I focused on the shortcomings of other systems, on the brutal nature of regimes outside of Canada. I spoke out against the persecution and imprisonment of dissenting political voices abroad. While I knew there was a great deal of injustice in this country, I judged life in Canada relative to life under more repressive regimes.

When I began working more intimately with people who were moving through the nightmare that is the Canadian immigration and refugee system, my thinking began to shift. Though I grew up in an immigrant community and have done community work with migrants in the past, it was not until a couple of years ago that I began to critically examine the immigration and refugee determination procedure. I was stunned to find a system that so openly and unapologetically propagates racism and intolerance.

Immigration detention is arguably the most brutal form of so-called short-term detention in Canada. (In reality, "short term" frequently means several months or even years of confinement.) Under this system, thousands of people from vulnerable, racialized communities are deprived of their liberty and separated from their family and friends, sometimes indefinitely. The Immigration and Refugee Protection Act authorizes the detention of foreign nationals on nearly limitless grounds, including the suspected inadmissibility of a family member – a fact that the detainee might not even know of and certainly can't control.[1] In addition, the standards for assessing grounds for detention are often based on cultural norms specific to the Global North. Unsatisfied with explanations as to why a document cannot be produced, for example, immigration authorities may apply an unrealistic standard of what constitutes "reasonable proof" of identity.[2] Officials might then see those who have difficulty providing documentation as uncooperative, and therefore more likely a flight risk; this perception often leads to ongoing detention.[3] Even those immigrants who do comply with these rules feel the hand of the state blocking their path forward and directing them to the exit.

The shock I felt during my summit detention echoed my initial astonishment at the sheer injustice of the Canadian immigration and refugee system. I simply had not anticipated the brazenness, the enormous scale, and the decidedly pre-planned nature of state repression during the G20. But while I was in detention, memories of immigrants and refugees I had worked with and the lessons I had learned from their experiences returned to me. I remembered families who had been stripped of their freedom and dignity, and the impact this had on communities and relationships. I still draw strength from the stories of resilience shared with me by survivors of this unjust system.

Forced to Bow to the Power of the State

At about the same time that the realities of immigration detention in Canada were becoming clear to me, a good friend began working in a men's correctional facility. We spent a great deal of time sharing our thoughts on incarceration; our conversations about the trauma of segregation resonate with me still. The stated legislative purpose of administrative segregation (isolation from the general prison population) is the inmate's own safety, the safety of other inmates, or the security of the penitentiary.[4] My friend's experience of visiting an inmate who had been placed in segregation made some of the other, more punitive reasons for segregation clear. To speak to each other, both my friend and the prisoner had to kneel at a slot at the bottom of the door to the small cell. I remember my friend describing how sick this episode made her feel, how degrading and humiliating this experience was both for the inmate and for herself. While safety is the ostensible reason for segregation, forcing inmates to kneel to communicate or to receive food and water does nothing to protect the safety of the other inmates. Rather, it serves as a forceful physical and psychological reminder that the prisoner is ever at the mercy of the state.

This intent to make prisoners feel powerless was evident in several

Connecting Carceral Spaces

forms during my G20 detention. To ensure we knew who was in control, police forced us to beg for basic necessities such as food, water, and medical attention. I knew that the purpose of imprisonment is to strip you of your dignity, strength, and willingness to fight. Given this awareness, I can't help but wonder why I was still so surprised at what happened to us that weekend. Sharing my experiences with friends and family has been difficult but also healing. I have been reminded that systems of oppression are all fundamentally rooted in the same ugly things – exposing these roots strengthens my resolve and makes me realize how many allies we have in the fight for justice.

Injustice Across Borders

In 2009, while carrying out a research project on the sexual and reproductive health rights of prisoners, I had the opportunity to speak with prisoners and prisoners' rights organizers in Malawi. As in most countries, the rights of prisoners in Malawi are seen as somehow separate and different from human rights, and prisoner rights are low on the list of societal concerns and government priorities. Malawi prisons are starved for resources. There is virtually no legal representation for prisoners and, as a result, most prisoners are waiting on remand; some are incarcerated for five or six years without ever having had a trial. I spoke to many women who, not knowing how to plead self-defence, were sentenced to several years for defending themselves against abusive partners. Many prisoners I spoke to had not even heard of bail. Extreme overcrowding causes food shortages and health issues, particularly HIV/AIDS, tuberculosis, and hepatitis.

One prisoner I interviewed in Malawi had been behind prison walls for several years but remained warm, open, and kind – I couldn't help but marvel at the kind of strength it must have taken him every single day to keep moving forward. I kept in touch with him after I left Malawi, and I thought about him constantly while I was detained in Toronto – his resolve inspired me, but his story also reminded me that, as horrible as it was in detention, at least I was not being detained in India or Malawi. As much as my own experience felt endless, and as terrified as I was, I knew that eventually I would get out. My very small taste of the loss of freedom and dignity through state violence has given me a sense of solidarity with ongoing struggles worldwide, which I would never have gotten otherwise.

The Power of Experience

After about fifteen hours in detention, I hit what was my ultimate low. I had just spoken to duty counsel, and he had told me that I might be held indefinitely and that he could not help. One woman in my cell had a serious panic attack and the guards simply watched, refusing to give her medical attention until she fell to the ground unable to breathe. They forced us to carry her to the door of the cage before they would provide her with assistance. At this point, we all cracked. I felt that no one could help me and that I was utterly power-less. After about an hour, we calmed a little. We told each other that there would be accountability and retribution – that this experience would not defeat us, but make us stronger – that if after we got out we didn't fight harder than ever, then the whole time in detention would have been in vain.

The more I reflect on the events of that week in June, the clearer it becomes to me that what happened at the G20 has afforded us a unique opportunity to increase the traction of existing community mobilization against various forms of state repression. It shouldn't have taken the arrest of eleven hundred mostly upper-middle-class, mostly white people to bring public attention to ongoing police vio-lence and the criminalization of poor and racialized communities. The anger and frustration felt by some that the G20 arrestees have suddenly taken centre stage is well justified. But people around me have had their eyes opened by this experience and are ready to join the fight for change. Activists are meeting and strategizing about how to use the G20 moment to call attention to the larger issues from which it arose, including the fight for migrant justice, ongoing anti-prison and anti-poverty work, and the collective struggle against police and state repression. If we continue to focus on whether or not the police oppression we encountered during the G20 was a valid experience of state oppression, we risk losing our momentum. To let this experience pass without harnessing its potential power would be a grave mistake.

Resilience

When I think about my time in detention now, it is the moments of resistance that stand out the most. Throughout our confinement, detainees would periodically begin shaking their cages, making a very loud noise, like thunder. When one cage shook all of our connected cages shook. This happened in waves – a group in one cell would yell and start shaking their cage, and others would follow, like a ripple, until it was deafening. It was simultaneously the most disturbing and the most intensely beautiful and powerful thing that the prisoners could do. It was something we could control; it was something the guards hated. It was something we could do collectively without seeing each other, and it was a form of physical resistance. The women in my cell would frequently get up and shake the cage very loudly and violently for long periods of time. Though I didn't join in, I would close my eyes and listen to the fierce sound of resistance – it soothed me, in a strange way. Increasingly, it is these memories of resistance, rather than the brutality and repression of the police, that resonate with me in my work and my life. I carry them forward.

16

Caught in the Crossfire

Elroy Yau

Update: September 2010

SOME OF YOU MAY HAVE HEARD OF ME. MY NAME IS ELROY YAU. I AM the Toronto Transit Commission (TTC) employee who was arrested, while in full uniform, on my way to work at the Queen's Park subway station on Saturday, June 26. I was tackled to the ground by two police officers and detained for over thirty hours – all for going to work.

So the update so far is I've been off work since July 4. The Ontario Workplace Safety and Insurance Board (WSIB) has more or less denied my claim because I refuse to sign a waiver that forbids me from suing Toronto Police Services or the City of Toronto for their blunders. I am not prepared to give up my civil rights for that. I cannot believe WSIB is denying me benefits because I won't promise not to sue a third party.

I am under the care of a primary physician. I see him once a week. For six sessions I saw a psychotherapist offered by the TTC Employee Assistance Program but he was of no help. I am on a variety of medications: Imovane for sleeping, Clonazepem and Ativan Sublingual (both tranquilizers) for anxiety, panic attacks, and flashbacks, Percocets for back and body pain. None of these pills are really working. I look at the sick benefits forms my doctor fills out for my Company Sick Benefits Association. I have never before seen words such as "debilitating," "not improving," and "poor" used to describe my condition.

I see a chiropractor three times a week. The soft tissue damage and back, lower lumbar, and shoulder damage caused when I was tackled to the ground is consistent with police hard arrest tactics.

Everyday, I wake up, sit in a chair, and look out the window. If it weren't for my dogs, I wouldn't leave the house. I have lost my appetite and don't eat much. I've gone from a healthy 160 pounds to 142 pounds. I've lost friends and I feel isolated.

I missed out on summer. I missed out on my favorite summer activities. Anxiety, panic attacks, flashbacks, and a sense of mental uncomfort kept me from going out unless I really needed to. I grocery shop once a week, go to doctor and chiropractic appointments three times a week, and walk my dogs. I look out the window with a blank, mindless stare, watching workers build a condo in front of mine. That is what my days look like.

My summer was ruined. My life has changed forever. No BBQ, no beach, no sitting on a patio enjoying some of the best summer weather in Toronto history. Some people dream of having the summer off – I had it, and I hated it. All I wanted to do was go back to work, back to my old life – to live a normal life. Unfortunately, that is something that will never happen.

Update: February 2011

In October, I finally got the chance to see a psychiatrist at St. Michael's Hospital. After our second weekly session, she diagnosed me with major depression resulting from post-traumatic stress disorder. Her treatment was to wean me off the Clonazepam. The withdrawal symptoms from getting off Clonazepam were wicked and harsh. My hands shook, my body shook; I was unable to sleep and the panic attacks and anxiety increased. I am still slowly weaning off of it, and now I know how a drug addict feels when he doesn't get his fix.

The psychiatrist put me on Risperidone (an anti-psychotic drug) and Zoloft to treat depression. Both had harsh side effects. From headaches and lethargy to sleeplessness, from constipation to diarrhea and loss of appetite, I had it all. Unfortunately, most people don't understand depression and mental illness. People couldn't understand what I was going through because they couldn't see it. A broken arm or leg, people can see and emphasize with, but mental illness they can't see, so it doesn't exist. I had no support network of friends who understood, so essentially I was alone.

As of now, I am getting better. I am back to work and slowly getting back to a normal life. I suffered months of depression, terrible side effects from various medications, and social withdrawal. I don't think I can ever forgive the police for doing what they did to me, or what they did to one thousand others. We are taught to obey the law and look to police for help. I did that throughout my life. But what do you do when the same people you were taught to trust and believe in turn on you and ignore the fundamentals of their own laws?

Police arrest a photojournalist at the Queen's Park "designated speech area," June 26, 2010. Photo by Vincenzo D'Alto.

Part Three

After the G20

Critical Reflections, Moving Forward

17

Martial Law in the Streets of Toronto
G20 Security and State Violence

Neil Smith and Deborah Cowen

A Police Riot

THE FIRST SIGN THAT SOMETHING WAS AMISS CAME QUICKLY, AS more than fifteen thousand demonstrators against the G20 left the Queen's Park staging area and chanted their way south on Toronto's University Avenue, turning westward along Queen Street. An empty police cruiser sat askew in an intersection, its windows down, keys in the ignition, and a pair of sunglasses atop an otherwise bare dashboard. Odd. Marchers pondered its presence and purpose and wondered why it was so exposed amidst a demo long hyped by police and politicians alike as sure to have a sinister outcome. A few curious protesters photographed the car with their cell phones as they walked by.[1]

Led by dozens of labour unions and supported by various provincial and national labour federations, the demonstration on Saturday June 26, 2010, marched to the theme "People First!" and it was loud and militant. Marchers protested the oppressive and exploitative neo-liberal policies the G20 stands for: the destruction of work conditions and wages that come in the wake of neo-liberal capitalism; the racist and class discriminatory policies this mode of production promotes; global poverty and starvation; gender and sexual oppression; the rapacious and persistent theft of land and resources from Indigenous people, not least the longstanding grievances of Canadian First Nations people; wholesale environmental destruction when nature gets in the way of profit; the acidic corrosion of already meagre social support for means of reproduction (health care, housing, education, etc.); and the outrageous cost of the G20 to Canadian taxpayers. Unions were joined by a wide array of other groups ranging from Free Tibet to 9/11 conspiracy theorists.

Within an hour or two, the abandoned police cruiser on Queen Street – along with several others – was set on fire, and it wasn't too long before the police responded in overwhelming fashion. Eleven hundred people were arrested and detained. This represented by far the largest mass arrest at any single event in Canadian history (more than even the 1919 Winnipeg General Strike) and in the aftermath personal stories documenting widespread police brutality filtered out, appearing not just in the city's newspapers but globally. The conditions inside the temporary detention centre on Eastern Avenue were deplorable, and police-inflicted injuries were widespread. The Toronto Street Medics, an independent group of volunteer health care workers who treated the injured, reported that police confiscated some of their medical supplies and prevented them from accessing injured protesters behind police lines. According to their account, "All of the serious injuries we treated were inflicted by the police. While violence against property received a great deal of coverage, violence against people – broken bones, cracked heads, and eyes filled with pepper spray – has yet to feature prominently in any mainstream media. Our teams of medics witnessed and treated people who had been struck in the head by police batons, had lacerations from police shields and had been trampled by police horses."[2]

The figures speak for themselves: of more than eleven hundred arrested, 827 were released without charges within seventy-two hours and 263 were released pending charges. Twenty of the original arrestees were held for bail hearings. What was the unspoken police strategy and intent if more than three-quarters of those arrested were released without charges?

The G20 and Global Capitalism

The G20 is the latest in a long line of ostensibly globe-spanning organizations intended to stabilize and restructure the world capitalist economy. Following in the footsteps of the now-superseded G7 and G8, it has a twofold rationale. First, the G20 resulted from the perceived need to manage a restructuring of the global economy, which in turn had three major elements, extant or desired: (i) the globalization of capital (cross-border labour, commodity and financial movement), however uneven; (ii) the dramatic expansion of the Chinese, Indian, Brazilian, South Korean, and other national economies (erstwhile seen as "underdeveloped," now included among the G20); and (iii) the emergence of the European Union and the euro as a major economic force. With a nod toward diversity of representation and a pragmatic embrace of the short-lived "Washington Consensus," the G20's membership additionally came to include, among others, South Africa, Turkey, and Saudi Arabia.

The second rationale is related. The swath of Bretton Woods institutions produced in the late 1940s, such as the IMF, World Bank, and World Trade Organization (WTO, previously GATT), although revived in the 1980s as key institutions of a strategic neo-liberalism, had more narrowly defined remits and long-term agendas and were less adept at responding with alacrity to the scale of the global economic crisis. Accordingly, and as befits a conclave that came to maturity amidst the post-2007 crisis, the overarching goal of the G20 is the negotiated management and regulation of the global financial system. It brings together the leaders of national governments, but increasingly, too, national finance and treasury ministers, and whereas Bretton Woods institutions had policy-making authority the G20 has none, its informality making it more, not less, powerful. It is free to make coordinated decisions over the global economy while answerable to no global constituency.

In Toronto, not surprisingly, one issue dominated the agenda for the leaders of the G20: how to restore growth in an economy that had melted down to a near repeat of the global depression of the 1920s and 1930s. Despite tentative signs of revival, many economists feared that, as happened eight decades earlier, any recovery would be mild and presage a "double dip" in which the second crash was worse than the first. Economist and Nobel Laureate Paul Krugman was far from alone in suggesting that a new depression might already be in its early stages.[3] After all, the various national stimulus packages enacted in 2008 and 2009 (according to the Organization of Economic Cooperation and Development, such packages topped $7 trillion) had now largely run their course, and, while the GDP measures of many economies had stabilized or even begun to grow again rather than shrink, other danger signs were mounting: official unemployment rates reached or threatened double digit figures in most of the wealthier economies (standing at almost 20 per cent in Spain) with real unemployment much higher; the global financial system was drowning in debt and many smaller banks continued to go bankrupt even as many of the largest banks, especially on Wall Street, registered multi-billion dollar profits and again doled out record bonuses; and state fiscal deficits hit record and unsustainable levels. The central debate among G20 leaders heading into Toronto therefore pitted neo-liberal diehards against those stirring a Keynesian sweetener into the neo-liberal punch. The former sought to slash fiscal budget deficits largely at the expense of the poor and working class while cutting taxes for corporations and for the rich. The latter, chastened, however mildly, by the failures of neo-liberalism (to wit, the global economic crisis), sought to nurse it back to health with new rounds of state economic stimuli. Taking the first path, most European elites (especially in Britain) positioned themselves as the avatars of a neo-liberalism on steroids while the US government, itself having already instituted various budget-cutting measures, pushed the stimulus path.

This of course was a debate largely within the capitalist class more than between countries, and the interests of capital were very much to the fore. For protesters in Toronto and for a wider global resistance to the G20 and the broader class interests it represents, the emblems of neo-liberalism's supposed economic successes, measured in profits, stock prices, GDPs, and asset aggrandizement, were precisely the emblems of its failure. For neo-liberals the world was or would be made into a flat playing field, but this is increasingly revealed as at best a wan dream, at worst an ideological smokescreen. This depiction hides the fact that the global playing field actually steepened drastically for most of the planet's population as poverty escalated, more and more workers were precariously employed, wages for the majority failed to keep up with living costs, work conditions deteriorated, unions were attacked as antithetical to free market principles, environmental destruction robbed people of decent living conditions, and access to necessary social services such as healthcare, housing, and education deteriorated for hundreds of millions as states slashed budgets. Generally, the gap between rich and poor yawned wider than at any time in living memory. This pertained not just within the wealthier nations and between nations but also, perhaps especially, in those "new" economies admitted to the G20 – the apparent jewels of neo-liberal success. To cite one obvious case, the historically low level of social inequality in China, perhaps the paradigm of neo-liberal success since 1978, has skyrocketed to levels never before recorded.

At different scales, from the local and the urban through the national state to the global, the extent of such inequality and deprivation is highly uneven, but it accounts for the issues raised most prominently by G20 protesters in Toronto. Anti-poverty activists, unions, community movements, environmental organizations (BP's massive Gulf of Mexico oil spill was a prominent target), socialists, housing advocates, and a range of groups and movements put global neo-liberalism squarely in the dock. Drawing special ire was the range of national stimulus packages, which exposed the naked opposition of social interests at the root of capitalism: financial institutions, banks, and the "banksters" who ran them had caused the global crisis in the first place but were bailed out with billions in tax money while the victims – those experiencing layoffs, bank-led housing evictions, wage cuts, dismantled social services – were handed the invoice.

The question of geographical scale came to play a strategic role in the Toronto summit. Like all such previous summits, this was a major global event, hosted by a single national state, dominating the life of a metropolitan area and held in a dense, highly localized urban space. More important, and beyond the obvious, the state security strategy for the event was also politically scaled. The Toronto Police Department was centrally involved but so too were the Ontario Provincial Police (OPP) and, crucially, in addition to the Canadian military and security apparatus as well as private security forces, the federally authorized and powerful Royal Canadian Mounted Police (RCMP), which sent five thousand officers. In all, an estimated nineteen thousand Canadian police and security officers were sent into action. The entire operation was overseen by a shadowy new security umbrella group called the Integrated Security Unit (ISU), first established to coordinate anti-terrorist security for the Vancouver Olympics in February 2010. Adding to this mixture, each national delegation brought its own security personnel and the United States sent helicopters that were used not only to ferry some of the one thousand US delegates attending the summit but were also clearly visible in the skies above Toronto, patrolling and circling above the various marches and demonstrations.[4]

By the same token, protesters came not just from Toronto but from around Ontario, from other provinces, including British Columbia. As many as two thousand came from Quebec, including Montreal members of the Anti-Capitalist Convergence (CLAC). Security forces especially targeted Quebec protesters. Vehicles with Quebec plates were apprehended en route and people detained; of 450 who came by bus, 300 failed to catch homeward-bound buses, many presumably arrested. There were also international protesters from the United States, Europe, and elsewhere.

The Securitization of the City

On view in Toronto was a new phase in the *securitization of the city*.[5] The language of "Fortress Toronto" made banner headlines in the establishment press even before the event began.[6] Beyond the physical geography of Fortress Toronto, with its locked down "island of non-constitutionality"[7] (the yellow zone), the securitization of the city was obviously visible in the strategic street geography of the security forces and the broader social experience of the city during the G20. "For the past few days," editorialized a *Toronto Star* postscript on the entire "brutal spectacle," "the city has looked like a vast reality-TV set, where heavily garbed gladiators in black, burdened under bullet-proof vests, guns, walkie-talkie, shields and batons, try to chase down a wild, quick-footed band of anti-gladiators in black sweatsuits and bandanas."[8] Access to the city was also restricted in less tangible ways: border security at airports, and at international rail and car crossings was intensified; airspace was restricted below 5,500 metres within a thirty-kilometre radius of the city; access from Lake Ontario was likewise subject to security checks, as was pedestrian and road traffic into and around the downtown securitized zone. Most chilling perhaps, was the explicit suspension of civil rights: several protesters who objected to their arrest and asserted their right to be there were gruffly told by police, "You have no rights here today."

Historically, there are countless precedents for this insofar as most cities other than the newest were heavily secured military strongholds at one time or another. Walled cities were the norm in the feudal period, but today also many cities are militarized for greater or lesser time spans, from Medellín to Mogadishu, Belfast to Baghdad, Jerusalem to Guantánamo. Yet such securitization also has contemporary precedent in specific communities in Canada. There, too, the seemingly exceptional is the everyday: pre-emptive, militarized, "targeted policing" in poor and racialized neighbourhoods, and the explicit use of military force for policing Indigenous communities.[9]

And yet such public securitization of North American and European cities today does connote something new. In many ways it betokens, at the urban scale, the strategic political-geographic expression of neo-liberalism – its political wing, as it were. There are two ingredients to this contemporary securitization of the city, none of them especially unique to Toronto in 2010. First, while various security forces could claim with some plausibility that their purpose lay in the defence of civil rights, increasingly the issue today is less one of defence than of active social control. Of course the state has always been an instrument of social control, but at least in the era of Keynesianism from the 1930s to the 1970s many of these social control functions were, except under exceptional circumstances, sublimated into the cultural and economic apparatus. The broad social service, welfare, and social security systems of the mid-twentieth century did precisely this as generations of political activists – Black power, marxist, feminist, and gay and lesbian liberation – well recognized. The lesser or greater dismantling of such state provision in the subsequent neo-liberal era, comparative waning of opposition and resistance, and the shift toward marketization all opened a potential vacuum in the architecture of social order. This vacuum was quickly filled by direct and often militarized means of control. Direct repression broadly substitutes for the defter ameliorative hand of bureaucracy and bribery.

In addition to the shift in emphasis from defence to control, a second significant ingredient of the increasingly securitized city is the intensified *weaponization* of social control. Technological developments have always been harnessed to security strategies, or may have derived directly from military innovation, and from tasers to the Internet (itself born of the US military) today is no exception. In terms of weapons aimed directly at the body, the military makes the distinction between lethal and non-lethal, and recent innovations have focused especially on so-called non-lethal weapons. As the case of tasers vividly shows – their use has led to numerous deaths – any supposed distinction between lethal and non-lethal is a fiction; conversely, the use or threatened use of handguns is commonly non-lethal. For the G20, a new generation of weapons graced the Canadian police arsenal. A week before the event, as if to intimidate would-be protesters, shock a complacent public into recognizing the indispensability of a heavily armed police force, or to prescribe the public response to policing, the security forces rolled out for journalists a veritable weapons bazaar complete with glitzy demonstrations.

The jewel in the crown was a sonic cannon – the American Technology Corporation's Long Range Acoustic Device (LRAD). The "ear splitter" might be a more apt description. Initially developed for the US Navy following the 2000 attack on the USS *Cole* off the Yemeni coast, it has been in operation in the Persian Gulf since 2003. Since that time, its use has proliferated; LRADs were used to quell opposition demonstrators in Tblisi, supposed looters in New Orleans, striking car workers in Bangkok, and "pirates" off the coast of Somalia. Its debut on US soil came with the 2004 Republican National Convention in New York City. Intended for "fending off insurgents, dispersing crowds, and flushing out buildings,"[10] the LRAD is designed to induce nausea, vomiting, and abdominal pain. At its highest volume it can cause human bones to resonate. It can be used to deliver thunderous crowd control commands in public space or switched to an elevated "alert" function, which delivers high-pitched ear piercing blasts measuring as high as 135 to 155 decibels. The generally accepted upper limit of safe noise is eighty-five decibels, above which ear damage is likely. Indeed, according to the Toronto judge who sanctioned the ear splitter's use, a "very real likelihood exists that demonstrators may suffer damage to their hearing from the proposed use of the Alert function at certain distances and volumes."[11]

It is possible to date the new phase in the securitization of the city back to September 11, 2001, when New York's World Trade Center was stunningly demolished by suicide hijackers in two planes, a third crashed into the Pentagon, and a fourth crash-landed in Pennsylvania. This event unleashed a "war on terror," spearheaded by George Bush but joined willingly or under pressure by governing elites in the majority of the world's capitals. This perceived crisis of security certainly ratcheted up the securitization of the city. Yet intensified securitization of everything from national borders to the merest nooks and crannies of daily life was not simply the result of a single event but rather the outcome of more systemic shifts that were already in process. The securitization of the city is a response to the vacuum of social control attendant on the rise of neo-liberalism, as well as a lucrative multi-billion dollar business opportunity for the growing industry of private security provision. The city as shocking, in need of securitization, can be seen as one strand of the "shock doctrine."[12]

While it is obvious that September 11 was opportunistically used in this power grab, fostering deep-seated fears and insecurities, this event worked more as trigger rather than cause, and it came in many respects as a gift on a silver platter to a ruling class that had hitherto only been able to dream of the power thus conveyed. Staying a moment with the United States, if one compares the response to the Los Angeles riots of 1992, for example – an event precipitated by the brutal and wanton police beating of an innocent African American – with the response to the civil rights movement in the 1960s, it may be that the LA uprising represents a more accurate historical fulcrum for the advent of the securitized city. In the 1960s, although there was a violently repressive response from the state, an effort, however half-hearted, was made toward ameliorative repairs to the impoverished social fabric of the city and the bolstering of social welfare provisions, as represented by the Kerner Commission report and Model Cities program. In contrast, by 1992 repression was the sole response to the LA uprising. This stripped down securitization of the city acutely symbolizes the new and continuing pattern of state response.

Violence and the State

In the aftermath of the Toronto G20, as city workers began dismantling the security fence, replacing removed trash cans and newspaper boxes, opening the downtown again to vehicle and pedestrian traffic, and planting sapling trees to replace the ones ripped out by security forces claiming they were potential weapons, the erstwhile no-go zone came back to life. Yet as revelation after revelation emerged, public outrage continued to mount over who to blame for the "cascade of failures," as a city councillor for downtown Toronto called it. The city police chief weighed in heavily, describing a "large and dangerous demonstration" and attributing the violence to "a mob," while Mayor David Miller concurred that the police "distinguished themselves" in handling the protests. *Maclean's* magazine was even more incendiary, blaring "LOCK THEM UP" across a doctored cover photo composite of a gas masked, guitar-toting protester in front of a burning police car.[13] Throughout the corporate media a certain hysteria took over concerning the "black bloc," who were invariably portrayed as violent anarchists conspiring to bring the city to its knees.

In fact, this script was effectively pre-written. In preparation for the G8 and G20 meetings, security forces fuelled the mainstream media with sensational stories about coming "violence." Obliging journalists fixated on the skyrocketing sale of gas masks at local army surplus stores, even donning the devices themselves to provide a graphic glimpse of a coming alien invasion. The anticipation of imminent mayhem was intensified by heavily publicized pre-emptive measures to protect property and by daily lists of closures mandated or leveraged by security forces, or else out of fear. Roads, schools, museums, banks, restaurants, parking garages, commuter train stations, shops and businesses, bars, universities, a sports stadium were all shuttered. What could be moved was moved; what couldn't be moved was locked down. (Several corporations even fortified their "plop art" – large, heavy art installations often plopped into forecourt space by helicopters.[14]) At the same time the media picked up on the unprecedented cost of the G8 and G20, an extraordinary $1.2 billion (Canadian), of which almost $1 billion was devoted to security. The media scratched their collective head when comparison was made with other such summits. The London 2009 G20 summit, for example, cost a total of US$30 million, while the security portion of the Pittsburgh summit later the same year came in at only US$12.2 million.[15] By way of context, this budget for the G8 and G20 was almost as high as Canada's annual budget for the Afghanistan war.

Ideologically collapsed in the corporate media was the not-so-subtle distinction between plans to commit violence and preparations intended as defence against violence, thus amplifying the singular police narrative of imminent *protester* "violence." Nowhere was this clearer than in the media's gas mask fetish, which evacuated the crucial distinction between activists preparing for police violence and the pro-corporate state, with all its sophisticated military weaponry, preparing to inflict violence. Activists' defensive preparation for police assault was morphed into a form of violence in and of itself. In fact, gas masks were not only paraded as weapons at a subsequent police press conference, but their use was itself treated as an act of aggression. On Sunday June 27, asthmatic protester Nat Gray donned a painter's respirator after riot police carrying tear gas guns confronted a jail solidarity protest on Eastern Avenue (see chapter 10 for Nat's story). Nat would later hear police explaining that they had made Nat a target for rubber bullets and arrest precisely for using the respirator.

The resulting jumble of media images and vignettes, from gas masks to ear splitters to multinational banks fortifying their fixed capital, all added up to an impending threat of violence on the streets. A symmetry of violence was written over a quite asymmetrical contest of powers. As if to cement the collusion of policing and the media, as many as four hundred security personnel were based in the Canadian Broadcasting Corporation (CBC) building inside the yellow zone.

When the G20 protests began in earnest and the police moved into action, the same media outlets seemed genuinely surprised at the fulfilment of their own prophesy, and the tenor of coverage changed. While many TV news stations played *ad nauseam* the same footage of a burning police car, the print media often sported side-by-side accounts of police brutality and protester vandalism. Reporters and editors often seemed taken aback by what they saw, as if working without a script. In the days after the delegates had left for home, the issue refused to die as press reports of police brutality continued to emerge, and defenders of the security forces in turn escalated their own rhetoric. The script of danger and threat was thereby "post-written" as well as pre-written, and the press gingerly began talking about the whole episode as a "riot" while right-wing politicians tried to argue that the event only proved that the suspension of rights and the expenditure of $1.2 billion was justified.[16] But the language of "riot" was a risky gambit insofar as mounting evidence now existed to suggest that if in fact it constituted a riot it was surely a police riot.

At the same time, as the clamour rose for an independent investigation, the security forces themselves became increasingly defensive. Two days after the close of the summit, the Toronto police held a news conference to display the cache of "weapons" they claimed to have confiscated from protesters. In truth, the haul looked more like yard sale bric-a-brac than the makings of urban terror. Apart from the obligatory gas masks, it included water bottles, bamboo tomato canes, a suit of chain mail, vinegar-soaked bandanas, a stapler, penknives, tennis balls, cameras, handcuffs, chains, an activist publication (*Upping the Anti*), goggles, a saw, a motorcycle helmet reading "food not bombs," an alternative media ("Media Co-op") logo, notebooks and pens, and so forth.

It is challenging to isolate a single object here that could legitimately be identified as a weapon, an object designed to inflict bodily injury, or at least a serious threat to the heavily armoured police. In fact, this display did more to affirm the self-justificatory desperation of the police than to convince anyone of a violent conspiracy. Like the gas mask, the inclusion of the "food not bombs" helmet, an object intended to *protect* from injury rather than inflict it, simply showed that the police evidential cupboard was bare. And it is tempting to assume that by including a pen, the Toronto police were claiming to have settled a two-century-old debate: whether mightier or not, the pen is indeed a violent weapon just like the sword. The inclusion of both Media Co-op, a democratic and grassroots alternative media group, and the journal *Upping the Anti*, published by a radical anti-capitalist group, are more serious. Executing another false symmetry of violence, it equates the power of ideas, in this case radical ideas of anti-capitalism, anti-oppression, and social equality, with the physical violence of guns, tear gas, rubber bullets, and ear splitters in a way that drowns out the very real police violence of the Toronto G20.

However, there were on the table some real weapons including a crossbow and some arrows. Challenged, the police chief conceded that some of these had been apprehended prior to the G20 in completely unrelated cases and did not really belong on the table. The crossbow, it was later revealed, came from the car of a farmer with a mental disability, who was in Toronto for a dentist's appointment. It was also conceded later that the safety-protected archery arrows, which the police chief claimed were incendiary devices, had no arrowheads and, along with the chain mail, belonged to a young man stopped on his way to the far suburbs for a role-playing medieval fantasy game. Likewise, the tomato canes were anything but weapons, but rather the masts for rainbow flags confiscated from a professional middle-aged gay couple en route to a Stonewall anniversary celebration. Even the penknife turned out to belong to a passerby who used it to cut fruit and who had no involvement in the protests.[17] The subsequent Bonnie-and-Clyde style most-wanted tableau issued by the police was easily understood as a desperate police PR effort to blunt their public humiliation.

However uncertain at times about its script, the establishment media persistently conflated "violence" (injury to a person) with small-scale property damage, yet remained largely silent about the systemic, global violence perpetrated by free market capitalism, which the G8 and G20 sought to shore up. In every basic category of everyday life the figures are sobering:

- Medical care: almost 200 women in the developing world die every day from backstreet abortions.
- Housing: the major factor behind the deaths of an estimated 225,000 people in the 2009 Haiti earthquake was unsafe housing.

- Wages: in China the urban proletarianization of rural workers since 1978 combined with continued state control of the economy has led to record levels of worker suicide.
- Clean water: an estimated 884 million people lack access to clean water while almost 9,800 people, disproportionately children, die every day from water related diseases.
- Starvation and hunger: 30,000 people (85 per cent of them children under five) die daily from hunger, malnutrition, and hunger-related illnesses.

The point here is less to evoke liberal lament than to take a further step toward analytical comprehension. The juxtaposition of this very real global violence with attempts to claim minor attacks on a building as comparable highlights starkly the ideological work done by the latter claims. This equation of attacks on property with violence is a hallmark of liberal capitalism, variously compounded in a neo-liberal era whereby corporations in various legal systems have been granted the legal status of individual persons. A particularly cruel irony resides in this shift. In the transition to capitalism "corporations" were formed via the incorporation of a group of individuals precisely to *limit* (hence "Limited") their legal responsibility, while today the positing of corporations as legal individuals provides the corollary, an *expansion* of corporate right. There is, however, a long alternative political tradition, harking not just to anarchists and marxists but also to multifold worker and peasant movements, past and present, which have resisted the privatization of land and property previously possessed and used in common. Private property, they adduced, and as Proudhon said, is theft. Put differently, "violence" is an ideological keyword that can only ever be fathomed in the context of the social, spatial, and categorial order of things.

The classic discussion of the state and violence, and certainly the best known, is that of Max Weber. For Weber, a monopoly on legitimate violence is not simply a feature of the state; this authority over violence is precisely what defines statehood. A "compulsory political organization with continuous operations will be called a 'state,'" he argues, "insofar as its administrative staff successfully upholds the claim to the monopoly of the legitimate use of physical force in the enforcement of its order."[18] Thus for Weber, it is not simply the state's capacity to mobilize and deploy violence, but to define the *legitimate use* of violence that matters. The state mobilizes and deploys police and military forces, and yet at the same time stands above itself as the arbiter of any distinction between (legal) force and violence. State violence, following Weber, *is the law*. Lenin would not so much have disagreed except to specify the source of state power in class relations and class struggle. Equally compatible is Walter Benjamin: "the law's interest in a monopoly of violence vis-à-vis individuals is not explained by the intention of preserving legal ends but, rather, by that of preserving the law itself; that violence, when not in the hands of the law, threatens it not by the ends that it may pursue but by its mere existence outside the law."[19]

This argument was expressed too in the stance of the Toronto protesters. Quick to point out that the contempt for democratic rights, hostility towards free speech, the criminalization of dissent (even the prospect of dissent), and the aggressive use of force were far from exceptional, activists refused the equation of violence with attacks on property and emphasized the continuities of state violence between Toronto city streets and oppressive conditions around the world. Economic violence and repressive political violence represent the everyday experience for so many people around the world who are subject to G20 actions and the policing of its member states. Right-wing commentators often portrayed these activists as naive and spoiled middle class white youth, but in truth their anticipation of state repression represented an astute analysis of the state.[20] "There's nothing safe to me about ten thousand fully armed cops," observed Syed Hussan, a TCMN organizer, several days before the G20 curtain rose.[21] Protest organizers understood the behaviour of the state not as exceptional but as systemic and they maintained an emphasis on commonalities across struggles. Quite reasonably, the actions of the G20 security forces shocked many in the middle class, but should also be seen as a microcosm for the workings of the G8 and G20 around the world.

Introducing the cache of weapons ostensibly stripped from protesters, Toronto police chief Blair explained that he wanted to drive home "the extent of the criminal *conspiracy*" his police faced.[22] To charge people openly committed to collective action aimed at transforming the status quo with conspiracy verges on tautology of a sort that Weber, Lenin, and Benjamin would readily recognize. There is no question that the protesters "conspired" to organize a series of events, some of which might become disruptive, and the police knew this well ahead of time. As became clear, police had infiltrated meetings of the TCMN in Toronto and meetings of organizers in several other cities, masquerading as activists. Needless to say, as regards conspiracy the security forces conspired secretly with others to execute their own plan. But with its billion-dollar G20 "security" budget, the state's own conspiracy, from the ISU, US forces, and the RCMP to the city level, took place at a whole different level of magnitude, and for hundreds of thousands in Southern Ontario, it disrupted everyday life for more than a week. Using high-tech hand-held, mobile, building-based, and airborne cameras, they conspired to provide surveillance of every minute movement made by protesters and by anyone in and around the yellow zone. Using their considerable institutional power, they conspired (quite transparently and not very successfully) to spin news accounts in their favour. They clearly conspired too in an effort to deny basic civil rights, and to commit seemingly criminal acts against demonstrators. With mass, arbitrary, and pre-emptive arrests on trumped up charges that were later dropped, they conspired to clear the streets of protesters until the summit was over. (They borrowed this tactic from New York police who arbitrarily rounded up 1,800 demonstrators during the 2004 Republican National Convention, holding them illegally for as long as seventy-two hours until the Republicans left town, only then releasing them, there too mostly without charges.) "The key was to take these people out of play," explained a senior police officer.[23] They conspired to construct a sophisticated command centre to coordinate the surveillance and the movement of security forces, as well as a logistics depot in Barrie, Ontario about ninety kilometres away. While a civilian review board member likened police behaviour to that of the black bloc,[24] community organizer Farrah Miranda, announcing an activists' investigation of the police, turned the police rationale back on itself: "We are aware that the rogue officers displayed here . . . were not acting alone. . . . They were part of a coordinated conspiracy by police chiefs and politicians."[25]

The choice of downtown Toronto for the G20's location is also mysterious. It has never been adequately explained why the Ottawa cabinet suddenly moved the G20 from its rural location to the city, nor why the initial choice of the Exhibition Ground several kilometres from the centre was suddenly passed up in favour of the downtown. Even before the G20 arrived, it was widely conjectured that Prime Minister Stephen Harper, whose governing Conservative Party had won not a single parliamentary seat in the Toronto metropolitan area, was cynically orchestrating a payback. Perhaps not accidentally, the Harper government's surprising announcement of the relocation to Toronto came on December 7, 2009, the first day of the Copenhagen climate change conference coordinated by then Toronto Mayor David Miller, who criticized the Harper government for refusing to act on climate change. The Harper government has resolutely blocked all efforts at a federal-level G20 inquiry.[26]

Leading up to the G20, many Torontonians reasoned that with so much publicity given to the astronomic cost of the event, the security forces would have to provoke a confrontation in order to justify the security expenditure and their own mass presence. The unfolding of events did nothing to contradict that expectation and much to support it. On the Saturday protest, marchers began to speculate that the mysteriously abandoned police cars in the middle of streets and intersections were deliberately left as bait, and later that police provocateurs masquerading as black bloc cadre participated in the first assaults on the cars. Others reported that one targeted car had already been stripped of valuable accessories such as computer and radio. So widespread was such speculation that the Toronto police felt forced to rebuff it directly: "Those cars were abandoned because officers' lives were in danger," insisted police superintendent Jeff McGuire. "We didn't leave these there intentionally."[27] But officer McGuire was entirely out of the loop or absent from the event, or else lying: thousands of protesters, some with young children, peacefully passed one or more of the abandoned cruisers a good hour before any confrontation, so it would be a sad commentary on the Toronto police force if the erstwhile drivers were indeed scared for their lives by people walking in the street. Further, various press accounts reported that frustrated frontline officers were directly ordered by superiors "not to get involved," not to defend the vehicles or properties under attack. Several officers confided that "they could have rounded up all, or most of them, in no time." Another claimed: "It was awful. . . . There were guys with equipment to do the job, all standing around looking at each other in disbelief. . . . The Montreal riot guys were livid. . . . They just wanted to get in there and do the job."[28]

The Fallout

Throughout the summer of 2010, three sets of public inquiries dominated national debate in Canada. Intimately connected as lenses into the world of state violence, taken together they dramatize the events of the G20 summit as everyday rather than exceptional. The first, addressing the 2007 RCMP taser murder of arriving Polish passenger Robert Dziekanski at the Vancouver airport, found clear evidence of outrageous police misconduct and culpability. Second, were the multiple inquiries into police violence against protesters and passersby at the 2010 G20 summit in Toronto, while a class action lawsuit was also launched on behalf of as many as eight hundred people arrested during the event. The third, addressing systemic police neglect of the disappearance and serial killing of mostly Indigenous women from Vancouver's Downtown East Side, finally began to receive serious consideration after exhaustive lobbying by the Union of British Columbia Indian Chiefs and the B.C. Civil Liberties Association.

Except within activist networks, few direct connections were initially drawn across these three major public controversies, even though they frequently appeared side by side in print media. In each case, national and/or local police forces committed violence, including violence by neglect, against the citizens they are ostensibly paid to protect. Together these cases offer a diagnostic not only for the strength of the security arm of the Canadian state or its hyperactivity in cities but also for the selectivity of its targeted violence: the foreigner who doesn't speak the language, the Indigenous sex trade worker, the political opposition criminalized as "black bloc." If Dziekanski was accosted "in a paranoid space where security officials are terrified that every foreigner is a terrorist,"[29] then the murdered women were in necropolitical space where sex trade workers and Indigenous people alike are "third class citizens,"[30] their lives valued as a percentage of some norm. These cases provide a vital parallax for understanding the systemic rather than simply episodic nature of G20 state violence during the G20 summit.

Yet "events belie forecasts," as Henri Lefebvre once observed. They "may even overturn strategies that provided for their possible occurrence."[31] But, as he also quickly says, however much discrete events upset the day-to-day flow of expectability, they may also "become reabsorbed into the general situation." Preventing that from happening is crucial. Lefebvre, of course, was reflecting on far more momentous events than the 2010 Toronto G20 police rampage, namely the May 1968 uprising in Paris, but his analysis travels well in time and space, if at a different scale. In the case of Toronto, the strategic complicity of the federal government, the quivering response by local politicians, the superordinate aggressiveness of the various police forces, all lay unusually bare the fact that however predictable the police assault, state strategy is both changing and yet contested from within. Similarly, the stunned response by many in Toronto to police suppression of rights and the confused response by a press that seemed not to know its script, suggest a political opening and at least in the short term a critical eschewal of innocence concerning the interests involved in state policing. Further, the various inquiries, the launching of the class action suit over widespread suppression of rights, and the broad failure of the G20 summit itself to tackle the economic crisis, will not only keep "the event" under the microscope but will also embolden the opposition. The prospect is there that, as Lefebvre puts it, this and related events can "reactivate the movement of both thought and practice."[32]

18

Marching with the Black Bloc
"Violence" and Movement Building

Tammy Kovich

The state is a mafia that has won control over society, and the law is
the codification of everything they have stolen from us.
— Peter Gelderloos, *Anarchy Works*

I WILL NOT SOON FORGET THE EVENTS OF SATURDAY, JUNE 26. WHAT
I experienced that day has been burned into my memory. My day
began, far earlier than intended, with a police raid on my Toronto
house. I was woken up at 5:00 a.m. (after only an hour of sleep) by
police officers descending the stairs to my basement bedroom. Once I
figured out what was going on, I quickly got out of bed, only to wit-
ness the fifteen or more officers who had broken into my home round
up my housemates, friends, and close comrades. I watched in outrage
as the police cuffed all of the men in the house, while more or less
ignoring the women. After we had been detained for almost an hour,
a close friend of mine was dragged away and forced into a waiting
police van. While I stood on my front porch, staring in disbelief, the
van drove away with my friend trapped inside. Needless to say, my
day did not begin well.

I spent the rest of that morning preparing for the afternoon march
and dealing with more bad news. I arrived at the Toronto Community
Mobilization Network convergence space to hear that the raid on my
house was not the only one. Police had raided another house in the
early hours of the morning and arrested more comrades. As I digested
that news, I heard rumors of further arrest warrants. People began to
discuss the increasing possibility that our groups had been infiltrated
by undercover police officers. As the weekend progressed these suspi-
cions were confirmed: our groups had been infiltrated. The pre-emptive
morning arrests were only the beginning of what became the largest

mass arrest in Canadian history. By the time Sunday night rolled around, almost everyone I knew was in police custody. I had personally been temporarily detained several times and was wary of leaving my house.

Despite the troubling experiences of that morning, there were moments over the course of the weekend that I found both beautiful and inspiring. For a few hours on Saturday afternoon, as I marched with the black bloc anything seemed possible and – for the only time all weekend – I felt safe. I was with friends, I was with comrades, and I was with people who would struggle alongside me, regardless of whether I knew them or not, and protect me if the need arose. The tactics of the black bloc are often described as confrontational, but they are also defensive. Demonstrators come prepared to protect themselves from police violence: they wear bandanas to protect themselves from tear gas and they dress in black to protect their identities and make it more difficult for police to find them in the crowd. That afternoon I witnessed black bloc actions that were destructive, but I also witnessed countless examples of black bloc demonstrators defending themselves and others from police. When police approached an unmasked couple I saw the bloc encircle and protect them. I watched people from the bloc help a young woman who was simply passing by and fell during a commotion. I saw black bloc demonstrators take care of each other as they made their way through the city.

From the moment the bloc broke away from the main march to the time that we dispersed a few hours later, my relationship to the city was transformed. For that short while the streets did not belong to the politicians or to the CEOs, but to us. We did not confine our dissent to the state-sanctioned "protest pen" in Queen's Park. We were taking back space, not asking for it. As we marched down the streets of Toronto, led – contrary to popular media images – by a small group of unmasked women of colour, I contemplated what seemed like the limitless potential of our movement. We were self-organized, we were full of rage, and our actions were not limited by the state's laws. The sound of breaking glass was for me a reminder that the value of property need not trump human life. Since that afternoon I've often reflected on how we might extend this transformative moment beyond the summit demonstration. How can we build on the sense of empowerment we felt that afternoon?

The Black Bloc Debate

The events of that Saturday, and in particular the actions of the black bloc, have become one of the most hotly debated moments of the Toronto G20 protests. Both within the mainstream media and within the left, this debate has followed the habitual pattern of post-summit protest fallout in which commentators question the legitimacy of black bloc tactics and the line between vandalism and violence: are bricks hurled through windows, rocks thrown at riot police, or fires set on the streets legitimate protest tactics? Do they constitute violence? Can violent tactics be justified? For over a decade – since the 1999 "Battle of Seattle" – the debate about violence, vandalism, and the black bloc has divided social movements. A staple of planning discussions leading up to major mobilizations, this debate has followed a predictable pattern of pacifists versus militants and has grown stagnant and counterproductive. To paraphrase Raoul Vaneigem, it has become a corpse in all of our mouths, and desperately needs to be put to rest.[1] In the face of growing environmental destruction and systemic global exploitation and in preparation for the coming austerity measures and the necessary intensification of social-movement struggles, we need to find a way to discuss the issue of protest "violence" constructively, and we need to leave behind dogmatic baggage – pacifist, militant, or otherwise – in order to strengthen our movements and expand the breadth of what we can accomplish.

Contextualizing Violence

As early as the mid-nineteenth century, radicals on the left began to debate the merit of "propaganda of the deed," with some arguing that bold, violent actions could be more effective than words in winning support for anti-capitalist struggle. Over a century and a half later, the question of violence continues to be one of the most controversial and polarizing issues in activist discussions. While historical debates concerning political violence involved questions pertaining to armed insurrection or the assassinations of state leaders and capitalist bosses, contemporary discussions primarily concern the use of direct action tactics during protests and focus almost solely on property destruction and confrontations with the police.[2] In the wake of the Toronto G20 protests, many people have criticized the black bloc for their so-called violent actions. This charge needs to be fleshed out.

At least within the North American context, "violent" actions at demonstrations are overwhelmingly directed at inanimate objects, and, if they are directed at people, are generally defensive in nature (engaging with the police to free someone from arrest, for example). Acknowledging this fact, it's important to be frank that when people talk about violence and criticize the black bloc, they are more often than not criticizing small-scale property destruction – nothing more, nothing less.

But does property destruction constitute a violent act? Over the last decade, this question has arguably been as controversial as the more general question of political violence. For some the destruction of property is necessarily a violent act. For others it is crystal clear that violence cannot be committed against an object, and that distinctions must be made between attacks on people and attacks on property. Either way, it is crucial to consider the context in which such actions take place.

Our society is based upon, maintained, and reproduced by widespread violence. Structural violence – in which our social structures and institutions systemically prevent people from meeting their basic needs – defines society's daily workings and implicates us all. From the food we eat to the clothes we wear, from the land we live on to the resources we consume, violence plays an integral role in all of our lives. The hamburger arrived on our dinner plate via the slaughterhouse. The clothes we wear were likely produced in a sweatshop. The land we live on is stolen – it was forcefully and often bloodily expropriated from Indigenous populations. This violence is for the most part hidden, but this does not make it any less real. In the face of this violent reality, indifference is a form of violence. Passive participation implies passive consent to this social order of violence.

This wider social context should help us to keep protest "violence" in perspective. Rocks thrown through windows and fires set to property pale in comparison to day-to-day structural violence. The corporations that profit from the decimation of the environment and the exploitation of their employees are violent. The state leaders who steal Indigenous lands and implement policies that criminalize immigration and institutionalize poverty are violent.

Acting Strategically

I believe that aggressive confrontations on the streets and unapologetically militant campaigns are of great importance to our movement – they empower participants and illustrate that it is unnecessary to petition to higher powers, parliamentary or otherwise, to bring about social change. We do not need to march alongside police escorts; we do not need to ask for permits to take to the streets; and we certainly do not need to restrict our demonstrations to designated "free speech zones." Claiming space in which to express our collective anger is a valid pursuit. In my experience, targeted property destruction and altercations with the police can be worthwhile endeavors, if only for therapeutic reasons.

That said, it is important to act strategically. It is absolutely crucial for those engaging in social struggle to choose their tactics wisely and to acknowledge the importance of context and timing. The black bloc is a tactic plain and simple; it is a tool that exists within a varied toolbox of potential tactics available to activists. As with any tactic, it makes sense to use the black bloc tactic in some situations but not in others.

However, in current debates within the left over the black bloc, many proponents of non-violence argue that the use of violence is in every circumstance wrong – that the master's tools cannot be used to dismantle the master's house. Some maintain that actions that include property destruction should not even be considered. Such tactics will alienate broad segments of the population, they argue, and thus reduce participation in protests and hinder mass movement building. Proponents of more confrontational actions, on the other hand, argue that, as Bakunin said, "the passion for destruction is a creative passion, too."[3] Some of these militants argue that only by attacking and tearing down the structures and institutions that oppress us can we create space to build alternatives and inspire and empower others to join our movements. Some offer unquestioning support of the black bloc tactic regardless of the circumstances. With heels firmly dug in the sand, many on each side of the debate refuse to budge, stunting the possibility for meaningful engagement and cooperation between activists from the two perspectives and ignoring the voices of those activists whose position falls somewhere between.

We cannot build social movements, or support each other's actions, or even stand in true solidarity with each other while claiming to know the one and only best way to go about organizing. Clearly, no part of the left has all of the answers. Recognizing this means taking a modest approach to organizing – an approach that does not give unwavering primacy to any one tactic, strategy, or position, and instead respects a diversity of tactics. So many of the struggles we engage in as activists are perpetual works in progress, ongoing experiments that may or may not result in positive gains. It is crucial not to limit the tactical options available to us. The moment that participants take a dogmatic position, whether it is arguing for non-violent actions in every circumstance or arguing for the confrontational escalation of every event, they shut themselves off from other potentially fruitful possibilities. I believe that both "violent" and non-violent tactics can be of use, and that the fetishization of any one tactic is counterproductive. Constructive projects that seek to prefigure the world we want to live in can work hand in hand with those more destructive initiatives that seek to directly confront and tear down all that protesters struggle against. To act strategically is simply to acknowledge this fact, while articulating clear goals and then deciding upon the particular tactics best suited to these goals.

It remains unclear if the tactics used during Toronto G20 mobilizations were strategic. The destruction of property that occurred on the afternoon of the twenty-sixth was for many an inspiring expression of indignation at all the G20 stands for. The burning of a few cop cars did not lead to the abolishment of the Toronto Police Force, nor did it meaningfully address the many social justice issues around policing in the city. However, it did challenge in a very public manner the unquestioned social position of the police, and thereby attacked the very notion that police authority, and by extension state authority, must be respected. Business as usual in the city was brought to a halt and it was impossible for even the most disinterested and apathetic of citizens to ignore the demonstrations. A protest in the street is one thing; a fire set on the street is something else entirely. Reflecting upon the property destruction that occurred in city, and the extent to which it was "intrusive on life in Toronto," Ontario Premier Dalton McGuinty publicly stated that he would "prefer not to see another G20-type summit in Toronto ever again."[4] For better or worse, the black bloc made its mark on the city.

This is, however, only one part of the story – the use of confrontational, sometimes illegal, tactics has repercussions that we cannot ignore. The immediate consequences of these tactics include ongoing repression of activists and the further criminalization of dissent. Surveillance, infiltration, and pre-emptive arrests have been Toronto's G20 legacy. Long-time organizers face serious criminal charges and are entangled in lengthy and costly legal battles. Restrictive bail conditions, including debilitating non-association and no-demonstration clauses, as well as the threat of jail time, have removed some of the movement's most respected and skilled organizers from their communities.[5] This immeasurable loss is compounded by the fact that many remaining activists have had to make their central focus solidarity work to support the criminalized organizers. Time, energy, and resources that would have otherwise been directed at more productive projects have been redirected to legal defence efforts. Providing support for those facing charges is absolutely fundamental but so too is continued organizing work, and thus activists are left struggling to strike a balance between the two.

Beyond Property Destruction

We're left with the question of how to move beyond – or at least reinvigorate – the debates about the black bloc and the question of violence. The initial starting point for our discussions has largely remained a demand for the supporters of the black bloc tactic to justify the use of violence. The pacifist position is accepted without question, while advocates of more aggressive tactics are put on the defensive. We need to turn the debate on its head – given the severity of the situation we face, in light of the pervasive nature of the systems of domination and oppression that we oppose, and acknowledging the pressing need for an intensification of our struggles, we need to begin asking ourselves if *non-violence* can be justified.

If we agree that both confrontational and peaceful tactics can be useful and justifiable, we can expand the repertoire of tactics available to activists. In some instances the black bloc tactic has been successful in meeting activist goals, while in others it has become a performance of solely symbolic action overshadowing more constructive anarchist projects – for example, anti-poverty organizing, migrant justice work, workplace organizing, alternative education projects, and childcare collectives. Just as it is worthwhile to consider a broad spectrum of non-violent actions, so too is it worthwhile to consider a broad spectrum of more confrontational tactics. The accusation that the use of more forceful tactics alienates people and is detrimental to movement building ignores the fact that different tactics appeal to different people. To win the upcoming fight against the austerity regime, the left needs to find ways to sustain social movement struggles on all fronts, to support a broad array of actions, and to engage both a large and a diverse group of people. This means leaving space for a variety of types of organizing within social movements, and acting in a spirit of solidarity and mutual aid. The stagnant debate surrounding the black bloc and the use of "violence" has little to contribute to these efforts.

19

Forms of Protest Reflect Our Power
Radical Strategy and Mass Mobilizations

Clarice Kuhling

IN THE SAME WEEK THAT TORONTO WAS HOST TO THE G20 SUMMIT, people in the Toronto area witnessed a tornado, an earthquake, and – as the G20 talks commenced – the massive build-up of almost twenty thousand law enforcement officers. While a more fantastical imagination might have forecast an invasion of locusts or an outbreak of boils as the next calamity to befall Toronto, the police response to the anti-G20 protests, including the arrest of approximately eleven hundred protesters, and the ensuing discussions about the protests were enough to shock and horrify. For instead of a thoroughgoing analysis of how an estimated $20 trillion global bailout to rescue the financial sector would be (violently) achieved through the imposition of massive spending cuts and an increase in the rate of exploitation of the world's working class,[1] media commentators on both the right and left bemoaned the "violence" of the protests.

Of course, the likelihood of mainstream media formulating a deeper understanding of the current period (as a systemic crisis of capitalism rooted in the dynamics of capitalist production and over-accumulation) was about as likely as an invasion of locusts or a pandemic outbreak of boils. However, the commentary about the so-called violent protesters that came from many quarters of the left was surprising and disappointing. Ken Georgetti, head of the Canadian Labour Congress (CLC) released a statement that condemned the vandalism and attacks on private property as derailing the events. Many offered scathing criticism of protest tactics, condemning the smashed windows and burned out cop cars, and opining wistfully about lost opportunities. Still others sprinkled their analysis of the vandalism with denunciations of the "substitutionism" (when a small group of often well intentioned activists fight on behalf of others rather than assist others to act for themselves), "adventurism,"[2] and "inherently elitist and counter-productive"[3] actions of some protesters. Not many asked the crucial question of *why* property damage as a protest tactic repeatedly re-emerges, and few traced or attributed these tactics to the political and economic context or the low level of left resistance in Canada and the United States. And yet, understanding this context and the factors that created it – the general absence of mass social protest; the continued weakening of left politics oriented to mass struggle; the decline of working-class movement organizing both inside and outside the workplace; the growth of an increasingly passive, unaccountable, and bureaucratic labour leadership, along with union structures that reinforce such characteristics; and the decline of spaces to connect with working-class activism – is absolutely crucial to understanding why breaking windows has emerged as the most seductive form of protest for some. The repeated occurrence of "smashing shit up" is both an expression of this context and a direct reflection of the low level of struggle and resistance on the left, particularly within labour unions. Ultimately, isolating particular protest tactics for criticism without a larger critique of strategies of left resistance inhibits our ability to learn the lessons that this round of protests could teach us about building for the next.

Looking Back: Union Transformation and the Decline of Infrastructures of Dissent

In the years since the end of the mass anti-war protests of 2003 in Canada and the United States, the strategy of "insurrectionism" has become more influential among some anarchists.[4] This approach favours attacks on property and conspiratorial actions over other kinds of anarchist action. With fewer mechanisms at our disposal to translate rage and opposition into an effective challenge to the current economic system, particular protest tactics such as smashing the "symbols of capitalism" – the windows of certain corporations (Adidas and Starbucks, for example) as well as the repressive state apparatus (police cars) that buttress this system – will inevitably appeal to some people. These tactics keep reappearing precisely because they represent a wholesale departure from the forms of passive politics and bureaucratically controlled resistance that have increasingly monopolized the political terrain of working-class struggle in the last half-century in both Canada and the United States.

As a crucial mechanism and expression of working-class power, labour unions should be one of the most obvious institutions from which a challenge to global capitalism could be mounted by the left. However, the Cold War greatly weakened radicalism within working-class movements: many leftist radicals were purged from unions, and some unions, like the Canadian Seaman's Union, were destroyed outright through these purges. And while the legal protection won in the 1940s did grant workers the freedom to organize and bargain, with these new rights came restrictions. For example, workers could no longer legally engage in sympathy strikes, strike during the life of a collective agreement, or strike in support of political demands. Union officials were now obliged to police their own members by discouraging them from undertaking illegal strike action. The new collective bargaining process thus imposed a host of regulations and requirements on workers, which dramatically circumscribed their activities.[5] The site of struggle shifted increasingly away from the streets and workplaces and over to the sterile boardrooms of bargaining tables – and thus into the hands of the union officials, bureaucrats, and professionals who increasingly dominated these spaces.[6] As David Camfield notes, the union officialdom that emerged as a distinct social layer became increasingly preoccupied with "preserving stable union institutions and bargaining relationships with employers."[7] Labour militancy was sacrificed in exchange for labour peace, and gradual incremental gains in the welfare state were won (for a time) at the expense of further struggle for more profound social transformation. And while radical movements did emerge in the 1960s and 1970s, aside from in Quebec they failed to build a new radical left of any significance inside the working-class movement.

Additionally, previous historical periods had more openings for people to connect with working-class politics and activism. These openings were crucial, and provided the organizational forms and the physical and intellectual spaces through which people could plug into militant working-class struggles. These "infrastructures of dissent," as Alan Sears calls them, are "the means of analysis, communication, organization and sustenance that nurture the capacity for collective action" and for challenging the system.[8] Such infrastructures of dissent included various socialist and anarchist political formations, left-wing ethnic organizations, community and civil rights organizations, radical publications, and left oppositional currents within unions. But these also included actual physical spaces (the community halls, bars, sports clubs, and coffee houses), and the cultural and leisure activities that people shared (the choirs, plays, parades, picnics, and dance groups), as well as the informal networks that existed in people's neighbourhoods, communities, and workplaces. As Sears notes, all of these provided the spaces and forms of organization necessary to debate and analyze, to learn how to organize and fight, to dream, and to hope, and to offer visions of what kind of workplace or society should emerge.

The decline, co-optation, or destruction of such vehicles for working-class resistance, which occurred alongside the declawing of unions, has dramatically altered social life. Forms of collective action that were previously part of working-class experience both in workplaces and in communities have been replaced by individual coping strategies, and the openings once available to plug into militant working-class struggles have dramatically narrowed for young activists, not to mention anyone who is disaffected, disenfranchised, and disillusioned.

Thus younger activists have very little connection to and identification with unions in particular and radical working-class politics in general. Instead, we have a widening cleavage – first apparent during the 2001 Quebec City protests against the proposed Free Trade Area of the Americas (FTAA) – between newly radicalized younger activists who have had little exposure to radical working-class politics, and labour activists, who "are not connecting with the energizing experiences of more militant forms of direct action and who have yet to make a connection with anti-capitalist ideas."[9]

Moving Forward: Effective Protests and Mass Militancy

The decline and retreat of working-class activism (which includes the structural separation of workers arising from the reorganization of work and the gradual replacement of more collective forms of action with individual coping strategies) is an objective problem, as David McNally notes – a real historical development emerging from a historically specific social context.[10] And the present day separation between labour movement activists and radicalizing youth – between workplace struggles and street protests (which are largely disconnected from union struggles) – is a direct expression of this historical development and context. As a participant and activist in various global justice and anti-poverty protests for over a decade, I have been disheartened to see a bureaucratic union leadership repeatedly mobilize members solely for marches that lead to empty parking lots (the FTAA protests in Quebec City in 2001, for example), or away from the fences behind which policies are made (take your pick from multiple examples including the anti-G20 protests in Toronto).

However, union leadership control goes beyond simple orchestration of these contained mobilizing efforts and, sadly, extends toward inhibiting the formation of more militant fight-back strategies that might provide alternative spaces for collective action. During the 2001 Quebec City protests, I was part of a group that organized to encourage participants in the labour march to change course and head toward the wall to support the thousands of protesters (many of them young) already there, who faced tear gas and water cannons – and eventually rubber bullets. Most labour leaders failed to tell their members what was happening at the wall; they didn't give them a choice of whether to march to the fence that encircled the FTAA meetings or to march miles away to a large field and empty parking lot. We tried to give union marchers that choice, but in response to our shouts of encouragement to turn left towards the fence – "À gauche, à gauche, pas à droite! To the left, to the left, not to the right!" – we were verbally chastised and in some cases physically obstructed by union marshals.

Then, as now, the top leadership of the CLC was centrally involved in orchestrating (and policing) the form that labour protests were to take. Compare Ken Georgetti's statement in April 2001 – "It's a good symbolic act to walk away"[11] – with his press release on the Saturday of the anti-G20 labour march: "We cooperated with police in choosing the route and had hundreds of parade marshals to maintain order."[12] The Toronto union marshals did not (from what I could observe) prevent marchers from undertaking a breakaway march to get closer to the fence, yet statements like Georgetti's provide evidence of how a bureaucratic labour leadership, rather than serving as a force for social change, increasingly has acted, to paraphrase John Clarke, to inhibit more militant formations within the unions and stymie working-class resistance, or has refused to act at all.[13]

Forms of Protest Reflect Our Power

The commonly heard chant, "Whose streets? *Our* streets!" aptly captures the exhilaration we feel when we register our dissent by taking over the streets during a demonstration – especially when the takeover ruptures the tightly choreographed boundaries of typical protests. The experience of being part of a mass crowd in opposition can be inspiring and can challenge previous assumptions about the world. But this heady feeling doesn't last long if opposition is not translated at some point into something more, some tangible result. The awe and inspiration we experience from being part of such events is quickly dulled when all we do is march in circles or to empty parking lots and when attempts at more oppositional forms of protest and more militant actions are immediately shut down or managed from above, like a faucet turned on and off (mainly off!).

Dismissively tossing accusations of "adventurist" at the tactics employed by some protesters in response to such manoeuvrings from above tends to obscure the ongoing reality of the simultaneous passivity and collusion of labour leaders in repeatedly shutting down militant struggle. It also fails to acknowledge the sheer anger that many feel at the failure of various community and labour organizations to adequately mount an effective fight-back strategy in the face of an ongoing onslaught by capital against the working class.

This onslaught is not felt equally across generations or across the whole working class, and it reflects the emergence of new and complex forms of working-class differentiation. It also presents new obstacles and challenges to building solidarity. The role of capital and the state in reorganizing the labour force and redistributing wealth to favour capital (controlled by some segments of older adults) at the expense of youth wage-labour can clearly be seen in the explosive growth of subordinate service occupations and temporary, part-time, contract work held by younger non-unionized workers (as well as workers of colour, particularly women of colour) and in the setting of minimum wage standards (not to mention "flexible" labour markets). According to one report, two-thirds of minimum wage earners are under twenty-four years of age. While in the mid-1970s minimum wage would have placed a worker approximately 40 per cent above the official poverty line, it now positions workers 30 per cent below that line.[14] Similarly, the unfortunate tendency of some unions to protect their own members at the expense of the larger working class or even to bargain differential protections for workers within the same collective agreement (seen in the increased incidence of two-tier contracts, which guarantee benefits to older generations of workers but diminish or outright eliminate these provisions for newer, younger workers) has further complicated efforts at bridging the yawning gap between radicalizing youth and labour movement activists.

We need to have honest, open, respectful discussions – without self-righteous name calling or accusations – that begin to grapple with the level of anger that the intensification of neo-liberal capitalism has generated and that begin to strategize about how we can translate anger into a resistance movement actually capable of turning the tide. Unless we contend with the reality that some young activists will turn to particular forms of direct action as a substitute for any other kind of power, then we will continue to have militant breakaway marches and smashed windows. As long as a servile, passive politics takes the place of (indeed "substitutes" for) active militant resistance, then we will continue to see part of the public expressing their frustration in ways that are not easily contained.

And yet, an analysis of strategies and tactics *is* desperately needed. The unfortunate reality is that smashing a window, even many windows, does not challenge the power of capital in any fundamental way, let alone overthrow the power of capital. Profits are not impeded when insurance can cover the cost of replacing windows, and capitalism does not grind to a halt – or even turn tail and run – when specific meetings are shut down or interrupted or when the "symbols of capitalism" are smashed. Changing the world would be so much easier if this were the case! Rather, the inequality inherent in capitalist production derives from the fact that the value of the work we perform is more than what we are paid in wages, and the difference (the profit) goes to the employer, not us. Disrupting this social relation (between people who sell their ability to work and those who purchase other people's ability to work) means getting at the core of what makes capitalism function as an economic system. Because the profit taken from us relies on our continuing to work, effectively challenging capital would require disrupting this chain of profit acquisition through stopping work. And going from challenging capital to ultimately overthrowing capital would involve seizing control of, and paralyzing the production of profits in, these very workplaces.[15]

Forms of Protest Reflect Our Power

This dauntingly far-reaching task of seizing control – collectively and democratically – of our workplaces and other institutions will thus obviously require large mobilizations. But it will also require large numbers of us actively working together, self-organizing – in stark contrast to more passive forms of political engagement (such as electoral politics) undertaken by isolated individuals. And this mass self-activity must be capable of disrupting the immobilization, powerlessness, and cynicism that we often feel, so that we begin to experience our world in new ways – as makers of history capable of changing our world rather than bystanders watching our world make or break us. Tactics like an occupation, blockade, militant strike, or sit-in, for example, are some of the methods that better enable us to begin to take power with our own hands. These three elements – mass mobilization, active self-organization, and collective empowerment (through forms of participatory democracy and direct action that enable us to experience and wield our power collectively) – are key ingredients in building our counter-power.[16]

Thus the process by which we struggle is absolutely crucial to building this counter-power. It might be useful, then, to ask ourselves if the tactics and mobilization strategies we currently embrace are indeed contributing to the process of building our counter-power. However convincing our arguments might be that property destruction and window smashing is not actually "violent," particularly when compared to all the other forms of systemic violence routinely enacted through the structures of power, we would have a more difficult time making the case that window smashing builds our counter-power. Regardless of how empowering it might feel in the moment to smash shit up – and it may indeed be an immense release to show the world one's profound discontent – it does not generally mobilize mass numbers of people, and it does not enable us to experience in any more than a fleeting way that sense of collective strength and power which is capable of changing both ourselves and the world around us. Equally as important, it also does not help us build our organizing skills, nor does it help facilitate forms of self-organization in workplaces or in communities that might eventually develop into an effective movement for change. Getting to the point where social struggle can hit profits will take time. In the interim it is essential to start building relationships and connections with workers (and others) upon whose labour power corporations depend and who toil away behind the very windows that some see fit to smash.

If part of our powerlessness and political disengagement derives from the feeling that our participation in the affairs of the world is meaningless, then it follows that we need to engage in methods of struggle that are effective and make a difference in people's lives. People are emboldened and radicalized through the actual experiences of gaining ground, of seeking and winning concrete gains in the here-and-now, in the process of struggle. In this way they begin to develop confidence and a sense of their capacities, and become active (perhaps for the first time) in creatively defining and fighting for their own interests. Winning at least partial victories, winning even defensive battles, can inspire higher levels of mobilization that could eventually tip the grossly uneven balance of social forces.

This is why it is so important to fight for and defend immediate improvements and reforms, and not impatiently reject this struggle as inadequately radical. We must fight for reforms, but in ways which are always "oriented towards the creation of new forms of democratic participation that challenge the limits and ultimately the existence of existing institutions. . . . We build a counter-power when people become active in their own cause: occupying, striking, or taking demands to the streets."[17] These forms of struggle would thus not be content merely with signing petitions and appealing through the courts or elections to be represented, nor would they be content with smashing windows. Rather, such forms of struggle would go further, would seek to translate our opposition into something more enduring. They would strive to challenge things like property rights and the legitimacy of governments by building new forms of popular power that wear down or partially replace existing forms of capitalist and state control over communities, neighbourhoods, and workplaces – a situation that is often called "dual power."[18]

Translating our opposition into more enduring forms of social organization that remain behind after the protests are over and the streets are empty, that sink roots into communities, that create new institutional forms that are democratic and express the power and will of the majority, then, involves much more than just expressing discontent at a protest. Even the most extraordinary of strikes and protests have often come up against the difficulty of reordering social relations and generating new institutions of popular power that are

Forms of Protest Reflect Our Power

broad based and oppositional and that can enable people to begin to "take control of social life."[19] This is why it is so important not to counter-pose forms of resistance understood as mass but not militant against those seen as militant but not rooted in mass numbers. Social gains have only been won through collective action in the form of mass *and* militant struggle; individual acts by tiny groupings have never successfully challenged the power of capital or won significant social gains.

One of the benefits of the large social justice mobilizations starting with the 1999 World Trade Organization (WTO) protest in Seattle was that they provided an organizational structure that enabled layers of activists to gain a sense of our collective numbers and strength. They also provided a space to learn from others in the process of struggle – seeing and hearing what other actions were planned, experiencing the creative fusion and explosion of ideas, debating amongst ourselves and arguing for a particular strategy or about the lack thereof, sharing our struggles and our skills and our knowledge, and collectively working together to solve problems. We thus need to ensure that concerns about police surveillance and infiltration (all very justifiable given what we now know about how infiltration has occurred at the highest levels of militant organizations!) do not lead to clandestine and non-transparent organizational forms. Police infiltration and surveillance has occurred and will again occur regardless of how clandestine an organizational approach we take. Our best security lies in our numbers, for the more people we mobilize, the more difficult it is to manipulate, infiltrate, and control us.

The key challenge of the present, then, is that the recurring systemic crises inherent to the capitalist system have not been matched either by a fighting movement of resistance large enough to effectively challenge this system, or by a vision of what can and should replace it.[20] This simultaneous "crisis of capitalism alongside a crisis of resistance and opposition"[21] means that we need to engage in movement building (in our unions and our community organizations) as non-sectarian participants in struggle. We need to focus on building large-scale, democratic, and effective mobilizations and put forward comprehensive notions of what we are fighting for. This also means that we need to initiate efforts to reclaim and radically democratize our unions so that they once again serve as an extension and expression of our class power. This will require a seemingly contradictory combination of patience (building sustainable relationships on the basis of solidarity and open debate) alongside urgency (respecting the necessity for action in the here and now). Only by narrowing the gap between the forms that mass protest presently take and what is required to build broad-based working-class power will we be adequate to the task of turning the tide.

Police block intersection of Richmond St. W. and Duncan St., June 26, 2010. Photo by Vincenzo D'Alto.

20

Surveying the Landscape

Local Protesters and Global Summits

Lesley J. Wood and Glenn J. Stalker

FOR LOCAL ACTIVISTS AND ORGANIZATIONS INTERESTED IN BUILDING broader, deeper, and more sustainable movements, summit protests not only offer an important chance to confront transnational institutions in the glare of the international media. They also present opportunities for coalition building, networking, and experimenting with new forms of organization, disruption, media work, and education. To *not* protest the gathering of the global elites seems like a missed opportunity.

Although much of the writing on summit protests has focused on their transnational dimension, these mass convergences are built largely by local social movement activists, some of whom have worked for years on issues of poverty, environment, immigration, student concerns, or gender and sexuality. Preparation for such protests can transform the way local activists work together as they make new connections between their issues and campaigns, learn new skills, attract new participants and funding, and capture media attention. These preparations and the summit protest experience itself can build lasting alliances or harden existing divisions among activists. Summit protests can bring new people, technologies, and ideas to activist groups, but they can also bankrupt movements left facing extensive legal costs. In such ways, global summit protests transform local organizing and organizers and yet these processes are poorly understood and rarely written about.

Summit Protesters and Summit Repertoires

Many grassroots organizers tend to see summit protests as incompatible with local organizing goals. Summit protests tend to combine the arrival of activists from out of town with disruptive and creative forms of protest, and often involve large-scale but decentralized forms of organization. However exciting such protests can be, these events sometimes bring repression on the most vulnerable as the homeless are targeted, arrested, and displaced, and as organizers are surveilled or harassed. Often summit protests leave crisis in their wake, as organizers, exhausted and broke, are left to deal with legal costs, traumatized community members, and a hostile public. Summit protests can leave scars.

Over the past decade, as these costs have become increasingly understood and the benefits to activists made less apparent, the excitement that followed the wave of summit protests associated with the 1999 Seattle summit has dissipated. "Summit hoppers" are now disparaged and many of those who once attended summit protests now prioritize local organizing, networking, and skill building. In their critiques of summit protests, activists often cite Betita Martinez's account of the Seattle protests: "Where Was the Color in Seattle? Looking for Reasons Why the Great Battle was So White." Martinez depicts Seattle's summit protesters as white, middle-class, countercultural students and maintains that "the overall turnout of color from the U.S. remained around five percent of the total."[1] Local protesters of colour, according to Martinez's research, experienced "culture shock" when they first visited the protest convergence space set up by the Direct Action Network coalition. This critique was taken seriously by some and subsequently some summit protest organizers attempted to create protest spaces that were not so rooted in counterculture and were more accessible and welcoming to diverse communities.

Despite these efforts to rethink mass convergences, however, it remains unclear if they can provide opportunities for diverse local communities to come together and build their capacity for the long-term. Is it possible to create a protest organizing strategy that prioritizes local grassroots organizing over the established summit protest repertoire in which non-local participants – often white, youthful, and relatively privileged – attempt to disrupt a highly fortified summit? Can summit protests build local organizing that emphasizes the needs of poor people, migrants, Indigenous people, and people of colour? Or are they bound to be temporary – although often inspiring – moments of resistance, militancy, and countercultural experimentation?

Partly in response to such questions, the Toronto Community Mobilization Network (TCMN) – strategically named with the word "community" – attempted to build a summit protest for the 2010

Toronto G20 meetings that would prioritize long-term movement-building over the classic summit confrontation – they would use the summit protest opportunity to strengthen local grassroots groups.[2] The TCMN described itself as:

> a collection of Toronto-based organizers and allies, that will use the fleeting moment of the G8/G20 meetings in Toronto in June 2010 . . . to come together and share the work that we do every other day of the year. We will build the momentum for a movement for Indigenous Sovereignty and Self-Determination, Environmental and Climate Justice, Migrant Justice and an End to War and Occupation, Income Equity and Community Control over Resources, Gender Justice and Queer and disAbility rights.[3]

After agreeing that a key goal of the mobilization was to build the capacity of local activists and local struggles, the organizers worked hard to give primacy to these activists and their already existing organizations. TCMN meetings were structured to build alliances between these organizations. The central role played in the TCMN by No One Is Illegal – a group that locates immigration issues within an anti-colonial, Indigenous sovereignty, anti-poverty, queer, feminist, and disability rights perspective – made clear these efforts to bring local activism to the fore. In addition, organizers chose one of the themed days of action that were part of the week-long summit protests to focus attention on local issues and the connections between them – "Justice for Our Communities! No, to G8/G20! Yes, to Taking Back Our City!" declared the TCMN in its call for participants for the rally, march, block party, and tent city protests planned for that day.[4] Initially, with the intention of building a lasting network amongst organizations, the planning meetings for this day excluded activists that weren't organizing within a grassroots, community-based group. This strategy was driven by an analysis that argued that in order to build an effective and lasting anti-capitalist movement in the city, the demonstrations needed to involve a broad array of marginalized communities and prioritize their demands and leadership. As an increasing number of unaffiliated individuals began to attend TCMN meetings, this strategy was largely abandoned.

It is not easy to assess the success of these efforts to involve local participants and build local organizations or to determine whether or

Surveying the Landscape

not the Toronto G20 protest remained a largely non-local, globally-focused event. Our work here attempts to start such an evaluation through the results of a survey of demonstrators who attended Toronto protests. The data, limited though it is, suggests that local strategy and leadership can influence a transnational protest event.

The Data and the Method

Although there have been significant surveys of summit protesters in Europe through the protest survey project based in Amsterdam and through the work of Donatella della Porta and her collaborators, to date there has been relatively little data collected on the demographics of summit protesters in Canada and the United States.[5] The survey we used was designed by Rachel Kutz-Flamenbaum and Suzanne Staggenborg for the Pittsburgh G20 Research Project in September 2009 – one of the few projects to take account of North American mass protesters.[6]

Other than a few minor alterations (removing some US-specific details), we used the Pittsburgh survey. Our surveyors (trained undergraduate students) attended the four largest protest events during the week of action – the Wednesday environmental justice protest, the Thursday Indigenous sovereignty demonstration, the Justice for Our Communities event on Friday, and Saturday's "People First!" rally and march. Following a protocol used elsewhere for surveying at demonstrations, the researchers divided up the crowd before the marches began and asked every seventh person to complete a written survey. While this approach was systematic, it nonetheless cannot yield a completely random selection process and, therefore, we do not claim that the findings are completely representative of all G20 protesters, especially since cases were collected only at four selected protest events. Regardless, we have confidence in the approach compared to alternatives like convenience sampling, which often results in clusters of friends or organization members responding. Response rates varied from surveyor to surveyor but, overall, 56.3 per cent completed the survey. Although lower than some comparable surveys, we consider this a good result given the understandable wariness of some participants to fill in a survey, even an anonymous one. We suspect that participants who were more suspicious of surveillance and intelligence gathering would be less likely to complete the surveys, biasing the sample away from such participants.

The Protesters: What We Found

Local

From our survey results we found that 67 per cent of Toronto's G20 protesters resided in the Greater Toronto Area, with another 18 per cent from other places in Ontario. In contrast, 58 per cent of the protesters at the 2009 G20 protest in Pittsburgh were residents of the Pittsburgh area. In a survey of 1663 demonstrators at five global justice movement (GJM) events between 2000–2002 (one in the Netherlands, one in Canada, and three in the United States) Dana Fisher and her colleagues found significant variation in the proportion of local protesters at different summit protests. At the Canadian and American events included in the study local participation ranged from 24 per cent and 39 per cent at two World Bank/IMF protests in Washington DC in 2002 to 53 per cent at a G8 protest in Calgary in 2002 and 58 per cent at a World Economic Forum protest in New York City.[7] According to Mark Lichbach's study of the Seattle protests of 1999 – before the success of summit protesting had been broadcast – 47 per cent of participants were from the Seattle area or Washington State.[8] Toronto's G20 protests, then, involved a higher proportion of local participants than other summit protests.

Diverse Ages

The Toronto survey also asked participants about their age and found that 43 per cent were under thirty years old, another 30 per cent were in their thirties, and only 26 per cent were over forty. In contrast, at the Pittsburgh G20 protests, while a similar percentage were under thirty (43 per cent), only 10 per cent were in their thirties, but 35 per cent were forty or older.[9] In their survey of 243 protesters at an IMF/WB protest in Washington in 2002, Adler and Mittelman found that nearly 36 per cent of their sample were between twenty and twenty-four years old, more than 33 per cent were over thirty, and more than 20 per cent were over forty.[10] Compared to protesters surveyed at other summit protests, those surveyed at Toronto's G20 were more likely to be in their thirties.

Students and Workers

Forty per cent of Toronto's G20 protesters identified as students. This is surprising to some, but not that unusual. In Adler and Mittelman's Washington survey, more than 40 per cent of the participants at the 2002 IMF/WB protest identified themselves as students. Interestingly,

55 per cent of the Toronto protesters also said they were working full time, which may be explained by the summer date of the protests. The results of the Pittsburgh survey have not yet been analysed on this question.

Educated but Poor

The Toronto G20 protesters were highly educated; while only 37 per cent of Toronto residents are college graduates, 72 per cent of the summit survey participants were college graduates. Nonetheless, Toronto's protesters had low incomes, probably due to the high proportion of students. Thirty-two per cent had household incomes less than $20,000 per year, with 60 per cent reporting less than $40,000 per year, and 23 per cent reporting greater than $60,000 per year. The Pittsburgh data has not yet been run on this question.

Race

When asked about their racial identity, 27 per cent of Toronto respondents identified as people of colour. Broken down further, the results show that 73 per cent of attendees identified as white, 4 per cent as Indigenous, 5 per cent as Black, 6 per cent as Asian, 5 per cent as mixed race, and 2 per cent as Latin American. This is quite different to the results from the Pittsburgh G20 summit, where the researchers found that only 17 per cent of protesters identified as people of colour, with 83 per cent identified as white (compared with 67 per cent of the local population), 8 per cent as African American (compared with 27 per cent of the population), 3 per cent as Hispanic, and 2 per cent as Asian. According to Adler and Mittelman, almost 30 per cent at the Washington protests regarded themselves as members of minority groups – but the researchers argue that given the large number of foreign citizens at the DC protests, this doesn't mean that these protesters of colour represented engagement by American minority communities. Although they did not represent the demographics of the city, where 47 per cent of the population identify as a visible minority, Toronto's G20 participants were less likely to be white than summit protesters at other Canadian and American events.

New Arrivals and the Deeply Committed

The summit survey found that Toronto's protesters tended to be either new activists or very experienced ones – a result more polarized than that found in Pittsburgh. In Toronto, 27 per cent had never attended an activist meeting (versus 23 per cent in Pittsburgh), while 30 per cent had attended ten or more (versus 23 per cent in Pittsburgh). Thirty-six per cent had attended five or fewer protests in the past five years (a similar figure to Pittsburgh), while 34 per cent had attended more than fifteen (as opposed to Pittsburgh, where the figure was only 18 per cent).

In Pittsburgh, activists were most likely to be heavily involved with the environmental, human rights, and peace movements. In Toronto, protesters were most involved (that is, indicating they were *very involved* rather than *somewhat* or *not at all*) in the human rights movement (36 per cent), followed by the global justice movement (33 per cent), the peace movement (31 per cent), the environmental movement (28 per cent) and the labour movement (26 per cent).

In Toronto, the highest levels of activist experience (indicated in the survey by higher meeting attendance) were among protesters in the global justice movement – 58 per cent of those involved in global justice had attended ten or more activist meetings – followed by the human rights movement (52 per cent), the peace movement (49 per cent), the labour movement (39 per cent), and the women's movement (also 39 per cent).

Local and Global Scales of Activism

Interestingly, Toronto's G20 protesters tended to indicate that they believed the most important scales of activism are local (35 per cent) and international (33 per cent) scales. Only 10 per cent of protesters indicated that the national scale was most important to them; the same number indicated that they felt all scales of activism were important, while the remaining 9 per cent of protesters indicated a preference for a unique combination of local, national, or international scales of activism. The large proportion of Toronto G20 protesters identifying the local scale as a critical site of activism may, in part, be an indicator of the TCMN's success in mobilizing local organizations to build capacity during what is, almost by definition, a globally-focused event. Although the Pittsburgh data has not been fully analyzed, initial impressions suggest that those protesters also placed their faith primarily on the local and global scales.

Previous experience as a protester seemed to shape which scale of activism participants indicated was most important. The more protests respondents attended in the past five years, the more likely they were to identify the local scale of activism as the most important. Close to 33 per cent of protesters who had participated in one to

Surveying the Landscape

five protests in the previous five years believed that the local scale of activism is most important, compared to 42 per cent of activists who had attended fifteen or more protests in the same period. Thirteen per cent of protesters with the least experience felt that the national scale of activism is most important, while only 4 per cent of the most experienced protesters agreed. The international scale of activism was considered most important for 40 per cent of protesters with the least protest experience but for only 26 per cent of those with the most protest experience. Consequently, protesters with the most experience – and, potentially, a greater capacity to assume leadership within organizations – may be more supportive of organizing at the local scale or working to build linkages between movements that usually tend to focus their activism on one scale of action.

Did the Local Strategy Work?

Toronto's G20 protesters were more racially diverse, older, a more polarized group of new and experienced activists, and more local than their equivalents in Pittsburgh, New York, Washington, and Seattle. Most interesting are the contrasts with the relatively recent Pittsburgh summit, which had a similarly short period in which to organize, and used the same survey (see Table 1) – the Pittsburgh summit protest crowd seems to have been whiter, younger, and less local than demonstrators at the Toronto G20. The differences between the two events could of course be tied to differences in nation-state, local history, or demographics. But they might also mean that the organizing strategy and leadership of the Toronto mobilization influenced the protest turnout. Intentionally emphasizing local organizing and local issues and involving grassroots groups led by people of colour in the leadership might make a difference to the makeup of summit demonstrators. Summit protests, despite potential risks and costs, might be used to build local movements. While the summit protest repertoire has a certain solidity, it can be adapted and altered in ways that can bridge the gap between local struggles and global events.

However, despite this optimistic possibility, it is striking that, despite the strategy of emphasizing local community organizers, the summit protesters in Toronto were for the most part still white, young, and educated. In order to know how much this lack of diversity reflects everyday social-movement activity in Toronto, more

Table 1
Summary of differences between G20 protesters
in Toronto and Pittsburgh

	Toronto, 2010	Pittsburgh, 2009
Residents of the city	67%	58%
In their thirties	30%	10%
People of colour	27%	17%
New activists	27%	23%
Experienced activists	34%	18%

research would need to be done. Nonetheless, the survey results may suggest that an organizing strategy that emphasizes "the local" can only trump an established, transnationally-oriented strategy to a limited extent. Summit protests have accumulated certain symbolic meanings and have developed a particular (and relatively risky) repertoire of multiple days of action, which involve disruptive and creative protest and decentralized forms of organization; they tend to attract protesters who are invested in this repertoire.

Regardless of the interpretation of these survey results, however, it is clear from the stories of organizers told in this collection that the local ties that were built by summit protest organizers before, during, and after the Toronto G20 summit protest were transformative for many involved. These connections between community activists will be important ones for the struggles to come. Already, ties among local activists have been used to support those arrested, to raise money for legal defence, and to call for accountability for the decisions made by government and police during the summit. The decision made within the walls of the G20 summit to impose twenty years of austerity cuts to social spending will inevitably bring new communities into the streets, and the relationships built amongst local activist communities in Toronto through summit organizing and summit protest experience will be vital for shared campaigns of resistance.

Friends carry a man to safety after he is pepper-sprayed by police at Queen's Park, June 26, 2010. Photo by Richard Tang.

21

What Moves Us Now?

The Contradictions of "Community"

Clare O'Connor

In the contradiction lies the hope.   – Bertolt Brecht

IN EARLY 2010, I WAS PART OF A GROUP THAT ORGANIZED A TEACH-in called "Toronto vs. the G20: Community Action for Global Justice." Our goals were to familiarize participants with Toronto-based grassroots organizations and their various analyses, and to encourage participants to contribute to anti-G20 protests. Because the Toronto Community Mobilization Network (TCMN) had called for "themed days of resistance" during the week of the summit, we scheduled workshops to correspond with the planned themes. The day closed with a plenary workshop led by two TCMN organizers, entitled "On the Ground in June: Know Your Rights."

Speaking to a packed room, the first facilitator opened by saying, "I want to talk to you about *shock* and *awe*." Everyone smiled, understanding that he was describing the Canadian state's very public security plans for the upcoming global summit. Forecasting harsh police repression and documenting the growing police arsenal (which by then included sound cannons), media reports seemed aimed at discouraging people from taking to the streets. In the month leading up to the summit, the *Toronto Star* published alarming articles warning readers that, for instance, "the RCMP and Toronto police have strongly recommended that children should not travel through the downtown core . . . due to potential violence."[1] In another instance, they cited a US travel advisory: "Even demonstrations that are meant to be peaceful can become violent and unpredictable. You should avoid them if at all possible."[2] When the *Star* solicited advice from former RCMP officer and "security expert" Chris Matthers, he responded unequivocally: "Don't go."[3]

In the context of such widespread fearmongering, workshop participants couldn't disguise the excitement the facilitator's defiant message provoked: although they will try to shock us, we won't be awed. But this message took an unexpected turn. When one workshop participant (who appeared to me to be white, young, and middle-class) asked the second facilitator how activists could protect themselves from the state's weapons and whether wearing earplugs was a sufficient precaution against sound cannons, the facilitator replied, "I'm going to ignore you." Surprised and upset, the participant quietly walked out. For a few seconds, collective zeal was suspended and people were forced to assess the interaction; had the facilitator messed up?

In a context where police had been targeting the offices and events of groups mobilizing against the June summit, many of us were understandably cautious about contributing to the state's intimidation efforts. At the same time, however, we knew that state violence at prior anti-summit protests had been severe. In Quebec City, the use of rubber bullets left one anti-FTAA activist in need of an emergency tracheotomy.[4] Live ammunition killed an anti-G8 activist in Genoa.[5] With a budget of $1.2 billion, the Toronto operation was likely to exceed the militarization of previous summits. Such conditions made it important for organizers to undermine state intimidation – but never at the expense of empowering activists to protect themselves. Why, then, did the facilitator respond as he did?

When the activist who had asked the question walked out, the facilitator went on to describe what he felt to be the unique character of this particular convergence. Noting that "we all know what was wrong" with previous anti-summit protests, he made clear that – this time – we were doing "community mobilization." Most teach-in participants were too young to have been personally familiar with anti-summit precedents like the 2001 convergence against the Free Trade Area of the Americas (FTAA) in Quebec City or the 2002 convergence against the G8 in Kananaskis. Consequently, they were unlikely to have known about the tactical and political deliberations about movement demographics and dynamics of privilege to which the facilitator was referring. But even if they had been familiar with the key debates that marked the last decade of struggle, it would remain unclear how "community mobilization" could justifiably foreclose discussion of actual risk. Did the facilitator's decision to "ignore" his interlocutor reveal a new framework of organizing and a new set of activist expectations? If so, what was the strategic merit of this new plan? What was "community"?

Community?

As Toronto-based social movement theorist and TCMN organizer Lesley Wood explains, TCMN organizers "all wanted this convergence to be different from previous ones."

> Specifically, we wanted this convergence to build stronger, more militant, and well-connected movements. . . . In order to achieve these goals, and to build solidarity in the city, we needed a mobilization that would foreground local campaigns and organizations. . . . [We] named ourselves the Toronto Community Mobilization Network (TCMN) to highlight our strategy and our intention of providing space for community activists to network beyond their immediate organizations and issues and develop a joint strategy.[6]

Unlike previous anti-summit convergences like those that took place in Seattle (1999) and Cancun (2003), the priority this time was not to disrupt or prevent the meeting. Instead, the plan was to use the summit as an opportunity to strengthen the radical left by building relationships among grassroots organizers. And while this priority (summarized in the activist phrase "the action is in the organizing") was eventually overshadowed by endorsements of anti-globalization-style tactics like confronting the summit's perimeter fence, the early stages of the mobilization involved a clear emphasis on "local communities."[7] In an invitation to an early TCMN meeting, a few organizers noted that there was "an unclear sense" of what "local communities" could gain from the proposed mobilization.

> Many are unsure that there is resonance against the G8/20 in the place we organize in. . . . We know that each time there are large mobilizations anywhere in the world, they side step local demands and become about the "big" things . . . the things we are for, like justice, an end to capitalist exploitation and so [on] . . . but not in isola-

tion to our local struggles for access and dignity. We believe that if enough of us work together that we can change that, this year, here in Toronto.[8]

Organizers succeeded in making "community" the central mobilizing concept of the anti-G20 protests. But despite its frequent use, the word remained formally undefined.[9] What was clear, however, was that – in activist discourse – "community" appeared to be a self-evidently good thing.

Like most concepts, "community" is in fact politically ambivalent. Our enemies draw upon its promise as often as we do. In the lead-up to the G20, Sergeant Michele Paradis, Integrated Security Unit (ISU) director of public affairs and communications, explained how ISU officers were there "to protect the community. . . . We signed on because we want to make a difference. And whether that is protecting the Prime Minister or a head of state, or protecting a community, that's just part and parcel of our job."[10] "Community" also makes an appearance in the names and mandates of state agencies we oppose, like the Toronto Community Housing Corporation. In Canada, official recognition of "minority communities" has often been extended in order to restrict claims for freedom and self-determination. In *The Dark Side of the Nation*, Himani Bannerji explains how, under official Canadian multiculturalism, "community" often functions as a category of ruling. "Community," Bannerji explains, "is a political and cultural-ideological formation reliant upon social relations which are the base of social life, and not a spontaneous or natural association of people." By viewing community as "an ideological, that is, cultural and political practice," Bannerji proposes, "it becomes possible for us to develop a critique of the social organization, social relations, and moral regulations which go into the making of it."[11]

What does it mean for something to be an ideological practice? For Marx (whom Bannerji draws upon), "ideology" is not "a set of ideas," but rather a particular political practice that has the effect of obscuring empirical conditions.[12] Applying this formulation to the mobilization against the G20, we see that activist use of the concept "community" *shaped* – rather than merely *described* – our work. For instance, early on in the mobilization, activists recognized that there was a lot to gain from building relationships between "local" groups fighting for justice and self-determination for marginalized populations. This observation sounded true because it corresponded with activists' lived experiences of the benefits of political networking and their negative experiences of being systematically divided by state policy and policing. However, we then seem to have projected this empirical observation into the conceptual register and made it equivalent to "community." In this way, we made it possible to imagine (and assert) that, so long as activists were collaborating (specifically activists representing and advocating on behalf of marginalized groups), we had "community." Then, by giving primacy to the concept and conceiving of "community" as the basis for (and the equivalent of) collaboration among these specific activists, we went on to claim that – by definition – any instances in which such collaboration occurred amounted to victories.

It's therefore not surprising that, despite Wood's observations that the TCMN strategy inadvertently "marginalized" diasporic activists, "ignored the role of organized labour," and may have missed "opportunities for increasing the militancy and creativity of the actions," the group released a statement on July 26, 2010, entitled *The People Won*: "Since September 2009, we've worked to challenge, disrupt and abolish the G8/G20. . . . And we succeeded."[13]

Did we really win? Stephen Harper would have likely secured support for austerity measures even if there had been thirty thousand protesters on the streets rather than the fifteen thousand who showed up. Success is difficult to measure. However, even by the measures proposed by the TCMN (building and growing a network of radical activist groups, for example,) our success is not entirely clear. And, as Wood noted four months after the convergence, "It's too early to see whether the heralded connections between these different struggles will last."

In light of the state's brutal repression, and especially the repression targeted at key organizers, it's understandable that we focused on our accomplishments. But whatever immediate strategic value such an approach may have, there's no doubt that it poses analytic dangers. When we focus on our accomplishments, we produce a distorted record of our efforts – specifically, we understate the important lessons we can take from our attempt to use "community" as the conceptual basis for building an anti-summit convergence that resonated with marginalized people.

In Search of the Local

The TCMN was not the first group to have tried to shift the paradigm of anti-summit protest. As early as the anti-WTO protests in Seattle, activists were raising concerns about what came to be known as "summit hopping." For critics, "summit hopping" denoted the practice of travelling from one anti-summit protest to the next without ever becoming rooted in ongoing campaigns. Less than a year after Seattle, Naomi Klein flagged the dangers of becoming "a movement of meeting-stalkers, following the trade-bureaucrats as if they were the Grateful Dead."[14]

In her G20 reflections, Wood identified the critique of summit hopping as one of the TCMN's guiding motivations for emphasizing community mobilization. Citing a 2001 article by the Dutch activist collective EuroDusnie – entitled "What Moves Us?" – Wood concurred that "summit hopping" imposed limits on movement participation. "It is difficult for activists from poorer countries to take part in [summit hopping]," EuroDusnie wrote, "and this is one of the reasons that the protests are predominantly white, even though westerners are hit the least by capitalism."

> Travelling across the globe from summit to summit is very exciting, but you do need enough money to be mobile. Also, the one-sided attention paid to summits, means that westerners have a dominant role in the direction in which this movement is developing.[15]

Despite important insights, EuroDusnie's assessment could not account for the 2003 anti-WTO convergence in Cancun, Mexico, which confirmed that the anti-summit repertoire was not confined to the Global North. Nor could it explain why the movement found its home in Porto Alegre, Brazil, where the World Social Forum emerged in 2001.[16]

But, despite these shortcomings, EuroDusnie's critique of summit hopping gained wide support. Wood explained how, when the TCMN developed its strategy for the anti-G20 mobilization, "we used this critique to justify our emphasis on local organizing, anti-oppression politics, and coalition building."

We told a story that used the tension between summit hopping and local organizing to express our strategy and convince others about how the convergence should take place.[17]

But though it seemed to be grounded in lived experience, the opposition between summit hopping and local organizing remained remarkably abstract.[18] Although the local side of the local/global binary was presented as the logical resolution to the "summit hopping" problem, it had the effect of obscuring the actual conditions under which activists were organizing. Reflecting on her experience with the TCMN, Wood explained the challenges anti-G20 organizers encountered when trying to translate the local/global binary into practical lessons for mobilization. "By emphasizing grassroots people over summit protesters, local targets over global ones, and people of colour and more marginalized folks over white and more mainstream folks, the [TCMN] story made some dynamics and contradictions invisible." By "fetishizing the local" as the logical opposite to the summit hopping "global," Wood explained that the TCMN "did not resonate with immigrant organizations working on issues in their home countries – Iran, Palestine, Mexico, Sri Lanka or Chile" and unintentionally excluded these "diasporic activists."[19]

Even more instructive for future convergences was Wood's observation that, "from the beginning, those who were attracted to the meetings to plan for the G20 summit protests tended to be activists who didn't represent the TCMN's presentation of itself."

> Instead, most of those who showed up for TCMN meetings were white, many were students, and most were in their twenties and early thirties. Despite the repetition of the story that this was a network of marginalized people of colour and poor people in grassroots organizations, and despite the establishment of formal processes to prioritize the participation of such participants, meetings were increasingly comprised of these more typical "global justice" activists.[20]

What Moves Us Now?

Why We Fight

In her widely read article, "Where Was the Color in Seattle? Looking for Reasons Why the Great Battle Was So White," activist Elizabeth "Betita" Martinez recounted how, despite the fact that activists of colour (and some white activists) "made constant personal efforts to draw in people of color," their participation in the Seattle protests amounted to only "around five percent" of the total mobilization. Trying to explain these demographics, Martinez noted that "information about [the] WTO and all the plans for Seattle did not reach many people of color."

> Limited knowledge meant a failure to see how the WTO affected the daily lives of U.S. communities of color. "Activists of color felt they had more immediate issues," said Rashidi [Omari, an Oakland-based hip-hop artist]. "Also, when we returned people told me of being worried that family and peers would say they were neglecting their own communities, if they went to Seattle. They would be asked, 'Why are you going? You should stay here and help your people.'"[21]

While Martinez acknowledged "concern about the likelihood of brutal police repression . . . lack of funds for the trip, inability to be absent from work during the week, and problems in finding child care," she also noted that people of colour didn't attend on account of seeing "only white faces in the news." According to one activist Martinez interviewed, this "was a real deterrent to people of color." Activists of colour felt further deterred because of "a legacy of distrust of middle-class white activists" arising "from experiences of 'being used'" and "not having our issues taken seriously."[22]

But while the Seattle summit protest did not attract wide participation by people of colour, it did produce conditions for participants to reassess their assumptions about solidarity across racial and class lines. Sometimes this solidarity was even "liberating." Martinez interviewed protesters of colour about their first visit to the Direct Action Network's convergence centre. "Said one, 'When we walked in, the room was filled with young whites calling themselves anarchists. . . . We just couldn't relate to the scene so our whole group left right away.'"

In retrospect, observed Van Jones of STORM (Standing Together to Organize a Revolutionary Movement) in the Bay Area, "We should have stayed. We didn't see that we had a lot to learn from them. . . ." "Later I went back and talked to people," recalled Rashidi, "and they were discussing tactics, very smart. Those folks were really ready for action. It was limiting for people of color to let that one experience affect their whole picture of white activists." Jinee Kim, a Korean American with the Third Eye Movement in the Bay Area, also thought it was a mistake. "We realized we didn't know how to do a blockade. We had no gas masks. They made sure everybody had food and water, they took care of people. . . ." Richard Moore, coordinator of the Southwest Network for Environmental and Economic Justice, told me "the white activists were very disciplined."[23]

These positive accounts became buried as the critique of summit hopping unfolded. Instead of trying to answer Martinez's question – why *had* the convergence been predominantly middle-class and white despite efforts to broaden the mobilization and despite the real impacts of corporate globalization on people of colour – activists proposed that they could resolve the problem by shifting the movement's tactics. This approach informed subsequent protests, including the 2002 "Take the Capital" march on Ottawa, which was conceived as an alternative to the "summit hopping" convergence against the G8 in Kananaskis. In the context of our strategic reorientation to "the local," "community" became the logical site of revolutionary promise. This reorientation became explicit in the Toronto mobilization against the G20. In Wood's account, TCMN organizers believed that "the convergence was a space in which marginalized people would come together and win."[24]

The anti-G20 strategy outlined by Wood seems to be based on a sound premise: people on the margins *are* most exposed to (and, as such, most familiar with) the direct violence of capitalism and colonization. But this important moral premise doesn't have self-evident strategic implications. For instance, it's not obvious that it's in the best interest of society's most marginalized for the radical left to adopt a strategy that conceptually divides them from everyone who is not marginalized. In 2005, Toronto-based activist Justin Podur publicly commented on the radical left's reluctance "to come to grips with the composition of this country."

The median income is around $18,000. The median family income is around $50,000. There are about one million aboriginal people and another three million people who the census calls "visible minorities." There could be another million undocumented working people. That leaves twenty-five million white people. It also means that we have a huge chunk of the population that is getting by. It means that even after years of terrible cutbacks, there is still a significant social net. All this is to say we can't expect desperation or grinding oppression of the majority to work in our favor.[25]

Although anti-racist and anti-poverty activism might not attract most people on the basis of self-interest, Podur explained, it could attract them "on the basis of solidarity, if we started with the assumption that such a thing were possible." Of course, he noted, this requires us to carefully consider how solidarity might be inspired and sustained. But our success will be determined at least in part by our belief that "people who are not poor or suffer [from] racism or imperialism are capable of acting against poverty and racism and imperialism."[26] In the mobilization against the G20, however, the claim of "community" did not help us to envision such solidarity as the basis for an anti-capitalist and anti-colonial convergence. Instead, "community" seemed to have the effect of limiting meaningful engagement between marginalized and not-marginalized populations.

Of course, white and middle-class entitlement and ignorance are annoying and can be destructive. Inevitably, we'll encounter situations when we can't help but express our outrage and impatience with these traits. But if we measure our success by how well we persuade people to change their ideas and join us and not from the standpoint of an abstract ideological concept like "community," these reactions should be rare. "That doesn't mean we pander" to people with privilege, Podur insisted.

> It doesn't mean we don't challenge white supremacy or imperialism or capitalism itself. It doesn't mean we gloss over the horrors inflicted on Indigenous people. It just means that we don't assume people automatically know or have experience on these things.[27]

Instances when what Wood calls "mainstream" people have tried to set the terms of struggle for marginalized people have produced legitimate distrust of the left. There is no simple method for overcoming this distrust, although the principle of self-determination is a crucial step in the right direction. In a context marked by systemic and ongoing attacks on people of colour, women, and poor, working-class, Indigenous, queer, trans, and disabled people, self-determination demands that we strive to ensure that those directly affected by capitalist and colonial violence (whether inflicted by police or policy) can determine who leads their particular struggles, and how. But even the principle of self-determination can be obscured by the ideological use of "community." Speaking specifically of immigrants to Canada, Bannerji explains how "community" leaves people "marked by a difference which has less to say about us – our histories and cultures – than about a mode of socio-political interpretation within a pre-established symbolic and practical schema of a racialized or ethnicized colonial and slave-owning discourse." This "recolonizing" discourse implies that people immigrate as "communities" and "not as responses to national and international political economy."

> We can say, therefore, that there is nothing natural about communities. In fact they are contested grounds of socio-cultural definitions and political agencies. . . . From this point of view community is not only an ideological and social category, but also a category of the state.[28]

Asserting that we uphold "community self-determination" (an ideological claim) rather than saying that we uphold self-determination for migrants or other specific people (a political description) obscures the state's role in constricting political agency and does nothing to reveal the complexity of social relations within specific groups.

Ideological use of the term "community" also obscures the political role of people who are not marginalized. For the TCMN, the principle of self-determination meant that those who were not marginalized were to be allies to "communities." But despite a few notable exceptions, activists haven't figured out what such a role concretely entails.[29] For Australian Aboriginal activist Lila Watson, being an ally means recognizing that "if you have come to help me, you are wasting your time. But if you have come because your liberation is bound up with mine, then let us work together."[30]

Here, being an ally means having your own reasons to struggle, and solidarity is – by definition – reciprocal. But though radicals often invoke the support of allies, we rarely talk about what might constitute "liberation" for middle-class people and white people. As "allies," what conditions compel these groups to participate in revolutionary politics? What do they hope to gain? Anti-racist theorists have consistently pointed to the dangers of not considering white people's desires for "liberation." As bell hooks points out, white people's desires need to be acknowledged and understood so that they can be directed toward more genuine and less harmful resolutions outside of market capitalism.[31] When we fail to redirect these desires – desires to overcome what hooks calls a "crisis of identity" – white people tend to resolve them through commodity culture and, importantly, by "eating the Other."[32]

In light of this dynamic, it becomes clear that – for "allies" – "community" is seductive primarily on account of its promise of providing some more "grounded" or "real" experience. But this promise is a mythical distraction. There's no place more "real" than where we happen to find ourselves. In order to build a world that accords with our desires (rather than conjuring it into existence through ideological invocations of "community"), we have to start with the raw material of our own immediate conditions.

Even extending "community" to include those currently outside of its purview won't undo the concept's ideological character. But if this is the case, then how do we constitute a "we" capable of working and struggling together? One possibility arises from the fact that capitalism stimulates desires for self-realization that cannot be satisfied by commodities, which – from the standpoint of capital – are the only game in town. And while people experience this dynamic differently depending on where they find themselves, the fact remains that the dynamic itself is knowable, analyzable, and – ultimately – total. Rather than relying on the abstract universalism of "community" to constitute our "we," attention to this dynamic allows us to understand our collective implication in the social relations we seek to undo – colonialism, white supremacy, patriarchy, and capitalism.

We Are Bigger Than We Think

The severity of repression against anti-G20 protesters in Toronto was widely experienced and is now well documented. It caused the ranks of the movement to temporarily swell. But mass condemnations – most of which remained preoccupied with restoring the sanctity of Canadian democracy and decrying police violations of charter rights – subsided within a matter of weeks. For its part, the anti-capitalist and anti-colonial left is now only slightly larger than it was at the outset of the mobilization.

Struggling to ease the trauma brought on by staggering state violence, surveillance, infiltration, and criminal charges, Toronto activists quickly reoriented to the work of "strengthening our resolve."[33] But it has been difficult for us to engage with criticism. One year after the G20 summit, even people whose efforts appeared peripheral to the TCMN seem reluctant to reflect on weaknesses for fear that such an emphasis would overshadow accomplishments – of which there were many.

But avoiding critique is of no service to activists who are wrestling (or will eventually have to wrestle) with similar challenges. And it is of no service to Toronto activists who have much to gain from reconsidering the ideological character of our conception of "community." For, while the emphasis on "community" in the anti-G20 convergence allowed established activist groups to strengthen their relationships with one another, it also meant that those who did not fit into the concept were left without organizational guidance or support. According to Wood, "our refusal to recognize the actual rather than the proclaimed demographics [of the TCMN] meant that some of us didn't always pay attention to our actual resources, connections, strengths, and weaknesses."

> This was evident in our outreach. Although we presented ourselves as a network of grassroots organizations connected to a wider range of community groups and neighborhood, in reality we remained limited to smaller and more particular sections of these communities. Seeing this, other groups became wary of engaging in the summit mobilization in any significant way.[34]

In a context such as this, "community" could not help but generate contradictory situations, like the one that took place at the June 5 teach-in when the facilitator refused to discuss the risk of state violence despite its likelihood. At its worst, our ideological use of the concept either inadvertently or explicitly led us to reject willing participants in anti-capitalist and anti-colonial struggle because they were not who we had in mind when we said "community." To honour the work that went into the anti-G20 mobilization, we must view these contradictions as opportunities for strategic reflection. Ideological claims prevent us from testing the bounds of our capacity. We must start with political *descriptions* of what and who we truly are, and continue – through analysis – to reveal the best strategy for building anti-colonial and anti-capitalist movements that are unapologetically dedicated to winning it all.

22

Social Protest in the Age of Austerity
Prospects for Mass Resistance after the G20

David McNally

Expect more rage if the rich and poor divide gets bigger.
— Chris Blackhurst, *Evening Standard*

A whole new generation has tasted the power and energy that comes with effective rebellion. — Jess Worth, *New Internationalist*

READERS MIGHT EXPECT THE TWO STATEMENTS ABOVE TO HAVE come from Tunisia or Egypt, where mass revolts have shaken the political order (and about which I shall have more to say below). Instead, they come from London, England. Published the day after a massive and insurgent student demonstration on November 10, 2010, they are eloquent testimony to what we can expect as the new age of austerity unfolds in the coming years.

To the delight of many and to the dismay of those in power, some fifty thousand students and their allies rallied in central London that November day to protest a tripling of university tuition fees and massive cuts to higher education funding. Toward the end of the demonstration, several thousand students occupied Conservative Party headquarters, overturning furniture and damaging the offices.

The statements above capture crucial elements of what happened on that day in London. But a statement issued by London's Metropolitan Police Federation was equally significant. It told reporters that Britain had reached "decision time" about policing, and it warned that what happened at Conservative headquarters would surely be repeated "as the public reacted to the spending cuts" imposed by the government.[1] In the context of planned cuts to social programs to the tune of $135 billion, and the accompanying layoff of half a million public employees, the prediction seems only reasonable.[2] It appears doubly so when one considers that the London demonstration was simply one among many waves of mass protest that swept over Europe in 2010, involving general strikes, demonstrations of tens and often hundreds of thousands, and combative street confrontations with police. Indeed, a few months later, on March 26, 2011, half a million people poured through London's streets to protest cutbacks and austerity, the largest such mobilization since the mass protests in 2003 against the war in Iraq.

Placing these two opening quotes alongside the one from the London police allows us to form an integrated picture of three key elements of the "age of austerity" initiated by the global bank bailouts of 2008–09: first, growing gaps between rich and poor; second, explosive outbreaks of social protest; and finally, ever more repressive forms of policing. All three of these interconnected phenomena were on display during the G20 meetings in Toronto in late June 2010. As representatives of the rich and powerful met behind closed doors to discuss how to slash social services in order to pay for rescuing banks, twenty thousand police carried out arbitrary mass arrests and egregious violations of civil and human rights, as authors in this volume document. But rarely do government and police spokespeople acknowledge the connection between austerity and police clampdowns as clearly as did the London police.

Having been completely overwhelmed by the size of the event and the militancy of participants, police in London vowed not to let this happen again. And in an effort to rally public support, they raised the spectre of more insurgent mass protests claiming the streets and disrupting the routines of everyday life. In so doing, they sought to prepare the ground for the repressive forms of policing they intend to deploy against mass movements of resistance.

Policing and Resistance in the Age of Austerity

What happened in the streets and makeshift detention centres in Toronto in June 2010 was, therefore, anything but an aberration. Arbitrary arrests, police violence, inhumane detention, the use of rubber bullets and tear gas – all of this is part of the *new normal* that governments are trying to create in the age of austerity.[3] They know that broad-based social protest will grow as a result of the global slump. Indeed, former US intelligence chief Dennis Blair told the Senate Intelligence Committee in early 2009, "Economic crises increase the risk of regime-threatening instability if they are prolonged for a one- or two-year period."[4] And in the same vein, the head of the International Monetary Fund has warned that "rising social and political instability" is likely to be an enduring feature of the landscape in the aftermath of the global crisis of 2008–09.[5] With governments unable to jump-start global economic growth and committed to policies of austerity that inflict immense hardship, police and security and intelligence agencies are promoting ever more militarized forms of policing, intrusive spying and surveillance, new laws designed to criminalize oppositional activism, increasingly violent tactics of establishing "public order," and heightened police powers across the board.

Recent episodes in Greece and the United States give us some sense of the progressively more repressive forms of policing that are being employed. No European country, with the possible exception of France, has seen such sustained resistance as Greece, where successive general strikes, mass demonstrations, and pitched battles with police have taken place since December 2008 in response to huge cuts to pensions and social programs, coupled with large hikes to sales taxes. But as social protest has mounted, so has police violence – to the point that doctors and surgeons have been provoked to speak out against police-inflicted head injuries as well as numerous ailments caused by chemical methods of "crowd control," while journalists have been moved to publicly denounce police violence against reporters.[6] But if police conduct in public spaces is the most conspicuous side of the law-and-order regime, equally decisive is a draconian regime of surveillance and legal harassment against known critics and dissenters, often aided and abetted by national security and "anti-terrorism" laws. In the United States, for instance, anti-war and Palestine solidarity activists have been subjected to FBI raids in which computers, passports, phones, notebooks, and even children's artwork have been seized. Moreover, those so harassed have frequently been summoned to appear before a Federal Grand Jury.[7] While Canadian security and intelligence forces have been slightly more subtle, they too have been deeply involved in spying on and harassing Indigenous activists, Arab-Canadian citizens and residents, and a variety of social justice organizers.[8]

It is true that an intensified "law and order" regime has been intrinsic to neo-liberalism for the past thirty years, particularly with respect to disciplinary policing and incarceration of members of racialized social groups.[9] But it remains the case that, as neo-liberalism undergoes a sustained economic slowdown, ever more alarming tactics are entering the arsenal of policing for the age of austerity. Even if these policing techniques have deep roots running through the entire history of capitalism, it is important not to lose sight of the ways in which government, courts, and police forces are "raising the bar" in their use of weapons, mass arrests, kettling of demonstrators, punitive bail conditions, inhumane detention, and intrusive surveillance as means of clamping down on social and political protest.

The political-economic context for all of this is crucial. Beginning with the global financial crisis of 2008–09, which toppled banks across the United States and Europe, we entered a sustained period of economic turbulence that I have called the *global slump*.[10] Rather than an ordinary recession from which the capitalist economy recovers quickly and dynamically, the global slump represents an era of high unemployment, deteriorating social services, declining incomes, and growing insecurity for millions. There are deep structural reasons for all this having to do with the contradictions of capitalism. But these are exacerbated by the effects of deliberate social policy, which saw governments direct $21 trillion to bailing out banks and giant corporations and to "stimulating" sagging economies.[11] By 2010, however, financial markets dictated that it was time to pay for these extraordinary bank and corporate bailouts. So, governments the world over turned to giant cuts to social programs and higher taxes on the poor in order to get their finances "in order," even though this was certain to de-stimulate the economy and decrease economic growth.[12] The dimensions of these cuts are staggering.

In Latvia one out of every three teachers has been fired and pensions have been slashed by 70 per cent. The government of Ireland has chopped wages of government employees by 22 per cent. The state of California has cut health insurance for nine hundred thousand poor children. Ohio has slashed community mental health services; Minnesota is eliminating health coverage for low-income adults. Some thirty-six US states have chopped higher education spending, twenty-four have reduced services to the elderly and the disabled, while twenty-eight have attacked health care. In all these settings, migrants and racialized workers experience the harshest effects. Astonishingly, four out of every ten African Americans have experienced unemployment during the Great Recession. And as a further reminder of the racialized character of labour markets, for Black and Hispanic workers the combined unemployment and underemployment rate (which includes those working part-time because full-time work cannot be found) is in the range of 25 per cent.[13] Equally damning, half of all American children now depend on food stamps at some point during their childhood – a figure that jumps to 90 per cent for Black children.[14]

All of this is just the beginning. Commentators are predicting a "decade of austerity," ten years or more of huge cuts to public sector jobs and to the social services on which poor and working-class people rely. The Institute for Fiscal Studies (IFS) in Britain estimates that by 2017–18 the average British family will be more than £2,840 poorer as a result of the combined effects of increased taxes and diminished social services.[15] Meanwhile, a presidential commission in the United States has recommended fully $4 trillion in cuts to federal spending in a plan that would eliminate 10 per cent of federal government jobs, cut in half community service block grants (which assist the work of grassroots groups in poor communities), raise the retirement age for all Americans, and gut a wide range of social programs.[16] Even before most of these cutbacks were in place, the World Bank was predicting that an additional sixty-four million people worldwide would be driven into poverty in 2010 as a direct result of the crisis.[17] This was also before wealthy investors poured billions of dollars in "easy money" provided by central banks into speculation on food, driving prices up 32 per cent in the last half of 2010 to their highest levels ever – and helping to ignite the wave of struggles for "bread and freedom" that have rocked regimes in Tunisia, Egypt, and beyond.[18] Those struggles, which are also rebellions against the G20's austerity agenda, are of immense significance for those fighting for social justice in the Global North.

"Tunisia Fever" and the Spread of Popular Rebellion

The epicentre of the crisis that broke out in 2008 was the United States and Europe, where the crescendo of bank failures occurred. As a consequence of the bank bailouts, many western capitalist societies are now subject to the equivalent of the Structural Adjustment Programs imposed on countries in the Global South throughout the neo-liberal period – huge cuts to social programs, reduced subsidies and assistance to the poor, privatization of public enterprises, and layoffs and wage cuts for public sector workers.[19] These austerity measures have provoked militant mass resistance in parts of the North, most notably in countries like France and Greece. Alarmed that ordinary people are taking to the streets and challenging governments, some right-wing commentators have cautioned that we are now witnessing the end point of all democracies – mob rule:

> Mobs have already taken to the venerable, iconic streets of European states, notably among them Greece, birthplace of Athenian democracy. . . . Already, hundreds of thousands . . . have thronged the streets of Paris and Rome, of Milan and Sarajevo, of Reykjavik and Bucharest (where demonstrators stormed the presidential palace, an insurgent act that invokes the spectre of revolution).[20]

But while the epicentre of the crisis and much of the first wave of resistance have been in the core capitalist states – indications of the *systemic* nature of the global slump – it was inevitable that much of the Global South would be hammered in quite profound ways.[21] As those effects took hold, forms of insurrectionary mass resistance have burst out in parts of the South.

The most dramatic and inspiring outburst of mass insurgency took place in Guadeloupe and Martinique in early 2009, just as the global crisis was nearing its worst point. The initial inspiration for these upheavals may have come from the mass strikes and demonstrations in France, but people in these former slave colonies (which are still in a semi-colonial relation with France) took the struggle to a much higher level.[22] Unemployment and poverty rates are twice as high on these Caribbean islands as on the French mainland, with youth unemployment well over 50 per cent. Equally significant, Guadeloupe and Martinique represent textbook cases of racialized, neo-colonial capitalism. The local ruling classes are almost entirely white – known as the béké, they are descendants of French slave-owners. Meanwhile, the working class is of African or mixed descent. Economic hardship in the context of racialized capitalism gave the general strike movement on these islands a massive popular resonance, similar to the convergence of class and racial struggles in Bolivia since 2000.

The battle started on January 20, 2009, when a coalition of fifty unions and social movement groups, known as "Stand Up Against Exploitation" (*Liyannaj Kont Pwofitasyon*, or LKP in the local dialect) initiated a strike with the central demand of a 200 euro (US$260) per month raise for the lowest paid workers. Under the leadership of the General Union of Workers of Guadeloupe, strikers shut down banks, schools, government offices, gas stations, hotels, the main shipping terminal, and the airport. Ten days into the strike, sixty thousand people demonstrated through the streets of Pointe-à-Pitre – a mobilization of 15 per cent of the island's population. Alarmed by the power of the movement, the French government sent five hundred police. But this only further inflamed things, prompting angry youth to occupy the city hall in Sainte-Anne, and others to burn local businesses. By this point, the strike had spread to the neighbouring island of Martinique, where twenty-five thousand people (out of a population of four hundred thousand) took to the streets with similar demands.

Not only did this Caribbean strike movement keep growing in militancy, it also spread to the French overseas "department" of Réunion in the Indian Ocean. At the same time, Olivier Besancenot, the popular spokesperson for France's New Anti-Capitalist Party, proclaimed the island strikes an inspiration "to follow." Sensing that its troubles were escalating, the French government caved in, agreeing on March 4, 2009, to raise salaries for the lowest paid by 200 euros, a 40 per cent increase, along with modest improvements of 3 to 6 per cent for better paid workers. As thirty thousand people marched through the streets of the capital, they learned that the government had also agreed to lower water rates, hire more teachers, aid farmers and fishers, fund jobs and training for unemployed youth, freeze rents, and ban evictions. While the workers of Guadeloupe and Martinique did not bring about all the political transformations they sought, their militancy, creativity, and determination achieved tremendous things, proving that one can make major gains in the face of a deep recession.

But no struggle in the Global South has more fired the popular imagination than the mass insurgency in Tunisia. The Tunisian uprising emerged around the interconnected demands for "bread and freedom," a sentiment that quickly resonated, inspiring upheavals in Jordan, Algeria, Egypt, Yemen, northern Sudan and beyond. Mainstream commentators typically saw these struggles as specific to the

Social Protest in the Age of Austerity

Arab world – and there are certainly features at work here distinctive to a number of Arab regimes. But serious analysis indicates their integral links to the effects of the global slump, particularly in terms of the intersection of mass unemployment, poverty, and rising food prices.

After all, neo-liberal structural adjustment has been a driving factor in all these respects. Trade liberalization and privatization have produced widespread job loss, while the creation of low-wage export-processing zones, such as the Qualifying Industrial Zones (QIZs) in Egypt, have intensified the poverty of workers. Fully 40 per cent of Egypt's population now lives on $2 a day or less. But workers have been organizing and fighting back; indeed the QIZs have been rocked by strikes in recent years. This is the volatile context in which rising food prices helped trigger large-scale revolt.

Soaring food prices are directly connected to neo-liberalism and the global slump. Liberalization of world trade, intense competition from the heavily subsidized agro-industries in the North, and removal of subsidies for poor farmers in the South have all conspired to drive millions of peasant-farmers off the land from India to Mexico and beyond. And national indebtedness causes governments to pressure farmers to grow export crops (like cotton or coffee) rather than food-stuffs. As a result, fewer countries today are capable of feeding themselves – all of which creates rising prices and profits for global agro-business. The onset of the global slump briefly arrested the escalation of food prices that had produced riots in 2008. As layoffs and unemployment swept the United States and Europe, demand slumped and food prices came down. But now, as the crisis changes form, they are on the rise once again and reaching unprecedented heights. Indeed, the UN's Food and Agriculture Organization's food price index has hit an all-time high, having risen a staggering 32 per cent in the last half of 2010. As a result, food is now more expensive than ever, aggravating economic hardship across the Global South and throwing fuel on the fire of popular resentment.

One part of the story here has to do with new flows of "hot money" generated by the worldwide bank bailouts and economic stimulus programs. With trillions pumped into the banking system and interest rates pushed down to record lows, investors and speculators have a huge incentive to borrow on the cheap to purchase commodities (and currencies) that look set to appreciate. Add into the equation two further factors – the increasing use of arable land for the production of bio-fuels rather than food, and speculative gambles that a poor Russian harvest or floods in Australia will damage food supplies and further drive up prices – and we have all the ingredients for huge price spikes. Wagering on exactly this, investment bankers and managers of pension and hedge funds have funnelled over $200 billion into bets on food since the financial crisis first broke, driving up prices in a frenzy of speculation.[23]

All of this made "food riots" inevitable. But other ingredients are necessary for food protests to develop into insurgent political uprisings against governments. If immediate economic grievances and political demands for democracy are to be fused into a popular upheaval, there must be sufficiently robust grassroots networks (independent unions, social movements, student groups) capable of organizing hubs of resistance. In Tunisia, a critical role was played by labour unions. Local and regional organizations of the General Union of Tunisian Workers (GUTW/UGTT), quiescent for years and its leaders initially hesitant to join the struggle, became key hubs of resistance thanks to pressure by rank-and-file members who had spearheaded independent workers' protest in recent years. Spurred into action and radicalized by events, the labour movement began organizing rallies and launched general strikes, proving itself, as one commentator put it, "to be a serious political force with currently-unmatched organizing capacity and national reach."[24] Alongside strikes, the revitalized GUTW has organized sit-ins and a "Caravan of Liberation" in its efforts to sweep away all political officials linked to the regime of former dictator, Zine el-Abidine Ben Ali. If it continues on its radical course, which is not a given, union activism could make common cause with students, street vendors, and the unemployed, and thus give the insurgency a vital organizational forum and an increasingly working-class character.

The Tunisian Intifada sparked waves of mass actions for "bread and freedom" throughout the region, as I have noted. Without a doubt, the most significant of these in terms of its possible effects on world politics has been the uprising in Egypt, which toppled former President Hosni Mubarak in February 2011. The insurgent crowds in the streets of Cairo, Alexandria, Suez, Mansoura, and beyond displayed levels of courage and determination that are utterly inspiring – and which pose immense problems for government and liberal opposition efforts to derail the movement. Even when violently attacked, as they were on February 2, 2011, by thousands of undercover police and goons of the ruling party wielding guns, knives, Molotov cocktails, and more, they held their ground and fought back, holding Tahrir Square in downtown Cairo. In the process, they extended their grassroots self-organization, as reporters for the *Washington Post* noted: "Refusing to end their ten-day old demonstration, protesters set up makeshift hospitals in alleyways off the square to treat their wounded, and fashioned a holding cell in a nearby travel office to detain those they suspected of inciting the violence. Organizers said they had captured more than 350 'thugs of the government' among the pro-government demonstrators, some carrying police identification cards, and turned them over to the Egyptian army."[25] In this spirit, the movement has formed People's Protection forces to provide safety and security in neighbourhoods and in the mass marches and assemblies. And from early February 2011, the Egyptian Revolution, whose roots lie in years of determined labour activism, gave rise to an enormous strike wave demanding a new minimum wage, the firing of autocratic managers and bosses, and the recognition of independent unions.[26]

These forms of popular self-organization are linked to new practices of radical democracy. In Cairo's historic Tahrir Square, which was at times jammed with well over one million protesters, the crowd engaged in direct decision-making. Organized into smaller groups, people discussed and debated, and then sent elected delegates to consultations about the movement's demands. As one journalist explained, "delegates from these mini-gatherings then come together to discuss the prevailing mood, before potential demands are read out over the square's makeshift speaker system. The adoption of each proposal is based on the proportion of boos or cheers it receives from the crowd at large."[27]

"Swimming in the Sea of the People": Challenges for the Radical Left

It is too early to say what the revolts in Tunisia and Egypt will bring. But they are clear evidence that we have entered a new period of mass protest, one in which popular uprisings of a radically democratic character are on the agenda and in which militant working-class movements can develop. Moreover, as we have seen, waves of popular mobilization are now a fact of life in the Global North too, as both government leaders and police spokespeople recognize. All of this poses unique challenges for movements of the anti-capitalist left.

For almost four decades, the radical left lived through a period in which retreats and defeats predominated. Counter-insurgency, police brutality, union busting, and the destruction of radical movements contributed to a counter-revolutionary wave in global politics that saw Central American revolutions undermined, left-wing activists in Latin America and the Middle East murdered and imprisoned, the American Black Power movement largely destroyed, militant unions crushed (as in the cases of the tin miners in Bolivia and the coal miners in Britain), and social movements derailed. Neo-liberalism thus created a political climate in which radical protest seemed the futile exercise of marginal eccentrics. It was to the credit of thousands of global justice campaigners, and activists in anti-war, feminist, anti-racist, trade union, sexual rights, anti-poverty, and environmental movements that they kept organizing and resisting. But generally deprived of even a small mass influence, radical movements did not gain the experience of working closely with thousands upon thousands of ordinary people, or of learning how to avoid the political jargon of the initiated and how to assist masses of people in self-mobilization.

The confining experience of the neo-liberal period legacy now poses serious challenges. For in the age of austerity the radical left needs to relearn some old lessons about mass politics, even while blending them with new·practices. Radicals need to recognize that whole new layers of people are likely to enter into resistance, but that this will only give rise to larger and sustained anti-capitalist movements if we can develop a new political language and forms of activism and organization that resonate with large numbers of people who are not today part of activist groups and circles. In particular, it means recognizing the need to build a movement of the exploited majority, a working-class movement – something many activists have shunned during the period of neo-liberal retreat by working-class movements. But the upsurges in Guadeloupe, Martinique, and Tunisia have reaffirmed the utterly decisive role workers' organizations can play in galvanizing and coordinating mass resistance. To be sure, unions are often afflicted by a paralyzing bureaucratic reformism. But this was largely true in Tunisia as well – until dedicated rank-and-file activists fought to reclaim and reorient their unions. What is crucial in the here and now is that radicals work together to learn how to relate to much wider layers of working-class people and to assist in the building of a class struggle movement. To this end, as Andrej Grubačić has put it, the "most crucial challenge" for anti-capitalist activists is to develop a genuine "class sensitivity and class analysis" as part of learning "to swim in the sea of the people."[28]

Moreover, this is the key to undermining police tactics of surveillance and repression. No small groups of people, no matter how disciplined, can effectively counter all the resources at the disposal of the police. But mass movements can paralyze the apparatus of police repression, as we have seen from time to time in Tunisia and Egypt, where police stations and vehicles have been attacked and police arrested by the people for crimes of violence.[29] As a result, the battles for civil and human rights – for freedom of expression and assembly in particular – are inextricably connected to the building of mass movements for bread and freedom, for both economic and political rights. This is the key lesson of the latest wave of mass struggle against austerity and for democracy and economic justice. Anti-capitalist movements now have to decide if they will be equal to the challenge.

Notes

Foreword: G20 Trials and the War on Activism

1 Toronto City Council, "City Council Decision to commend the outstanding work of Chief Bill Blair, the Toronto Police Service and the Police Officers working during the G20 Summit in Toronto," Toronto City Council Meeting No. 51, July 7, 2010, http://app.toronto.ca/tmmis/viewPublishedReport.do?function= getCouncilMinutesReport&meetingId=3291.

Introduction: From the Great Recession to the Streets of Toronto

1 For a full schedule of events see http://g20.torontomobilize.org/schedule.

2 Although the establishment media referred to this entire contingent as the black bloc, this description is incorrect. The contingent was an anti-capitalist break-off from the "People First!" march; it was composed of a variety of radical people who were united in their desire to confront the G20 summit directly at the security perimeter. Some of these protesters marched in a black bloc with faces covered, while many did not. Some engaged in property destruction, while many did not.

3 The Toronto G20 was estimated to cost $857 million (see "G8/G20 costs top $857M," *CBC.ca*, Nov. 5, 2010, www.cbc.ca/news/canada/toronto/story/2010/11/05/g20-costs-tabled.html). With the addition of the G8 summit in Huntsville the day before, the total cost was closer to $1 billion (see Pav Jordan, "Canada braces for 'G' summits with C$1 bln plan," *Reuters*, June 2, 2010, www.reuters.com/article/2010/06/02/g20-canada-protests-idUSN02138 55620100602.

4 See Dave Seglins, "G8, G20 police raked in bonuses, OT pay," *CBC.ca*, May 30, 2011, www.cbc.ca/news/story/2011/05/29/g20-police-bonus-pay.html, and Robyn Doolittle, "G20 a big boost to police pay," *Toronto Star*, March 30, 2011, www.thestar.com/news/article/966792--g20-a-big-boost-to-police-pay.

Chapter 1: Building a Protest Convergence

1 Thanks to the other TCMN organizers, particularly Jean Margaret and Lesley Wood, for their helpful comments on this chapter. The opinions expressed here are solely those of the author and do not necessarily represent any other TCMN organizers or the TCMN itself.

2 For an excellent account of the origins of the TCMN in the context of recent Toron-

tonian social movement organizing, see Lesley Wood, "Bringing Together The Grass-roots: A Strategy and Story from Toronto's G20 Protests," *Upping the Anti* 11 (2010): 85–98.

3 See "Toronto Community Mobilization Network: Solidarity and Respect," Toronto Community Mobilization Network, http://g20.torontomobilize.org/SolidarityRespect.

Chapter 2: Community Organizing for a Global Protest

1 Elizabeth (Betita) Martinez, "Where Was the Color in Seattle? Looking for Reasons Why the Great Battle was So White," *Monthly Review*, July-August, 2000, 141–148.

Chapter 3: Collective Movement, Collective Power

1 What I know about organizing, I've learned from women of colour and Indigenous organizers. What I write is one etching of our ideas. This is not an objective telling; no such thing exists. Rather it's my memory of people's struggle and victories, and a remembering of why we took to the streets and some of what we achieved as a result.

2 Though the Crown subsequently had to drop the charges for Harsha Walia from Vancouver, Jaggi Singh from Montreal pled guilty to a lesser "counselling" charge in exchange for having his more serious conspiracy charges dropped.

3 No One Is Illegal–Toronto, Vancouver, Halifax, Montreal, and Ottawa, "Joint Statement," June 18, 2010, http://toronto.nooneisillegal.org/node/472.

4 Elizabeth (Betita) Martinez, "Where Was the Color in Seattle? Looking for Reasons Why the Great Battle was So White," *Monthly Review*, July-August, 2000, 141–148.

5 Lesley J. Wood, "Communities Converging: A Story and a Strategy of the G20 protests in Toronto," *Upping the Anti* 11 (2010), 85–98.

6 No One Is Illegal–Toronto, email message to community groups, Feb 10, 2010.

Chapter 4: "Canada Can't Hide Genocide"

1 Martin Cooke, Daniel Beavon, and Mindy McHardy, "Measuring the Well-Being of Aboriginal People," Research paper for the Strategic Research and Analysis Directorate, Indian and Northern Affairs Canada, October 2004.

2 Section 74 of the Indian Act, for example, is currently being used to force a westernized election system on the Algonquins of Barriere Lake, quashing a traditional election system that has been working for generations.

3 Canadian Press, "First Nations children still taken from parents: Analysis finds more First Nations children in care than at height of residential school system," *CBC.ca*, Aug. 2, 2011, www.cbc.ca/news/politics/story/2011/08/02/pol-first-nations-kids.html.

Chapter 5: Labour's Role in Opposing the G20

1 This chapter is dedicated to my siblings in the trade union movement – you know who you are! – who live and breathe their commitment to making a better world for all everyday of their lives. Without their friendship and fellowship, I could not believe in what I do. The views expressed in this chapter are my own, and are not endorsed by CUPE.

2 Jane McAlevey, "Labor's Last Stand," *The Nation*, Feb. 16, 2011, www.thenation.com/article/158640/labors-last-stand.

3 CUPE, my own union, represents over six hundred thousand public sector workers in Canada and the average CUPE wage is just $40,000 a year.

4 Canadian Civil Liberties Association, *Breach of Peace: G20 Summit: Accountability in Policing and Governance* (Ottawa: NUPGE and the CCLA, 2011).

Chapter 6: Unions, Direct Action, and the G20 Protests

1 CUPE Ontario, "Statement on G20 Protests and Aftermath by CUPE Ontario," June 30, 2010, http://cupe.ca/rights/statement-g20-protests-aftermath.
2 Sid Ryan, "Thousands Stood Up for Humanity," *Toronto Star,* June 29, 2010, www.thestar.com/opinion/editorialopinion/article/829904--thousands-stood-up-for-humanity.
3 Ken Georgetti, "Georgetti Responds to Sun Media's Misleading Attack on Unions," *Canadian Labour Congress,* July 8, 2010, www.canadianlabour.ca/news-room/editorials /ken-georgettis-letter-editor-response-attacks-journalist-union-activities.
4 "Open Letter to Ken Georgetti and the Canadian Labour Congress," www.g20.torontomobilize.org/node/422.
5 "CUPE signs on to Direct Action," *Socialist Worker* 358 (June 20,2001), www.web.net/sworker/En/SW2001/358-03-CUPE.html.
6 Jeff Shantz, "The Limits of Social Unionism in Canada," *WorkingUSA: The Journal of Labor and Society* 12, no. 1 (2009): 113–130.
7 Ken Georgetti, "Statement by Ken Georgetti, President of the Canadian Labour Congress on Vandalism Surrounding Toronto G20 Meeting," *Canadian Labour Congress,* June 26, 2010, www.canadianlabour.ca/national/news/statement-ken-georgetti-president-canadian-labour-congress-vandalism-surrounding-toron.
8 Georgetti, "Statement," June 26, 2010.
9 John Clarke, "The Labor Bureaucracy and the Fight Against the Ontario Tories" (unpublished manuscript, 2002).
10 Upping the Anti Editorial Committee, "With Eyes Wide Open: Notes on Crisis and Resistance Today," *Upping the Anti* 10 (2010): 27–40.
11 See www.workersassembly.ca/contact.
12 Herman Rosenfeld and Carlo Fanelli, "A New Type of Political Organization: The Greater Toronto Workers' Assembly" *The Bullet,* Socialist Project E-Bulletin No. 400, August 6, 2010, www.socialistproject.ca/bullet/archive4.php?f_arch=4.
13 Rosenfeld and Fanelli, "A New Type."
14 Clarke, "The Labour Bureaucracy," 1.

Chapter 7: Presenting the Movement's Narratives

1 CTV.ca News Staff, "Day blames G20 travel alert on 'small group of thugs,'" *CTV.ca,* June 20, 2010, http://ottawa.ctv.ca/servlet/an/local/CTVNews/20100620/G20-travel-warning-100620.
2 I was interviewed by mainstream media outlets (CNN, CTV, and Global) on two occasions after police attempted to steal my flagpoles (and finally succeeded).
3 *The Dominion/Media Co-op* has been awarded the Canadian Federation of Worker Co-ops' Best Practice Award for "outstanding contributions to democratic engagement." See "Media Co-op Wins Best Practice Award from National Federation of Cooperatives," *Toronto Media Co-op,* Nov. 1, 2010, www.mediacoop.ca/blog/editor/5029.
4 See http://g20.torontomobilize.org/getinformed and search "SOAR" on http://toronto.mediacoop.ca.
5 It could be argued that the stories produced by the mainstream press about the AMC

were used to distract viewers from the protests themselves and that this content was used to fill space and avoid reflecting substantively on the stories and messages of protesters.

6 G20 Alternative Media Centre, "Toronto Police Services visit Alternative Media Centre: Continues pattern of police harassment, intimidation and physical abuse of journalists," Toronto Media Co-op, June 27, 2010, http://toronto.mediacoop.ca/story/toronto-police-services-door-alternative-media-centre/3875.

7 Ali Mustafa, "G20 Profile: Independent Journalist, Daniel Adam MacIsaac," *Toronto Media Co-op*, July 5, 2010, http://toronto.mediacoop.ca/story/g20-profile-independent-journalist-daniel-adam-macisaac/4056; "Independent Journalist Amy Miller on Violence and Threats Against Women in Detention Centre," *Toronto Media Co-op*, June 28, 2010, http://toronto.mediacoop.ca/video/independent-journalist-amy-miller-violence-and-threats-against-women-detention-centre/3945, "Police attack journalists, public's right to know,"*Toronto Media Co-op*, June 28, 2010, http://toronto.mediacoop.ca/video/police-attack-journalists-publics-right-know/3903; and Dominion Stories, "Safety and Rights of Journalists in Canada," *Toronto Media Co-op*, October 26, 2010, http://toronto.mediacoop.ca/blog/vkauri/4964. The police have refused to return my bag of media gear (laptop, cameras, sound recorders, batteries, glasses, cash, etc.).

8 From Steve Paikin's Twitter account: "He talked too much and pissed the police off. Two officers held him. A third punched him in the stomach. Totally unnecessary. The man collapsed. Then the third officer drove his elbow into the man's back." CBC News, "Police beat journalist covering G20: report," *CBC.ca*, June 28, 2010, www.cbc.ca/news/canada/story/2010/06/28/g20-rosenfeld-police.html.

9 Christie Blatchford, "Self-Anointed G20 'Journalists' Should Get Real," *Globe and Mail* (Toronto), June 26, 2010.

Chapter 8: Got Your Back!

Epigraph: Ching-In Chen, Jai Dulani, and Leah Lakshmi Piepzna-Samarasinha, eds., *The Revolution Starts at Home: Confronting Intimate Violence in Activist Communities*, (Cambridge, MA: South End Press, 2011), i.

Chapter 9: Police Violence and State Repression at the Toronto G20

1 *Brown v. Durham Regional Police Force*, (1998), 43 O.R. (3d) 223 at 249 (C.A.).

2 "Blair displays seized weapons," *Globe and Mail* (Toronto), June 29, 2010, www.theglobeandmail.com/video/blair-displays-seized-weapons/article1622963/.

3 Jill Mahoney, "'Weapons' seized in G20 arrests not what they seem," *Globe and Mail* (Toronto), June 29, 2010, www.theglobeandmail.com/news/national/toronto/weapons-seized-in-g20-arrests-not-what-they-seem/article1622761. See also CP Video, "G20 weapon haul revealed," *Globe and Mail* (Toronto), June 29, 2010, www.theglobeandmail.com/news/world/g8-g20/video/g20-weapon-haul-revealed/article1623061.

Chapter 10: They Sought to Terrify Us out of the Streets

1 This chapter originated as a rally speech for the 'Reclaim Your Rights' rally held in Vancouver on July 17, 2010. An earlier version was also published at www.mediacoop.ca.

2 I identify as genderqueer, and use the singular, gender-neutral pronoun, "they." Not all identities can be easily expressed in a two-gender, two-pronoun binary system.

Chapter 11: One Day in a Cage

1 Some of my video of the demonstration and the arrival of the police can be found at http://bit.ly/aEiNaV.

2 "Independent Journalist Amy Miller on Violence and Threats Against Women in Detention Centre," *Toronto Media Co-op*, June 28, 2010, http://toronto.mediacoop.ca/video/independent-journalist-amy-miller-violence-and-threats-against-women-detention-centre/3945.

Chapter 13: Women Resist, Police Repress

1 Conway W. Henderson, "The Political Repression of Women," *Human Rights Quarterly*, 26, no. 4 (2004): 1032.

2 Marjorie Whittaker Leidig, "The Continuum of Violence Against Women: Psychological and Physical Consequences," *Journal of American College Health*, 40, no. 4 (1992): 149–155.

3 United Nations, "Ending Violence Against Women: From Words to Action," study of the Secretary General (October 9, 2006).

4 Black feminist scholar Joy James points us in this direction when she acknowledges that the "policing gaze" is "informed by racial and sexual," as well as class, bias. Joy James, *Resisting State Violence* (Minneapolis: University of Minnesota Press, 1996), 27.

5 Catherine Porter, "Porter: When police stick to phony script," *Toronto Star*, June 26, 2010, www.thestar.com/News/GTA/TorontoG20Summit/article/828876.

6 Leslie Woods, "What Happened in Toronto? Policing Protest and Criminalizing Dissent" (lecture, Laurentian University, Sudbury, Ontario, Nov. 18, 2010).

7 Interviews with ten Toronto G20 summit demonstrators by Shailagh Keaney, November 2010 to March 2011. All interviews were conducted in confidentiality and the names of interviewees are withheld by mutual agreement.

8 Nicholas Hune-Brown, "How the G20 – with its burning cars, broken storefronts, violent beatings and mass arrests – ruined Bill Blair's popularity," *Toronto Life*, August 3, 2011, www.torontolife.com/daily/informer/from-print-edition-informer/2011/08/03/bill-blair-profile/.

9 Similarly, police targeted people who normally experience health concerns, queer bashing, racism, and anti-poor discrimination.

Chapter 15: Connecting Carceral Spaces

1 *Immigration and Refugee Protection Act (IRPA), Statutes of Canada* 2001, c. 27, s. 42.

2 UN Human Rights Council Working Group on Arbitrary Detention, "Report of the Working Group on Arbitrary Detention – Visit to Canada," UN ESCOR 62d Sess., UN Doc. E/CN.4/2006/7/Add.2 (2005) para. 75.

3 Refugee Law Office, Legal Aid Ontario, *Best Practices for Representing Clients at Detention Reviews*, Toronto: June 2008, 8.

4 *Corrections and Conditional Release Act, Statutes of Canada* 1992, c. 20, s.31.

Chapter 17: Martial Law in the Streets of Toronto

1 Originally written in August 2010, a longer version of this chapter was published in *Human Geography*, 3, 3 (2010). Thanks to the editors for their permission to reprint it here.

2 Andrew Pinto, Malika Sharma, and Michaela Beder, "Medics at G20 Protest Speak Out Against Police Brutality," *rabble*, July 5, 2010, http://rabble.ca/news/2010/07/medics-g20-protests-speak-out-against-police-brutality-0.

3 Paul Krugman, "The Third Depression," *New York Times*, June 28, 2010.

4 "G8/G20 Summit Security Map and 'Fortress Toronto'," *Toronto Star*, June 25, 2010. US helicopters were also used in the Vancouver Olympics under the guise that they were participating in a routine North American security exercise.

5 See, for instance: Jon Coaffee, "Urban Renaissance in the Age of Terrorism: Revanchism, Automated Social Control or the End of Reflection?" *International Journal of Urban and Regional Research* 29, 2 (2005): 447–454; Steven Graham, "Cities and the 'War on Terror'," *International Journal of Urban and Regional Research*, 30, 2 (2006): 255–276; and Peter Marcuse, "Security or Safety in Cities? The Threat of Terrorism after 9/11," *International Journal of Urban and Regional Research*, 30, 4 (2006): 919–929.

6 "Tourists Fleeing Fortress Toronto," *Toronto Sun*, June 19, 2010; Christopher Hume, "City Walls: A Modern Comeback," *Toronto Star*, June 26, 2010; "Graphic: Fortress Toronto," *National Post*, June 18, 2010, http://news.nationalpost.com/2010/06/18/graphic-fortress-toronto/.

7 Nathalie Des Rosiers, general counsel for the Canadian Civil Liberties Association, quoted in Ian Austin, "Toronto Summit Meeting Brings Curbs on Canadian Rights," *New York Times*, June 25, 2010, www.nytimes.com/2010/06/26/business/global/26canada.html.

8 "Editorial, "A Brutal Spectacle that Failed a City and its People," *Toronto Star*, June 28, 2010.

9 Amy Marie Siciliano, "Policing Poverty: Race, Space and the Fear of Crime After the Year of the Gun (2005) in Suburban Toronto" (doctoral thesis, University of Toronto, 2010). See also Leo Panitch, "Whose Violence? Imperial State Security and the Global Justice Movement," *Socialist Interventions Pamphlet*, 2 (Jan. 2005): 17.

10 Marine Capt. D.J. McSweeney, quoted in B. Baiker, "Master Blaster: A New Noisemaker," *Newsweek*, July 12, 2004.

11 Martin Lukacs, "Judge' Green-lights Sonic cannons," *Toronto Media Co-op*, June 26, 2010, http://toronto.mediacoop.ca/story/judge-green-lights-sonic-cannons/3818.

12 Naomi Klein, *The Shock Doctrine: The Rise of Disaster Capitalism* (New York: Metropolitan Books, 2007).

13 See David Rider, "Arrests, Tear Gas, Outweigh Glory," *Toronto Star*, June 28, 2010; Kelly Grant, "Police Chief Offers no Apologies for G20 Tactics," *Globe and Mail* (Toronto), June 28, 2010; Kelly Grant, "Toronto Mayor Backs up Police Chief," *Globe and Mail* (Toronto), June 29, 2010; *Maclean's* July 19, 2010.

14 G20 Street Team, "Photos: Chinatown graffiti and the Hockey Hall of Fame," *CBC.ca*, June 21, 2010, www.cbc.ca/canada/g20streetlevel/2010/06/photos-chinatown-graffiti-and-the-hocky-hall-of-fame.html.

15 Oakland Ross, "G20: "Canada's Billion-Dollar Summit Mystery," *Toronto Star*, June 24, 2010. The London and Pittsburgh figures are in US dollars but with the Canadian dollar hovering close to parity, they are reasonably comparable. The scandal around financial squandering on the events took an other worldly turn when it was revealed

that $1 million was spent on a fake lake for the pleasure of G8 journalists and delegates even though the picturesque Huntsville site of the earlier meeting sat amidst a landscape replete with glacially rather than politically inspired lakes.

16 Robert Benzie, "Rick Bartolucci: Riots Prove Extra Powers Were Needed," *Toronto Star*, June 28, 2010.

17 Jill Mahoney, "Weapons Seized in G20 Arrests Not What They Seem: Police Display Items Confiscated in Unrelated Incidents," *Globe and Mail* (Toronto), June 29, 2010.

18 Max Weber, *Economy and Society: An Outline of Interpretive Sociology*, Volume 1 (Berkeley and Los Angeles: UC Berkeley Press, 1978), 54.

19 Walter Benjamin, "Critique of Violence," in *Reflections*, ed. Peter Demetz (New York: Schocken, 1978), 281.

20 Christie Blatchford, "'G17' Defendants Mostly White Kids with Good Teeth," *Globe and Mail* (Toronto), July 6, 2010.

21 "With the G20 Ahead, Police and Protesters Prepare for Each Other," *The Torontoist*, June 23, 2010, http://torontoist.com/2010/06/police_and_protesters_g20.php.

22 Mahoney, "Weapons Seized."

23 John Intini, "The Fallout from Toronto's G20 Protests," *Maclean's* (Toronto), July 8, 2010.

24 Robyn Doolittle, "Chain of Command Questioned in G20: Toronto Police Wasn't Always in Charge," *Toronto Star*, July 10, 2010.

25 Wendy Gillis, "Anti-G20 Group Seeks Evidence of Alleged Police Brutality," *Toronto Star*, July 13, 2010.

26 Steven Chase, "Tory Filibuster Seeks to Block Hearings on G20 Policing," *Globe and Mail* (Toronto), July 12, 2010; Tomitheos Linardos, "Toronto's David Miller Joins 100 Mayors at Copenhagen Conference," *Now Public*, December 10, 2009, www.nowpublic.com /environment/torontos-david-miller-joins-100-mayors-copenhagen-conference.

27 Intini, "The Fallout."

28 Joe Warmington, "Warmington: Cops Had Hands 'Cuffed,'" *Toronto Sun*, June 30, 2010.

29 Dawn Moore, "Who or What Killed Robert Dziekanski," *rabble*, December 5, 2007, www.rabble.ca/news/what-or-who-killed-robert-dziekanski.

30 Marylin Kraft, mother of one of the Vancouver missing women, suggests that systemic neglect of their disappearance was possible because the women were "third-class citizens." Quoted in Robert Matas, "Revelations About Pickton's 1997 Arrest Fuel Calls for Inquiry," *Globe and Mail* (Toronto), August 5, 2010.

31 Henri Lefebvre, *The Explosion: Marxism and the French Upheaval* (New York: Monthly Review Press, 1969) 7, 33.

32 Lefebvre, *The Explosion*, 8.

Chapter 18: Marching with the Black Bloc

This chapter offers my reflections on my experience of the Toronto G20 summit protests. It is not an incitement to do anything illegal.

1 Raoul Vaneigem, *The Revolution of Everyday Life* (London: Rebel Press, 2001), 26.

2 Uri Gordon, *Anarchy Alive! Anti-Authoritarian Politics from Practice to Theory* (Pluto Press: London, 2008) 81.

3 Arthur Lehning, ed., *Michael Bakunin: Selected Writings* (New York: Grove, 1974) 58.

4 CTV Toronto, "Toronto Should Never Again Host G20: McGuinty," July 7, 2010, http://toronto.ctv.ca/servlet/an/local/CTVNews/20100707/g20_terrifying_mcguinty _100707/20100707.

5 Non-association clauses prohibit those facing criminal charges from having any con- tact with their co-accused (often their partners or closest friends) and restrict them from having any contact with known members of particular activist organizations. No-demonstration clauses prevent defendants from organizing and/or participating in any political demonstrations, broadly defined to include public events such as panel discussions, as well as traditional street protests.

Chapter 19: Forms of Protest Reflect Our Power

1 David McNally, *Global Slump: The Economics and Politics of Crisis and Resistance* (Oak- land: PM Press, 2011). See his endnote 4 for an explanation of how the amount is de- duced from a tally of all forms of financial sector support (which includes the rescue of the US auto sector, global fiscal stimulus plans, emergency funds, etc.).

2 Socialist Project, "The Mass Arrests, the Security State and the Toronto G20 Summit," *The Bullet* 377, June 28 (2010): 2.

3 See for example Ritch Whyman, "Reflections on Strategy, Tactics and Militancy," *The Bullet* 381, July 3 (2010): 4. While I agree with some of his analysis, I take issue with some key points.

4 Here I use the term "Canada" reluctantly, in recognition of its contested meaning. What we commonly understand as the region of Canada is in fact a multinational state composed of Canada, Quebec, and Indigenous nations.

5 David Camfield, *Canadian Labour in Crisis: Reinventing the Workers' Movement* (Win- nipeg: Fernwood, 2011), 69–73.

6 Clarice Kuhling and Alex Levant, "Political Deskilling/Reskilling: Flying Squads and the Crisis of Working Class Consciousness/Self-Organization," in *Sociology for Chang- ing the World*, eds. Caelie Frampton et al. (Halifax: Fernwood Publishing, 2006), 214.

7 David Camfield, "The Working-Class Movement in Canada: An Overview," in *Group Politics and Social Movements in Canada*, ed. Miriam Smith (Peterborough: Broadview, 2008): 80.

8 Alan Sears, "Creating and Sustaining Communities of Struggle: The Infrastructure of Dissent," *New Socialist* 52, July-Aug (2005): 32.

9 David McNally, "Mass Protests in Quebec City: From Anti-Globalization to Anti-Capi- talism," *New Politics* 8, 3, Summer (2001): 80.

10 David McNally, public speech, 4th Greater Toronto Workers' Assembly, Bahen Cen- tre, Toronto, ON (July 17, 2010).

11 Reported in McNally, "Mass Protests," 79.

12 Ken Georgetti, "Statement by Ken Georgetti, President of the Canadian Labour Congress on Vandalism Surrounding Toronto G20 Meeting," *Canadian Labour Congress*, June 26, 2010, www.canadianlabour.ca/national/news/statement-ken-georgetti-president-canadian -labour-congress-vandalism-surrounding-toron.

13 John Clarke, public speech, Greater Toronto Workers' Assembly Workshop: "Under- standing and Resisting the G-20," Oakham Lounge, 63 Gould Street, Ryerson Univer- sity, (June 20, 2010).

14 James E. Côté and Anton L. Allahar, *Critical Youth Studies: A Canadian Focus* (Toronto: Pearson Prentice Hall, 2006), 54.

15 McNally, "Mass Protests," 83.
16 David McNally, *Another World Is Possible: Globalization and Anti-Capitalism*, 2nd ed. (Winnipeg: Arbeiter Ring, 2006), 355–357.
17 Alan Sears, "Notes Towards A Socialism For The Times," *New Socialist* 63, (2008): 7.
18 "Dual power" is Lenin and Trotsky's term for a situation where alternative centres of popular power are created alongside and in opposition to ruling class power (such as governments, courts, army), with the goal of paralyzing and then ultimately replacing the traditional institutions of power. This alternative centre of popular working-class power might be mass democratic assemblies in neighbourhoods and communities or workers' and community councils, and would facilitate the expression of democratic forms of self-rule. See McNally's *Another World Is Possible* chapter 7 and *Global Slump* chapter 6 for further discussion and examples.
19 McNally, *Global Slump*, 163.
20 See David McNally, *Another World Is Possible* (particularly chapter 7) for a detailed discussion of political alternatives and visions of a different society.
21 John Clarke, public speech, (June 20, 2010).

Chapter 20: Surveying the Landscape

1 Elizabeth (Betita) Martinez, "Where Was the Color in Seattle? Looking for Reasons Why the Great Battle was So White," *Monthly Review*, July-August, 2000, 141–148.
2 Lesley J. Wood, "Communities Converging: A Story and a Strategy of the G20 protests in Toronto," *Upping the Anti*, 10 (2010): 85–98; Toronto Community Mobilization Network, "Who We Are," http://G20.torontomobilize.org.
3 Toronto Community Mobilization Network, "Who We Are."
4 "Toronto Community Day of Action," www.g20.torontomobilize.org/june25.
5 Donatella della Porta, "Making the Polis: Social Forums and Democracy in the Global Justice Movement," *Mobilization* 10:1 (2005).
6 We must sincerely thank Rachel Kutz-Flamenbaum and Suzanne Staggenborg for their survey and their data from the Pittsburgh G20 Research Project.
7 Dana R. Fisher, Kevin Stanley, David Berman, and Gina Neff, "How Do Organizations Matter? Mobilization and Support for Participants at Five Globalization Protests," *Social Problems*, 52, no.1 (2005): 102–121.
8 Mark Irving Lichbach, "Global Order and Local Resistance: Structure, Culture and Rationality in the Battle of Seattle," 2002, http://depts.washington.edu/wtohist/Research/documents/Lichbach.pdf.
9 Rachel Kutz-Flamenbaum and Suzanne Staggenborg, "Summary Sheet," G20 survey data, unpublished, University of Pittsburgh, 2009.
10 Glenn Adler and James H. Mittelman, "Reconstituting 'Common-Sense' Knowledge: Representations of Globalization Protests," *International Relations* 18, no. 2 (2004): 189–211.

Chapter 21: What Moves Us Now?

1 Editorial, "Darts, No Laurels," *Toronto Star*, June 19, 2010.
2 Jesse McLean, "U.S. G20 Travel Alert for Toronto an Overreaction, Mayor Says; Peaceful Demonstrations Can Turn 'Violent, Unpredictable,' Washington Advises U.S. Citizens," *Toronto Star*, June 18, 2010.
3 Katie Daubs, "G20 Fashions for the Militant and Fabulous," *Toronto Star*. June 23, 2010.

4 Eamon Martin, "Trade Summit Disrupted as Protesters Battle Police in Quebec City Streets," *The Free Press*, July 1, 2010, http://freepress.org/journal.php?strFunc=display&strID=70&strJournal=12.

5 Simon Jeffery, "Protester Shot Dead in Genoa Riot," *Guardian* (London), July 20, 2001.

6 Lesley Wood, "Bringing Together the Grassroots: A Strategy and a Story from Toronto's G20 Protests," *Upping the Anti* 11 (2010): 86.

7 TCMN, "Get off the Fence," June 26, 2010, http://g20.torontomobilize.org/getoffthefence.

8 TCMN, "G8/G20 for community organizations . . . ," email from TCMN organizers, February 11, 2010.

9 Activists confidently used the term "community" because we felt it was clearly defined. However, the term merely referred us back to the abstract concept; it didn't *explain* the material basis for the concept. In his *Economic and Philosophical Manuscripts of 1844*, Marx critiqued a similar ideological use of "economy." Marx wrote: "Political economy starts with the fact of private property; it does not explain it to us. It expresses in general, abstract formulas the *material* process through which private property actually passes, and these formulas it then takes for *laws*. It does not *comprehend* these laws – i.e., it does not demonstrate how they arise from the very nature of private property."

10 Tonda MacCharles, "Impromptu, But Rarely Ad Lib; No Aspect of Summit Protection for G20 Leaders Is Left to Chance," *Toronto Star*, June 22, 2010.

11 Himani Bannerji, *The Dark Side of the Nation* (Toronto: Canadian Scholars' Press, 2000), 154.

12 Marx describes the tricks of ideology in his critique of German "true socialism":

> First of all, an abstraction is made from a fact; then it is declared that the fact is based on the abstraction. A very cheap method to produce the semblance of being profound and speculative in the German manner.
>
> For example:
>
> *Fact:* The cat eats the mouse
>
> *Reflection:* Cat–nature, mouse–nature, consumption of mouse by cat = consumption of nature by nature = self-consumption of nature.
>
> *Philosophic presentation of the fact:* Devouring of the mouse by the cat is based upon the self-consumption of nature.
>
> Having thus obscured man's struggle with nature, the writer goes on to obscure man's conscious activity in relation to nature, by describing it as a *manifestation* of this mere abstraction from the real struggle.

Karl Marx and Friedrich Engels, *The German Ideology* (Amherst, NY: Prometheus Books, 1998), 508.

13 Email Subject line: "[g8/g20mobilization] JUNE 2010: THE PEOPLE WON," sent from the community.mobilize@resist.ca mass email account, July 26, 2010.

14 Naomi Klein, "The New Statesman Essay: Does protest need a vision?" *New Statesman* July 3, 2000, www.newstatesman.com/200007030017.

15 EuroDusnie, "What Moves Us?" (2001), www.gipfelsoli.org/Home/Seattle_1999/4962.html.

16 For a good treatment of the movement's international temperament and scope, see British journalist Paul Kingsnorth's classic *One No, Many Yeses: A Journey to the Heart of the Global Resistance Movement* (Washington: Free Press, 2003). Kingsnorth's index re-

veals that his account of the global movement takes him to the following locations: the African Social Forum, Amazon tribes, Asian Social Forum, Bangladesh, Barcelona, Bolivia, Brazil, Britain, Canada, Chiapas (and Mexico more generally), Delhi (and India more generally), Denmark, Durban and Chatsworth township, the Durban Social Forum, Ecuador, European Social Forum, Genoa, Ireland, Japan, Johannesburg, Nigeria, Oaxaca City (and Mexico more generally), Paraguay, Philippines, Porto Alegre (and Brazil more generally), Qatar, Sacramento, Santa Cruz, South Africa (Durban and Soweto in particular), Thailand, West Papua.

17 Wood, "Bringing Together," 88.

18 In *Black Bloc, White Riot,* author AK Thompson explains that "advancing a universal category like 'the global' actually becomes an *impediment* to grasping the whole picture. A concept, after all, cannot do the work of investigation." AK Thompson *Black Bloc, White Riot: Anti-Globalization and the Geneaology of Dissent,* (Oakland: AK Press, 2010), 93.

19 Wood, "Bringing Together," 95.

20 Wood, "Bringing Together," 94.

21 Elizabeth (Betita) Martinez, "Where Was the Color in Seattle? Looking for Reasons Why the Great Battle was So White," *Monthly Review,* July-August, 2000, 141–48.

22 Martinez, "Where Was the Color," 141–48.

23 Martinez, "Where Was the Color," 141–48.

24 Wood, "Bringing Together," 88.

25 Justin Podur, "War Profiteering and Us," ZNet, January 23, 2005, www.zcommunications.org/war-profiteering-and-us-by-justin-podur. Note that, according to Statistics Canada, the national after-tax median income in 2008 was $24,900 and the median family income was $63,900. These numbers were based on census data collected before the 2009 economic crisis.
See www.statcan.gc.ca/pub/75-202-x/2008000/analysis-analyses-eng.htm.

26 Podur, "War Profiteering."

27 Podur, "War Profiteering."

28 Bannerji, *Dark Side,* 158.

29 Anne Bishop, *Becoming An Ally: Breaking the Cycle of Oppression in People* (Halifax: Fernwood, 2002). See also www.becominganally.ca.

30 Quote from an address by Lila Watson, an Indigenous Australian activist, delivered at the UN Decade for Women Conference in Nairobi, 1985. Web. Ret. February 11, 2011. www.yesmagazine.org/issues/a-conspiracy-of-hope/etiquette-for-activists.

31 "Masses of young people dissatisfied by U.S. imperialism, unemployment, lack of economic opportunity, afflicted by the postmodern malaise of alienation, no sense of grounding, no redemptive identity, can be manipulated by cultural strategies that offer Otherness as appeasement, particularly through commodification. The contemporary crisis of identity in the west, especially as experienced by white youth, are eased when the 'primitive' is recouped *via* a focus on diversity and pluralism which suggests the Other can provide life-sustaining alternatives." bell hooks, "Eating the Other: Desire and Resistance," in *Black Looks: Race and Representation* (Toronto, Between The Lines, 1992), 25.

32 hooks, 21.

33 "Strengthening Our Resolve after the G20: Movement Building and Ongoing Resistance to the G20 Agenda" was the title of a public activist event held on September

17, 2010 at Ryerson University in downtown Toronto.

34 Wood, "Bringing Together," 94.

Chapter 22: Social Protest in the Age of Austerity

Epigraph: Chris Blackhurst, "Expect More Rage if the Rich and Poor Divide Gets Bigger," *Evening Standard* (London), November 11, 2010; Jess Worth, "We Need to Support Student Direct Action," *New Internationalist* (blog), November 11, 2010, www.newint.org/blog/2010/11/11/supporting-occupatio/.

1 Elizabeth Rigley and James Boxell, "Rally Riot Blamed on Hardcore Few," *Financial Times* (London), November 12, 2010, paraphrasing a statement issued by the Metropolitan Police Federation.

2 See Doug Sanders, "Britain Unveils Harshest Budget in a Generation," *Globe and Mail* (Toronto), June 23, 2010, and Sanders, "Britain Braces for Sting of Austerity," *Globe and Mail* (Toronto), October 20, 2010.

3 For solid documentation on arbitrary and abusive use of police powers see Canadian Civil Liberties Association, *A Breach of the Peace: A Preliminary Report of Observations during the 2010 G20 Summit* (Toronto: June 29, 2010); Andre Marin, *Ontario Ombudsman Report: Caught in the Act* (Toronto: December 2010).

4 Stephen C. Webster, "US Intel Chief: Economic Crisis a Greater Threat than Terrorism," *Rawstory.com*, February 13, 2009,
http://rawstory.com/news/2008/US_intel_chief_Economic_crisis_greater_0213.html.

5 Ambrose Evans-Pritchard, "IMF Raises Spectre of Civil Wars as Global Inequalities Worsen," *The Telegraph* (London), February 1, 2011.

6 Apostolis Fotiadis, "Greece: As Austerity Bites, Police Get More Brutal," *Inter Press Service*, January 12, 2011, http://ipsnews.net/news.asp?idnews=54096.

7 For details see www.stopfbi.net.

8 Yves Engler, "Canadian Police Repression of Leftists," *Dissident Voice*, January 22, 2011, http://dissidentvoice.org/2011/01/canadian-police-repression-of-the-left/.

9 See for example, Christian Parenti, *Lockdown America: Police and Prisons in the Age of Crisis* (London: Verso, 1999); Ruth Wilson Gilmore, *Golden Gulag: Prisons, Surplus, Crisis and Opposition in Globalizing California* (Berkeley: University of California Press, 2007); and Todd Gordon, *Cops, Crime and Capitalism: The Law and Order Agenda in Canada* (Halifax: Fernwood Publishing, 2006).

10 David McNally, *Global Slump: The Economics and Politics of Crisis and Resistance* (Oakland: PM Press, 2010).

11 For data on the size of this spending see my *Global Slump*, 197n4.

12 Getting government finances in order in a capitalist world economy means pursuing those (regressive and neo-liberal) economic and social policies that keep wealthy investors and investment institutions happy. As for the effects of cuts, British economists estimate they will reduce growth by 2 per cent a year (see Sanders, "Britain unveils harshest budget").

13 Andrea Orr, "One in Four Black, Hispanic Workers Is Underemployed," Economic Policy Institute, January 8, 2010, www.epi.org/analysis_and_opinion/entry/one_in_four_black_hispanic_workers_is_underemployed/.

14 Agence France-Presse, "Half of US Kids Depend on Food Stamps During Childhood, Study Says," November 2, 2009.

15 Steve Schifferes, "UK economy 'faces decade of pain'," *BBC News*, April 23, 2009, http://news.bbc.co.uk/2/hi/business/8015063.stm.

16 James Politi, "Blueprint Seeks $4,000bn Cuts," *Financial Times* (London), January 11, 2011; Jacob Lew, "The Easy Cuts Are Behind Us," *New York Times*, February 6, 2011.

17 World Bank, *Global Economic Prospects 2010: Crisis, Finance and Growth* (Washington, D.C.: World Bank, 2010).

18 See Paul Waldie, "World Food Prices Hit New High, Raising Fears of Another Food Crisis," *Globe and Mail* (Toronto), January 6, 2011. And on the wave of food-related uprisings see David McNally, "A Night in Tunisia: Riots, Strikes and a Spreading Insurgency," http://davidmcnally.org/?p=245.

19 The literature on structural adjustment in the Global South is voluminous. For one very good overview see Eric Toussaint, *Your Money or Your Life*, updated edition (Chicago: Haymarket Books, 2005).

20 Neil Reynolds, "The Disintegration of the European Welfare State," *Globe and Mail* (Toronto), July 12, 2010.

21 See, for instance, Adam Hanieh, "Hierarchies of a Global Market: The South and the Economic Crisis," *Studies in Political Economy*, 83 (2009).

22 In what follows, my account draws from Rudolphe Lamy, "Price Protests Paralyze Martinique, Guadeloupe," *Associated Press*, February 11, 2009; Angelique Chrisafis, "France Faces Revolt over Poverty on its Caribbean Islands," *Guardian* (London), February 12, 2009; United Press International, "Protests Disrupt Life on French Islands," February 13, 2009; Richard Fidler, "Guadeloupe: General Strike Scores Victory, Spreads to Other Colonies," *Green Left Weekly*, March 3, 2009; and Richard Fidler, "Martinique General Strike Ends in Victory," *Green Left Weekly*, March 21, 2009.

23 Deborah Doane, "The threat of rising food prices," *New Statesman*, January 11, 2011.

24 "Tunisian Unions eclipsing parties as democratizing force?" *Democracy Digest*, January 24, 2011. See also Yassin Temlali, "Pourquoi l'UGTT a joué un role aussi important dans l'intifada tunisienne," *Maghreb Emergent*, January 25, 2011, www.maghrebemergent.com/actualite/maghrebine/1976-pourquoi-le-syndicat-a-joue-un-role-aussi-important-dans-lintifada-tunisienne.html.

25 Leila Fadel, Will Englund and Debbi Wilgoren, "5 Shot in 2nd Day of Bloody Clashes; Amid Outcry Egyptian PM Apologizes," *Washington Post*, February 3, 2011.

26 See especially Raphael Kemp, "First Democracy, Then a Pay Rise," *Le monde diplomatique*, March 2011; Mostafa Omar, "The Spring of the Egyptian Revolution," *Socialistworker.com*, March 30, 2011; and David McNally, "Mubarak's Folly: The Rise of Egypt's Workers," February 11, 2011, http://davidmcnally.org/?p=354.

27 Jack Shenker, "Cairo's biggest protest yet demands Mubarak's immediate departure," *Guardian* (London), February 5, 2011.

28 Andrej Grubačić in Staughton Lind and Andrej Grubačić, *Wobblies and Zapatistas: Conversations on Anarchism, Marxism and Radical History* (Oakland: PM Press, 2008), 24. While Grubačić addresses this remark to the anarchist movement, in my view it applies across the board of the anti-capitalist Left.

29 For one vivid and inspiring portrayal of these practices see "Video Report on the Battle for Tahrir: How Pro-Democracy Activists Reclaimed Tahrir Square after Attacks by Mubarak Forces, *Democracy Now*, February 4, 2011, www.democracynow.org/2011/2/4/video_report_on_the_battle_for.

Demonstrators walk past dislodged pavement stones on Yonge St. south of College St., June 26, 2010. Photo by Richard Tang.

Contributors

Deborah Cowen teaches in the Department of Geography at the University of Toronto. Her research explores the role of organized violence in shaping intimacy, space, and citizenship. Deborah is the author of *Military Workfare: The Soldier and Social Citizenship in Canada*, co-editor with Emily Gilbert of *War, Citizenship, Territory*, and a co-editor of the journal *Environment and Planning D: Society and Space*.

Lisa Currier is a lifetime activist and organizer from Nisichawayasihk Cree Nation who works in support of self-determination, social justice, and unity for Indigenous movements. She holds a Bachelor of Indian Social Work from the First Nations University of Canada.

Nat Gray is a poet, a member of *The Dominion* editorial collective, and a contributor to the Montreal Media Co-op. You may find Nat furiously biking around Montreal, attending too many glitter-themed dance parties.

Syed Hussan is a Toronto-based researcher, writer, and organizer in Indigenous sovereignty, anti-war, anti-poverty, environmental justice, and migrant justice struggles.

Shailagh Keaney is a student and independent media activist based in occupied Atikameksheng Anishnawbek territory in Sudbury, Ontario. She organizes with her community on a grassroots level on various fronts.

Dan Kellar is a Kitchener-based anarchist, organizing with AW@L, the KW Community Centre for Social Justice, and several other anti-poverty and anti-colonial organizations. He is a PhD student at the University of Waterloo, where he researches the application of Canadian environmental laws to un-ceded Indigenous territories.

Naomi Klein is an award-winning journalist, syndicated columnist, and bestselling author. Her most recent book, *The Shock Doctrine: The Rise of Disaster Capitalism* (2007), has been published in thirty languages and is an international bestseller. Her previous book, *No Logo: Taking Aim at the Brand Bullies* (2001), also an international bestseller, was named one of the 100 most important Canadian books ever published. She is a contributing editor for *Harper's*, a reporter for *Rolling Stone*, and writes a regular column for the *Nation* and the *Guardian* that is syndicated internationally. Her work has appeared in the *New York Times*, the *Washington Post*, *Newsweek*, the *Los Angeles Times*, the *Globe and Mail*, *El Pais*, *L'Espresso*, and the *New Statesman*.

Tammy Kovich recently received a master's degree in political science from York University with a research focus on anarchist social movements. She is a Toronto-based organizer, and divides her time between the library stacks and the streets.

Clarice Kuhling teaches sociology and contemporary studies at Wilfrid Laurier University and Ryerson University. She has been active in global justice, anti-poverty, and labour movements for over a decade.

Tom Malleson is an anti-authoritarian social justice organizer, particularly within anti-poverty and migrant justice movements. He is a PhD candidate in political science at the University of Toronto.

David McNally teaches political science at York University. He is a long-time activist in socialist and global justice movements and is the author of six books, including *Global Slump: The Economics and Politics of Crisis and Resistance*.

The Movement Defence Committee is an autonomous working group of the Law Union of Ontario made up of legal workers, law students, activists, and lawyers, which provides legal support to progressive organizations and activists in Toronto.

Clare O'Connor is a Toronto-based activist and writer. She is an editor of *Upping the Anti: A Journal of Theory and Action* and Volunteer Coordinator for the Ontario Public Interest Research Group at the University of Toronto.

Sarah Pruyn is a recent graduate of the University of Guelph, where she completed her MA in theatre studies, focusing on radical politics and performance. She lives, works, and organizes in Southern Ontario.

Archana Rampure is a researcher for the Canadian Union of Public Employees; she usually works on social policy and legislation in Ontario but often gets involved in special projects such as organizing around the G20 or the elections. She has a PhD from the University of Toronto and is a former chair of CUPE 3902, the academic workers' union at U of T.

Mac Scott is an anarchist working in law, go figure. He also works with No One Is Illegal (a migrant justice organization) and the Ontario Coalition Against Poverty. In his free time he likes science fiction, his collective house and family, beer, and bad suits (not necessarily in that order).

Swathi Sekhar studied law in Toronto. She has been doing anti-oppression activist work in Toronto and elsewhere for several years.

Jeff Shantz is a long-time union and community organizer, having been a member of the Canadian Union of Public Employees and the Ontario Coalition Against Poverty. He is the author of *Active Anarchy: Political Practice in Contemporary Movements*.

Neil Smith is Distinguished Professor of Anthropology and Geography at the Graduate Center of the City University of New York where he was the founding Director of the Center for Place, Culture and Politics. He is also Sixth Century Chair in Geography and Social Theory at University of Aberdeen. His numerous authored and edited books include *New Urban Frontier; American Empire: Roosevelt's Geographer and the Prelude to Globalization* (2004), which won several awards including the Los Angeles Times Book Prize for Biography; *The Endgame of Globalization;* and *Uneven Development.* He has written more than 200 articles, chapters, and essays, and his work is translated into more than a dozen languages.

Glenn Stalker is an Assistant Professor of Sociology at York University. His research interests include culture, political and environmental sociology, and work and family.

Nicole Tanguay is a mixed-race Cree two-spirit woman. She is a writer, poet, musician, and social activist. She was one of the organizers for the Indigenous day of action during the Toronto G20.

David Wachsmuth is a PhD candidate in sociology at New York University and was trained as an urban planner at the University of Toronto. He is an organizer with GSOC-UAW, the graduate employee union at NYU.

Lesley Wood worked with the Toronto Community Mobilization Network. She is an Associate Professor of Sociology at York University.

Monique Woolnough has organized in the feminist, queer, environmental, and decolonization movements in some way or another for the past ten years, mostly as a facilitator, trainer, fundraiser, kitchen coordinator, writer, and book nerd. The G20 was her first experience taking part in organizing for a mass mobilization.

Elroy Yau is a Toronto Transit Commission employee. During the G20 protests he was arbitrarily arrested while on his way to work.